www.wadsworth.com

wadsworth.com is the World Wide Web site for Wadsworth and is your direct source to dozens of online resources.

At *wadsworth.com* you can find out about supplements, demonstration software, and student resources. You can also send email to many of our authors and preview new publications and exciting new technologies.

wadsworth.com
Changing the way the world learns®

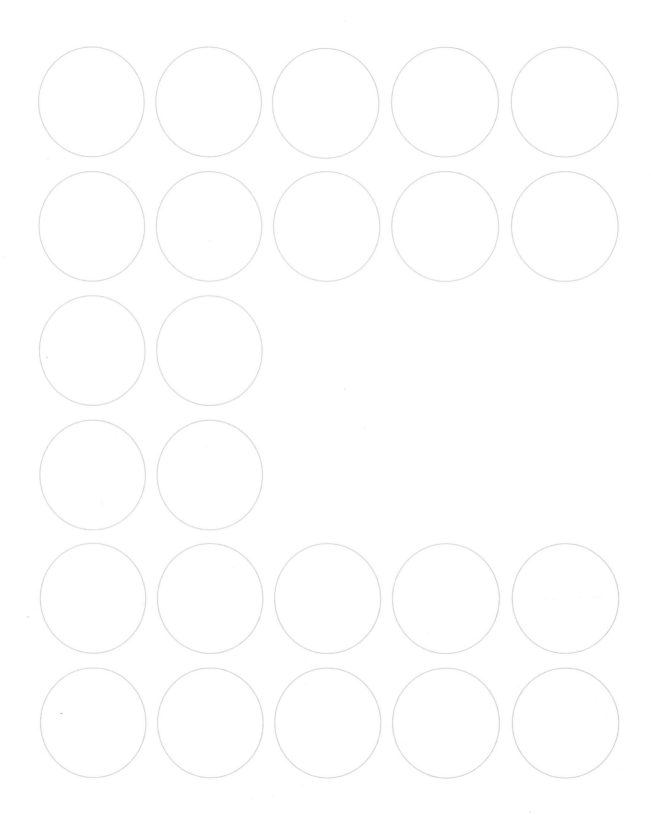

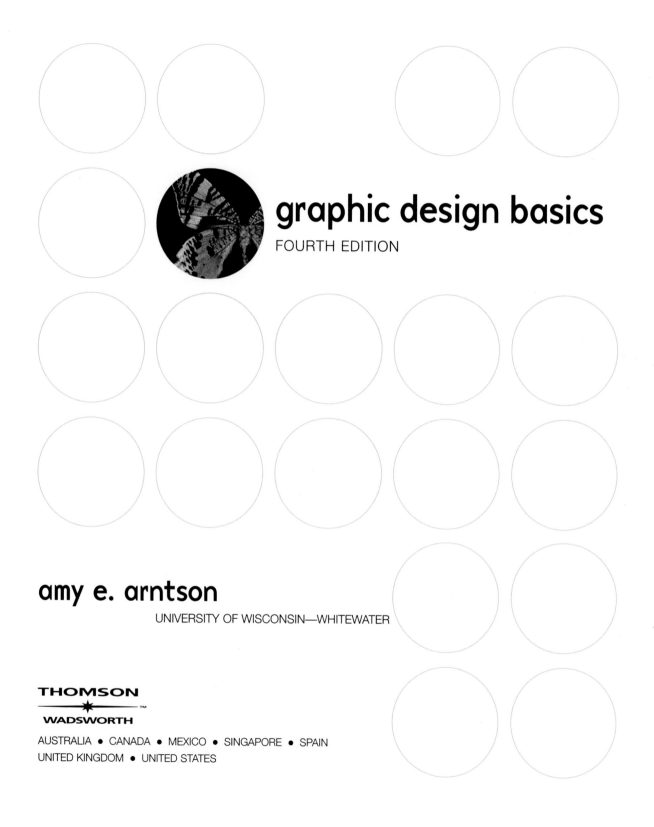

graphic design basics

FOURTH EDITION

amy e. arntson

UNIVERSITY OF WISCONSIN—WHITEWATER

THOMSON

WADSWORTH

AUSTRALIA • CANADA • MEXICO • SINGAPORE • SPAIN
UNITED KINGDOM • UNITED STATES

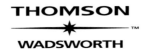

THOMSON

™

WADSWORTH

Publisher: Clark Baxter
Executive Editor: David Tatom
Acquisitions Editor: John Swanson
Senior Development Editor: Stacey Sims
Assistant Editor: Amy McGaughey
Editorial Assistant: Rebecca Jackson
Technology Project Manager: Melinda Newfarmer
Marketing Manager: Mark Orr
Marketing Assistant: Justine Fergusson
Advertising Project Manager: Vicky Chao

Project Manager, Editorial Production: Ritchie Durdin
Print/Media Buyer: Tandra Jorgensen
Permissions Editor: Joohee Lee
Production Service: Thompson Steele, Inc.
Text Designer: Preston Thomas
Photo Researcher: Amy E. Arntson
Cover Designer: Preston Thomas
Cover Printer: Transcon-Interglobe
Compositor: Thompson Steele, Inc.
Printer: Transcon-Interglobe

For more information about our products, contact us at:
Thomson Learning Academic Resource Center
1-800-423-0563
For permission to use material from this text, contact us by:
Phone: 1-800-730-2214 **Fax:** 1-800-730-2215
Web: http://www.thomsonrights.com

Library of Congress Control Number: 2002105844

ISBN 0–534–27399–8

Wadsworth/Thomson Learning
10 Davis Drive
Belmont, CA 94002-3098
USA

Asia
Thomson Learning
5 Shenton Way #01-01
UIC Building
Singapore 068808

Australia
Nelson Thomson Learning
102 Dodds Street
South Melbourne, Victoria 3205
Australia

Canada
Nelson Thomson Learning
1120 Birchmount Road
Toronto, Ontario M1K 5G4
Canada

Europe/Middle East/Africa
Europe/Middle East/Africa
Thomson Learning
High Holborn House
50/51 Bedford Row
London WC1R 4LR
United Kingdom

preface

Graphic Design Basics introduces students to an exciting and demanding field. Design is linked tightly to society as it both reflects and helps to shape the world around us. Designers are part of this dynamic, important process. To enter this field requires discipline-specific information, hands-on practice and an understanding of time-honored principles. The fourth edition of this text continues to weave a concern for design principles with specialized information about applications in the field of graphic design.

Students will find a comprehensive introduction to the field of graphic design that stresses theory and creative development. The fourth edition includes many new, beautiful, full-color visuals that reflect many stylistic directions. These new designs and illustrations are among the best work from the history of 20th century design. Although graphic styles are constantly evolving, the structural underpinnings of good design remain constant. Their application leads to successful design solutions.

The tools of the graphic design field are changing quickly, offering opportunities for new complexities of creation and delivery of content. The fourth edition of *Graphic Design Basics* integrates information about computer graphics throughout the text and provides a guide to generating successful files for electronic prepress. It also includes an entirely new chapter on web design, which has become one of the most powerful and exciting new tools for designers today.

Graphic Design Basics introduces the form and function of graphic design. It works well for courses in the field of design, as well as related courses dealing with visual communication and advertising. Projects and exercises challenge the student to internalize the lessons in the text and to learn by doing. Chapters 1 and 2 present an introduction to the design process and the last one hundred years of design history. Chapters 3, 4, and 5 discuss the vital principles of perception, dynamic balance and Gestalt, and how they relate to graphic design.

Chapters 6 and 7 focus on design principles and applied skills in the special areas of text type and layout design. Illustration and photography are combined in Chapter 8. The boundaries between these disciplines are less rigid than in the past, especially as electronic media makes photographic manipulation, drawing tools and typography available to a broad range of professionals. Advertising Design is covered in Chapter 9. Chapters 10 and 11 contain extensive material on computer graphics. Traditional and electronic color are discussed in Chapter 10 with information about color theory and its application both on and off the computer. Traditional and electronic prepress production are covered in Chapter 11 with a step-by-step guide for creating successful electronic prepress documents. A new chapter on Web design concludes the text.

The pedagogical features in *Graphic Design Basics* are useful for both students and instructors. The extensive Glossary explains technical terms while the bibliography opens the door to further discoveries and is helpfully arranged by chapter. The Index provides a ready access to locating topics. A new Web site accompanies the fourth edition.

Thank you to the following reviewers for their help in preparing this edition: David Andrus, John Brown University; Sarah A. Bauer, University of Minnesota, Duluth; Cheryl Gelover, Burlington Community College; Steven E. La Suer, Nossi College of Art; Tova Rabinowitz, Westwood College of Technology; and Linda Sanderson, Bradley Academy for the Visual Arts.

about the author

Amy E. Arntson is a Professor of Art at the University of Wisconsin–Whitewater, where she teaches graphic design and illustration. Her art is exhibited nationally and internationally. Her presentations on the nature of design and perception have been given in China, England, Spain, Peru, and Costa Rica, as well as in the United States, from New York to California. Professor Arntson has extensive experience as an artist, designer, and educator.

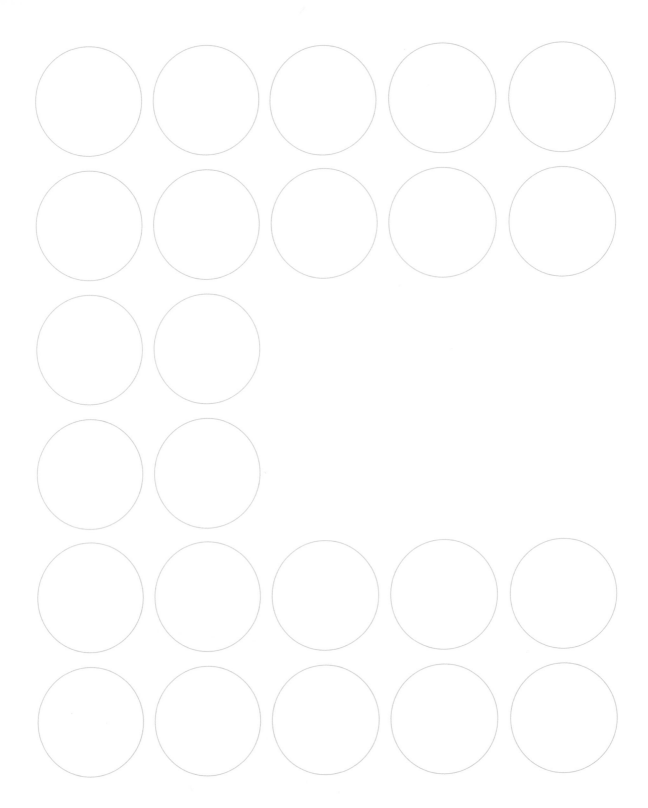

contents

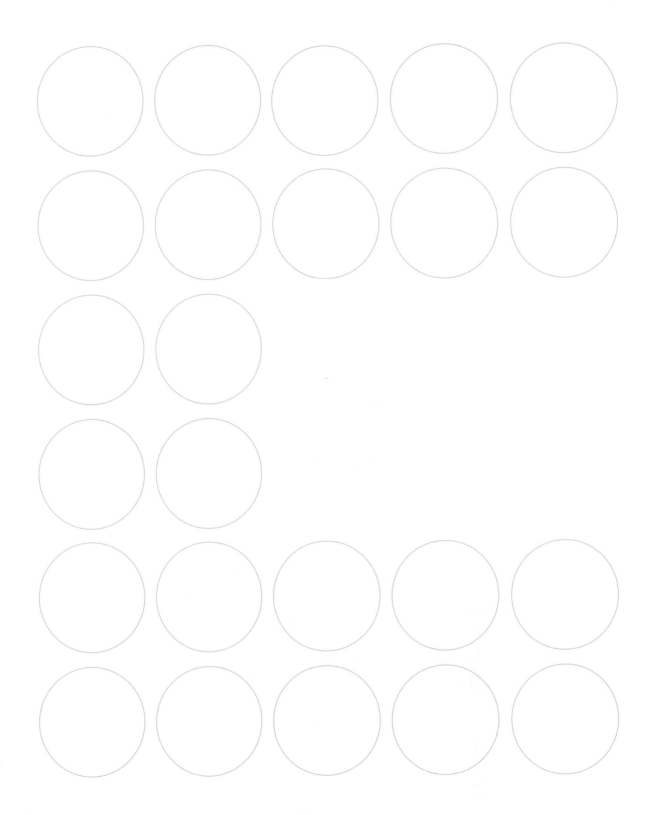

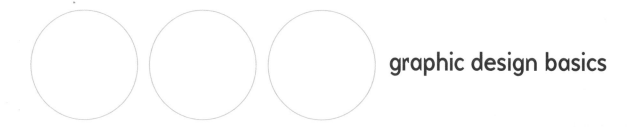

graphic design basics

Chapter 1 ⬚ applying the art of design

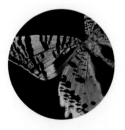

PRINCIPLES AND PRACTICES

This book is about applying the *principles* of visual perception to the *practice* of visual communication. The premise is that a course of study in graphic design should begin by applying the principles and theory of basic design. Interwoven with information about how we perceive and shape a two-dimensional surface will be its application to graphic design problems.

Information from one college class is still pertinent in the next. Although you will be learning special information and terminology in this text, you will discover how closely it ties in with the basic theory of design you already know.

Students often think a class in graphic design or computer graphics is about the hardware and software. It is not—just as graphic design in the precomputer days was not about rubber cement and Exacto blades. The computer is a tool that aids in the process of learning about and producing good design. It is a powerful, complex, exciting tool that must be mastered, but the end product is no better than the concept that defines it. This is true of all art and design media.

Problems in graphic design almost always relate to communication. There are methods of making a design hold together as a unit to communicate information. This text discusses them in simple and straightforward language and contains many fine illustrations throughout, from various periods of design history. You will discover how applying basic design principles can enhance visual communication. You will also explore the nature of visual perception, the role of visual illusion, and the contrast between visual and verbal communication, as well as the full range of basic design skills.

Visual arts in general, and two-dimensional disciplines in particular, share a common language. The study of shapes on a flat ground has yielded a great deal of information about how we see, understand, and interact with the image on the page. You will learn to apply this universal information to solve graphic design problems.

A designer is not in search of one solution, but of several. There is no one correct answer in graphic design, but a rich set of possibilities. This book presents principles like Gestalt unit-forming, balance, emphasis, and eye direction as tools, not as rules. Use them to increase your options and widen your vision. These methods may become intuitive after a while, but in the beginning you will need to study and consciously apply them. Later, you will learn to interpolate and experiment, combining formal study with a more personal, intuitive approach.

WHAT IS GRAPHIC DESIGN?

Graphic design is traditionally defined as problem solving on a flat two-dimensional surface. New fields of Web design and motion graphics expand the field into 3-D and time-based 4-D applications. New-media designers sometimes refer to themselves as "information architects," referring to the importance of organizational hierarchy. The design field's practitioners are

1-1
Julius Friedman.
The Louisville Orchestra.
Photograph from PW, Inc.
Courtesy of the artist.

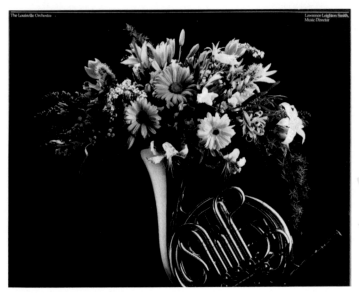

searching for contemporary definitions that reflect and help clarify the field's importance.

The designer conceives, plans, and executes designs that communicate a specific message to a specific audience within given limitations—financial, physical, or psychological. A poster design, for example, may be restricted to two colors for financial reasons. It may be physically restricted in size because of the press it will be run on or because of the mailing method. It may be restricted by the standard viewing distance for a poster in a hall or store window, by the size of a Web surfer's screen, or by the age and interests of the group for which it is intended. Nevertheless, the designer must say something specific to a given audience about a given product or piece of information. Communication is the vital element in graphic design.

It is this element of communication that makes graphic design such an interesting and ever evolving contemporary area. Designers must present current information to modern taste with up-to-date tools. They must stay informed about trends, issues, inventions, and developments. What is the societal impact of new technology? How will film, television, holograms, and computers integrate? Will print become obsolete? What is the relationship of medium and message?

Design education is a lifetime activity. Constant change requires constant renewal. It is not a career for a slow-paced, nostalgic person. To keep up with this fast-changing field you must approach the basic principles and practices with a flexible, curious mind.

Values

Our current society is based on processing information more than producing goods. This is the Age of Information, not the Industrial Age. The product itself, the information disseminated, the point of view illustrated, and the mode of communication used all contribute to shaping the world. It is a good idea to ask early in your career (now would not be too soon) where you stand on certain issues. You will be making career decisions that shape your life and the character of our society. Figure 1-1 is an example of design work that helps advertise and support a not-for-profit arts organization.

A successful designer vividly described one of his early career decisions. His first job out of college was as a junior designer at a small advertising firm, where he was put to work designing a hot dog package. After preparing several roughs, he presented them to the client, only to be sent back to the drawing board. Rejected time after time, the designer grew more familiar than he ever wanted to become with hot dogs. He persevered, learned the basics, and now has his own firm specializing in educational and service-oriented accounts. This allows him more creative freedom and work that is consistent with his personal values.

The Japanese artist Kazumasa Nagai created the design in Figure 1-2 for the UCLA Asian Performing Arts Institute. A pioneer of

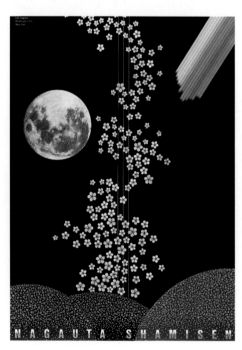

1-2
Kazumasa Nagai.
(Nippon Design Center, Inc.). Design for UCLA Asian Performing Arts Institute. *Courtesy of the artist.*

Japanese contemporary design, his style is recognizable and different from the U.S. style. Like the illustration in Figure 1–1, however, the nature of his client makes for an unusual degree of creative options.

Most design jobs do not offer many opportunities for the exercise of creative freedom. For the most part, we are designers working in a consumer society. Designers are integrally involved in the production and marketing of consumer goods. It is important that while acquiring design skills we consider our potential impact on society. The major artistic movements of the 20th century each had a theory of society that provided a structure and direction for their artwork. The futurists, constructivists, dadaists, and surrealists actively helped define their society and their role in relationship to it. As designers, we have a vital role that needs to be continually examined as it shifts and changes in the 21st century.

However, creating a design that is appropriate for a given product and its audience may not always give you an opportunity to exercise your own sense of aesthetics. (Laying out a motorcycle products catalog may not provide an opportunity to experiment with visual effects.) In addition to directing the visual to a particular audience, the individual client's preferences often also need to be considered. In the face of all the compromises that must be made, keep sight of your own goals and do not become frustrated early in your career. There are many different kinds of jobs in this field, and as a beginning designer, plan on staying at your entry position only until you have mastered the skills required and gained experience.

Each of us must satisfy our own values in our career path, as well as learn to satisfy the requirements of the workplace. Keep your goals in sight. Are there products or points of view you do not want to promote? Is there something you do want to promote?

1-3
Marianne Brandt.
Teapot. 1934. Brass, 7" (17.5 cm). Staalich Kunstammlunger, Weimar.

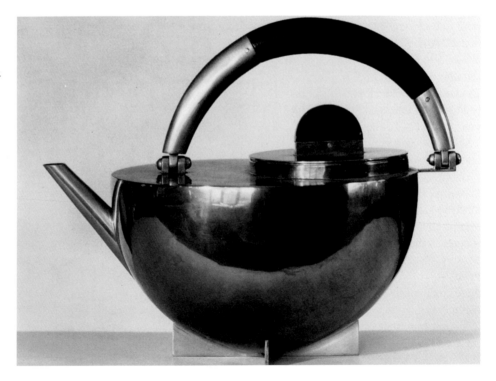

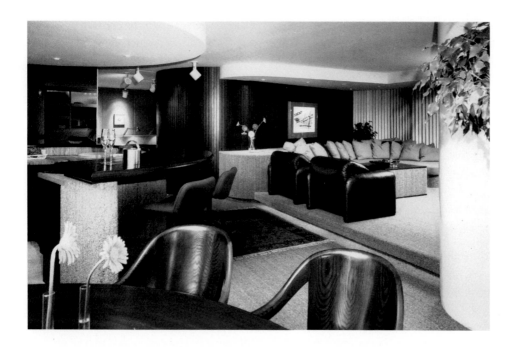

How important is salary? What will make this career successful for you? What kind of lifestyle do you want for yourself? How hard are you willing to work for it? Where do you want to be in ten years? How will you work to achieve these goals?

Design Fields

The field of applied design includes industrial design, environmental design, and graphic design. *Industrial design* is the design and development of three-dimensional functional objects. Figure 1-3 shows a beautifully elegant teapot, considered an important hallmark in the history of functional design. Machines, tools, kitchen implements, and other products are among those objects shaped by the industrial designer. Package design for these objects is often placed in the category of graphic design because it must be designed and printed flat before assembling. The industrial designer attempts to simplify the use and manufacture of objects as well as increase their safety and efficiency.

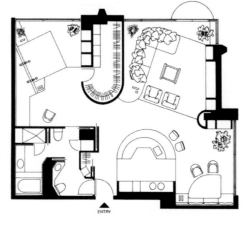

1-4, 1-5.
David Saylor.
(ASID). Interior and floor plan of the Cohen apartment, Milwaukee. Photo by Jim Threadgill. 1983.

Environmental design is a large general category that includes the design of buildings, landscapes, and interiors. Again, the designer attempts to fashion designs that are safe, efficient, and aesthetic. In the unified, flowing floor plan shown in Figures 1-4 and 1-5, curves and angles and varying levels are used as unifying elements.

Graphic design is the design of things people see and read. The field is constantly expanding. Posters, books, signs, billboards, advertisements, commercials, brochures, Web sites, and motion graphics are what graphic designers create. They attempt to maximize both communication and aesthetic quality.

Buildings, environments, products, and written communications will affect us whether they have been deliberately designed or not. Design cannot be eliminated. The printed piece will always communicate more than its words because it uses a visual language. It may, however, communicate exactly the opposite of the intended message. It can damage the image of a company or cause. Learning to apply the *theory* of design and information processing to the *practice* of graphic design will help you achieve the intended communication.

Designers must interface with fields other than their own. They must learn to address the basic marketing concerns of the client, the problems of special workers such as illustrators or photographers, and the difficulties of the printing process.

Some graphic designers do a whole range of work—typography, illustration, photography, corporate identity, logo design, and advertising. Others specialize in one area such as Web design.

Whatever area of design or illlustration you pursue, it is best to follow the design process.

THE DESIGN PROCESS

Research

The first step in preparing a design solution is research, determining the parameters of the problem. Who is the audience? What constraints are there in format, budget, and time? What is the goal of the project?

The next step is to gather and study all the related materials. Selling this design to a client (or an instructor) will be easier if it is backed with research and justified from a perspective the client will understand. In the future, you may work in a large firm or agency where most of the research and information gathering is done by marketing professionals. Visual research, however, both then and now, is the designer's area. It's important to know what has been done before and what is being created locally and nationally for this type of design situation. Develop a feeling for contemporary work by studying design annuals, periodicals, and Web sites.

Designers also keep a file of anything that is interesting or well done. A personal file of such samples can be useful to look through for ideas to build on. Subscribe to graphic design magazines and plan to save all the back issues. Never simply lift another designer's solution; that is unethical. Lifting isolated parts from someone else's work will not give a unified design, and lifting the entire solution will be immediately recognizable as plagiarism. Looking at how someone else solved a particular problem, however, is part of your education. Designers are expected to build on the work of others. We do not create in a vacuum. We are influenced by the hundreds of samples of good and bad design we are all exposed to every day.

Expand your visual vocabulary and plan to use that vocabulary to build new and reactive designs. A colleague describes the process as similar to that of an author using a verbal vocabulary developed over time. These elements are used to create an original story. An author does not have to create a new alphabet or a new language in order to create an original piece of literature. As part of the research stage, search for a creative approach to your design problem in as many ways as possible. Build your visual and conceptual vocabulary. Try looking up a dictionary definition of your topic. Look in an encyclopedia for additional background. Search the Internet for information on the

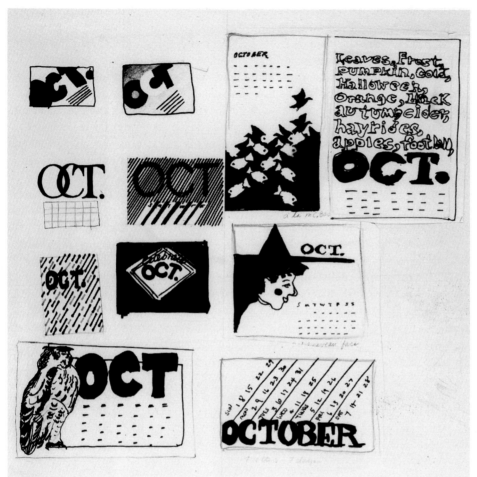

1-6
Amy E. Arntson.
Thumbnail designs for
October calendar
experiment with a wide
variety of solutions.

topic. Use a thesaurus. Make a word associ-ation list of everything you can think of that is associated with your topic. Save personally significant visuals and collectibles. *Approach your design as both prose and as poetry.*

Thumbnails

A designer needs to explore many alterna-tive solutions. Thumbnails are the second step in the design process. Thumbnails are idea sketches. They are visual evidence of the thinking, searching, and sorting process that brings out solutions.

Exercising the mind with thumbnail sketches is like exercising any muscle. The more it is exercised, the more powerful it gets. The more you work to develop ideas through small preliminary sketches, the richer the range of solutions available to choose from for the final design. Never short-cut this stage, because it determines the strength of the final solution. For a stu-dent, the thumbnails are more important than the final project, because they demon-strate thinking, experimentation, and growth. Keep these thumbnails. The ideas in them may be of use to you later in other projects. Prospective employers may wish to see evi-dence of the flexibility and tenacity of your thinking (Figure 1-6).

Thumbnails are usually small because they are meant to be fast and not detailed. They are around 2 × 3" (5 × 8 cm) and drawn in proportion to the dimensions of the finished piece. Fill a sheet of paper with ideas. Never reject an idea; just sketch it in and go on. Work through the idea with your pencil from every perspective you can imagine. Then try taking one good idea and doing several variations on it. Tracing paper or lightweight bond is excellent for this purpose. You may also want to cut and paste and recombine existing images for new effects. It may be faster to work at a size determined by existing elements. In that case the thumbnails may become larger or smaller. The principle of "sketching" through ideas holds true no matter what the size or format of your preliminary investigation. Be as neat and precise as is necessary to show the relationship between elements and their general shapes. The stages of thumbnails, roughs, comps, and camera-ready art, however, often blend together when executed on a computer. The danger with this blending is that, although software may help provide quick, workable solutions, it can be tempting to short-cut the planning stages. Thumbnails are vital to good design, no matter how they are produced, in whatever size or stage of polish. They must exhibit flexible, tenacious *visual thinking* (Figures 1-6 and 1-7).

Roughs

Once the range of ideas has been fully explored, select the best two or three thumbnails for refinement. You may want to talk this choice over with other designers

1-7
Amy Sprague.
Thumbnail sketches for wildlife advertisement.

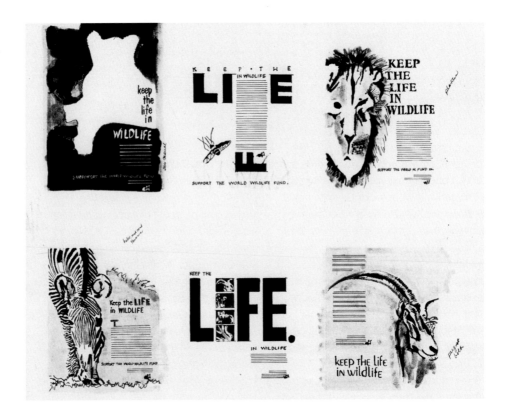

and with the instructor. Later, as a professional designer, you will present the roughs to an art director or a client for review. Or you may be the art director who is reviewing someone else's design. Often considerable redefining and rethinking occurs at this third stage. The thumbnail process may begin all over again.

On a computer, you may want to do a full-size rough. The purpose is to test whether the idea still works on a larger scale. Take this opportunity to work out small problem areas that you could not deal with or foresee at the thumbnail stage. The type style, the other shapes, the exact proportional relationship of these elements to the edge of the format, and the color and value distribution can all be refined at this stage. Computer programs make this relatively easy. Figure 1-8 explores logo development for a special zoo exhibition using a vector graphics program.

Comprehensives

The comprehensive, or *comp,* the fourth step in the design process, is the piece of art you present to the client for final approval. Based on the rough, it is much more carefully done. Once again, consult with art directors, editors, or the instructor before choosing the rough idea to refine.

The client is able to judge the design solution from the comp because it looks much like the finished printed piece. There is no need to explain "what would go there" or how "this would be smoother." A comp is usually computer generated with all components assembled and exactly positioned. It might include photographs, computer-generated type, silkscreen printing, tight electronic illustrations, and a scanned pen and ink rendering.

In most projects from this text, the comp will be the final step. These comps will be

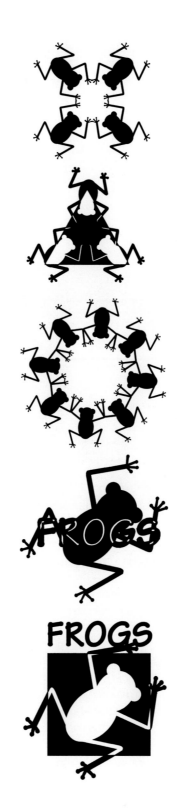

1-8
Angela McFarlane.
Computer-generated thumbnails/roughs for logo design investigate a variety of possibilities in a polished presentation created with Adobe Illustrator.

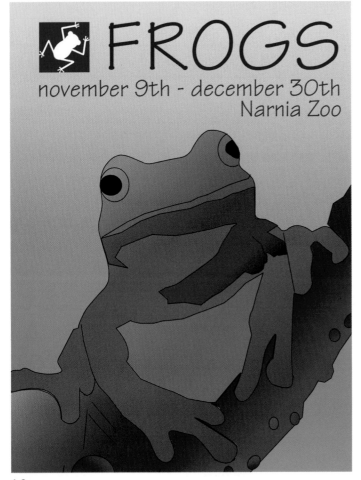

1-9
Angela McFarlane.
Poster comprehensive incorporating frog logo design.

the basis of your portfolio that you will continue to develop in future classes (Figures 1-9 and 1-10).

Comps take different forms depending on the media for which they are intended. Television and film ideas are presented as storyboards with key scenes drawn in simplified and stylized fashion or as abbreviated animation. The three-dimensional comp for a package design may be presented in multiples in order to demonstrate the stacking display possibilities of the package. A publication such as an annual report or a newsletter is usually represented by the cover and certain key pages in the layout design. A Web site is presented to the client with a flow chart and key pages completed. Computer

technology makes it possible to send a rough or a comp to a client for approval via disk, e-mail, or fax. This streamlines the process and makes the designer and client's locale a less important consideration.

Presentation

Practice selling the concept verbally before presenting it. Demonstrate that you understand the client's perspective and goals. Discuss your design enthusiastically in terms the client can understand. Be prepared, however, to listen and to compromise. If revisions are called for, note them carefully.

Ready for Press

The job is now ready for production. The comprehensive shown to the client may look exactly like the finished piece, but it cannot be used to produce the final printed product. Everything must be sent to the printer ready for press. Printer's inks must be indicated, as well as paper selection.

The file must be cleanly prepared, with all links and fonts included. Electronic files that print well inside a classroom may not "RIP" on an imagesetter (see Chapter 11). The disk that contains the file must be carefully prepared.

Base the designs you create on a sound knowledge of the reproduction and printing process. Develop a respect for tools and procedures, because no design is successful if it is flawed in execution. Begin your very first project with a respect for precision, accuracy, and cleanliness. There can be no compromise with perfection in this line of work.

Many designers are responsible for selecting and dealing with a printer. Often the work must be bid to two or three printers, giving each an opportunity to estimate costs. Selecting printing firms to bid for the work is often based on prior experience. If you are unfamiliar with a printing firm, ask to see samples of its work, especially samples with production problems similar to those of the new job. Quality in printers, like quality in designers, varies. Finding a good printer and establishing an easy working relationship is important. A good printer can be an excellent reference for answering tricky production questions and suggesting alternate solutions to an expensive design.

CAREERS

A variety of working environments occur in the design field, with varying advantages and limitations. What suits one person may feel like a limitation or undue pressure to another. You will want to have an idea of what the opportunities are before beginning your job search.

Design Studios

Clients with various needs and backgrounds may seek the assistance of a design studio. The studio will have designers, production artists, account service representatives, and often illustrators and photographers on staff or on call. Design studios hire freelance creative help when their regular staff is too busy or lacks specific skills to handle a project. Designers working in a studio generally have other artists around to discuss and share ideas. The number of working hours spent on each assignment is logged and the time billed to a client's account or to the studio itself. A high value is placed on an ability to work quickly and with a clear understanding of the client's needs and preferences. Clients consist primarily of various advertising agencies and large and small companies or institutions. The graphic design work prepared for these clients includes brochures, mailers, illustration and photography, catalogs, display materials, Web sites, and promotional videos.

Small studios are springing up as computers make it easier for one or two people to provide full-service design.

In-House Design

Many institutions employ their own in-house design staffs. These in-house designers

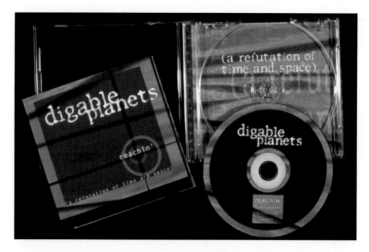

1-10
Jennifer Freson.
CD comprehensive. Inkjet prints with folding insert and plastic holder makes this student portfolio piece look very professional.

serve the particular needs of institutions ranging from hospitals, banks, newspapers, insurance companies, publishers, colleges and universities to large and small manufacturing concerns. In-house design organizations vary greatly according to the type of product or service their company provides. Designers work on projects that relate to the parent corporation's activities. Individual designers may keep track of their hours, if the design area bills its time to other departments. Many in-house operations offer services free to departments within the company. Individual designers may work closely with the client or receive all information and instructions funneled through an art director. It is sometimes possible to develop a corporate career by moving up within the organization. An in-house design organization may lack the presence of other artists and the challenge of interpreting and representing various clients that a design firm provides. However, an advantage to working in an in-house operation is the opportunity to get to know one company in depth by developing a relationship with it and its various departments. Oftentimes the deadline pressure is less and the job security better than in a studio. The growth of computer software has caused a boom in this area as more and more companies find it possible to meet many of their publication needs in house.

Many positions exist for designers at area printing companies. These companies sometimes have their own in-house design departments or hire graduates to do prepress work. A printing company can be an excellent place to gain valuable experience in the technical aspects of reproduction.

The Advertising Agency

Ideas and sales are the cornerstones of the advertising agency. It is dominated by people who deal in words. Account executives bring in the jobs and develop the advertising concepts with the creative director. The art director, designer, and copywriter execute the concepts, although the number of people involved and the exact tasks performed vary from agency to agency. Projects cover all forms of print and multimedia advertising, from film and video work to packaging, display, print ads, billboards, and Web sites. A good art director is versatile. He or she is skilled at conceptualizing and presenting ideas verbally and visually as well as directing others and organizing assignments. More money is spent on advertising than on any other area of graphic design, which is reflected in the salary a designer can expect to earn in this field.

Freelance

Working as a freelance artist allows a maximum amount of freedom, but calls for certain business-related skills. Personal promotion, networking, and a constant vigilance to find new customers will help establish a freelance career. Good organizational skills in billing and record keeping along with talent and hard work keep a freelance business going. Computers, modems, and fax machines make it possible to live outside a metropolitan area and still maintain client contact, once it is established. One of the drawbacks to a freelance career is the lack of company benefits. Health insurance and retirement benefits are not part of the package. It can also be comparatively lonely work.

New Opportunities

Every situation is unique, and this is a generalized description of the types of situations in which a designer can find employment. Many, many variations occur within these categories. A relatively new field for designers is in nonprint media. Web site creation calls for design skills with page layout, logo design, scripting, illustration, typography, and animation. Many companies now use the Internet to communicate with prospective clients, and designers play an important part in facilitating this informational and persuasive communication. Motion graphics and interactive and multimedia design are also exciting and rewarding new career directions.

THE CHALLENGE

The challenge of being a graphic designer involves working through the restrictions and demands of the design process. It involves visualizing the job, although the actual finished printed product will not be done by hand, but on a press with printer's paper and inks, with elements that may have been photographed or drawn by other artists, and with copy written by others. Or it may be shown on a Web site or via another electronic mode of presentation. It involves meeting personal design standards as well as the needs of the client and the audience. It calls for organization and self-discipline to meet the constant deadline pressure. In the classroom, students generally get one project at a time and a generous length of time to complete it. The emphasis in school is on learning. On the job, however, designers work on several projects at once and must uphold design standards while concentrating on time and money issues. A good education in design fundamentals that stresses theory and creative development as well as production techniques is important in this environment. Designers must constantly update their education and stay current with new technologies. Technology has made major changes in the design field in the past several years, and greater changes are on the way (see end of Chapter 2).

Your final challenge is to take a responsible stance in the world. Knowledge of current events and attitudes will help you create designs that reflect and responsibly affect society. Traditionally, it has been the fine arts artist who has set new visual trends and opened fresh creative ways to see ourselves. The designer now also plays this role (see Figure 1-11 by well-established designer McRay Magleby). One of the issues facing contemporary design is the impact of our printed product on the environment. Recycled paper products are part of an attempt to lessen the negative impact of printed materials on the environment. Online graphics are also helping. The aesthetic qualities of design affect our lives in many ways, but the total effect of a design solution has numerous varied and important impacts on our lives.

As designers, we are in the process of redefining our field (Figure 1-12). We need to examine how our culture functions, and how both our perceptions and our values shape and are shaped by the world around us.

Exercise

Research the types of employment opportunities in your geographic area. Find samples of a design firm, an in-house facility, and an advertising agency. Arrange a field trip to one of each. If there are none in your area, do the research on the Internet, sharing the information with your classmates.

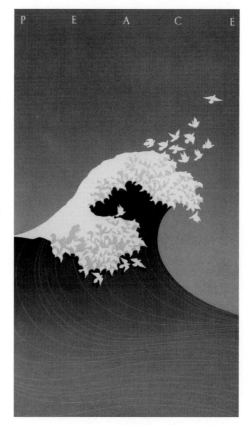

1-11
Wave of Peace poster design by **McRay Magleby.** *Courtesy of the artist.*

1-12
Diane Fenster.
LookListen. Fenster is the first artist to be inducted into the Adobe Photoshop Hall of Fame in September 2001. *Courtesy of the artist.*

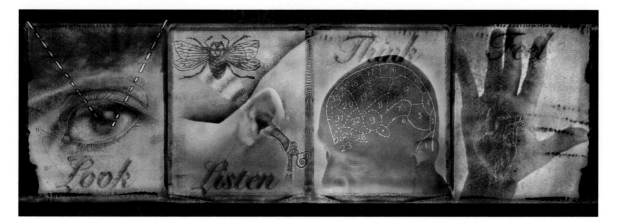

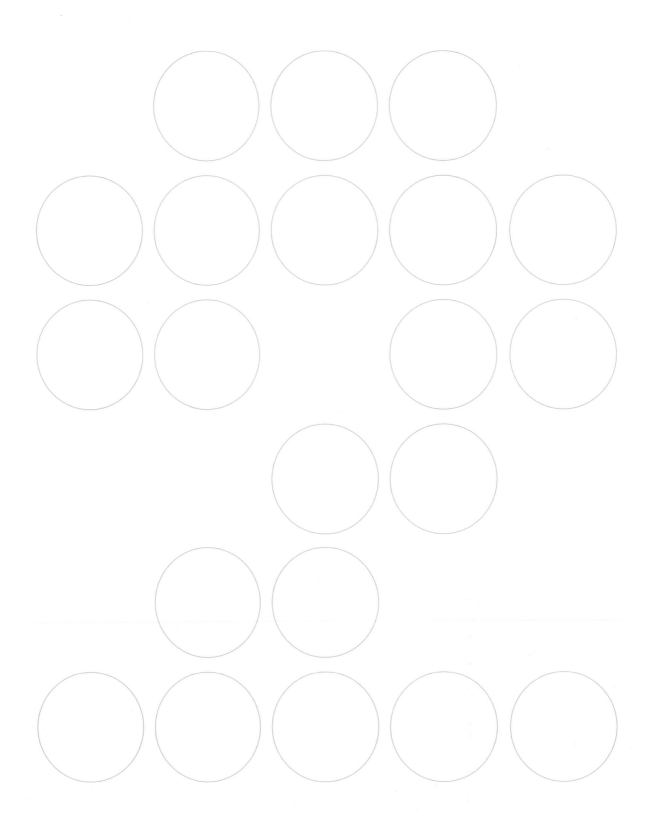

Chapter 2 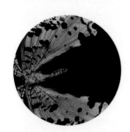 graphic design history

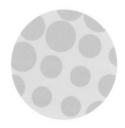

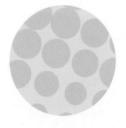

For a graphic designer, the movement of ideas is as important as changes in style. Design is affected by the fine arts as well as by scientists, psychologists, and by the development of new technologies. The study of design history is a relatively new discipline, but it can provide inspiration and insight into the future of design. This chapter's overview shows how design developed both as an art form and as a reflection of society.

THE BEGINNING

The birth of graphic design could be traced back 30,000 years to cave painting or about 550 years to Gutenberg's invention of the printing press. Whatever the origin, the explosive development during the last decade of the 19th century is a good beginning point for study. Fine art and design often inspire one another.

The Industrial Revolution brought about new attitudes and inventions, both of which contributed to the sudden growth of graphic design. A spirit of innovation and progress gave rise to a new interest in providing information to an entire culture rather than only an affluent elite. The growth of population centers, industry, and a money-based economy all increased the need for the dissemination of information. Advertising flourished during this exciting time, and great strides were made in printing. The first photographic metal engraving was invented in 1824; the first halftone screen was made in 1852. Color process work was first successfully printed in 1893. The first auto-

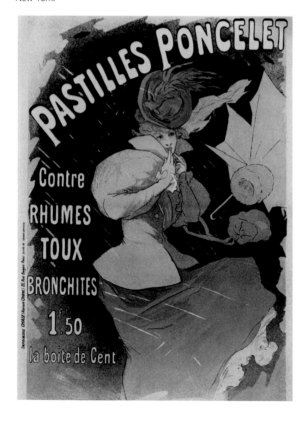

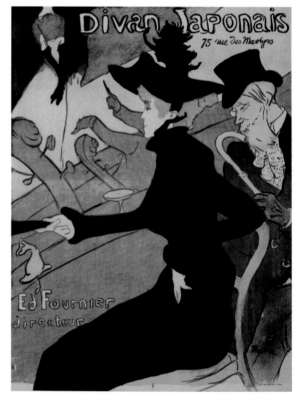

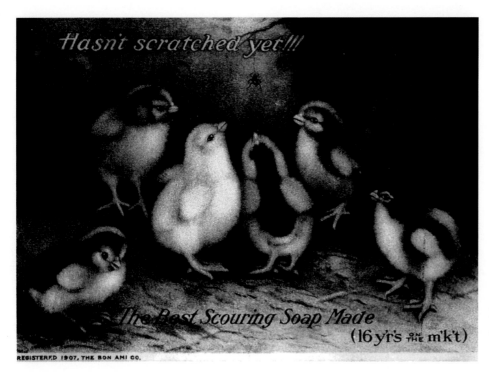

2-3
Trade card. Nineteenth
century. Wisconsin
Historical Society
Iconographic Collection.

mated steam press for lithography was
designed around 1868, and the first offset
press in 1906.

Advancement in stone lithography color
prints in the 1880s encouraged artists to
work directly on the stone for multiple repro-
ductions of large-scale posters. They were
freed from the stiff, geometric confines of
the letter press. The resulting burst of sensual and decorative images in the advertising posters of the time is classified as *art
nouveau.* The movement began in France,
and the names most closely associated with
its development are the Frenchmen Jules
Cheret (Figure 2-1) and Henri de Toulouse-
Lautrec (Figure 2-2), and the Czech
Alphonse Mucha (Figure 8-20).

Lautrec was primarily a painter and printmaker who produced only about thirty-two
posters, as well as music and book jacket
designs. Mucha designed furniture, carpets,
jewelry, and posters for the famous actress
Sarah Bernhardt. Jules Cheret is now called
the father of the modern poster. He produced over a thousand posters, some of
them close to 7 feet tall. This size was
achieved by joining sections mounted on
walls. Posters brought art out of the gal-
leries and into the streets and homes of the
working class. Art nouveau became an
international style that spanned the period
from 1890 to 1910. Its organic, decorative
style stressed the invention of original forms
that were often inspired by nature. These
forms and shapes were applied not only to
graphic design but also to product design
and crafts.

All of the functional arts grew during this
period. In the United States, Lewis Tiffany
created stained glass windows, lamps, and
glassware. The illustrations in Figures 2-3
and 2-4 show early U.S. advertising design
flourishing in the form of trade cards. Scottish
architect, designer, and watercolorist Charles

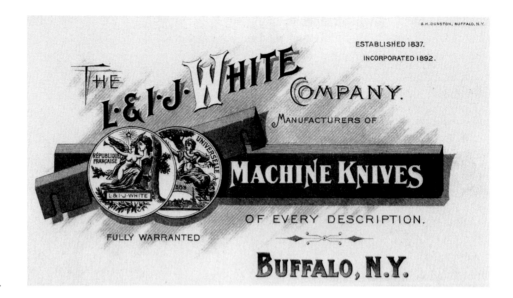

2-4
Trade card. Nineteenth century. Wisconsin Historical Society Iconographic Collection.

(bottom left)
2-5
C. R. Mackintosh.
Chair designed for the Rose Boudoir, Scottish Section, International Exhibition of Modern Decorative Art, Turin, 1902. The Hunterian Museum and Art Gallery, University of Glasgow.

(bottom right)
2-6
Aubrey Beardsley.
Pen and ink drawing for an illustration in *Salome*. 1894. $8\frac{13}{16} \times 6\frac{5}{16}$" (22 × 17 cm). The British Museum.

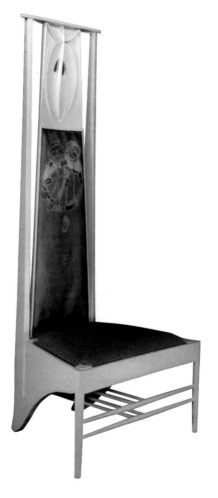

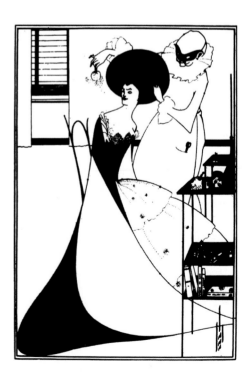

Rennie Mackintosh, his wife, Margaret Macdonald, and her sister Frances Macdonald developed furniture and cutlery designs as well as interior and graphic design (Figure 2-5).

An English artist whose work is an important example of art nouveau style is Aubrey Beardsley. A curving, sensual line and a compelling tension between the figure and background (Figure 2-6) characterize his illustrations for Oscar Wilde's *Salome* and other books. A prolific artist, with an enduring reputation, Beardsley died at age 26.

Among the many U.S. art nouveau artists is Maxfield Parrish, an illustrator for *Harper's* and *Life* as well as many other clients (Figure 2-7). Parrish worked as an illustrator for the first three decades of the 20th century, creating book, magazine, and advertising illustrations. The legacy of art nouveau is not only its stylistic surface treatments (Figure 2-8) but also its concern with the interrelationship of materials, processes, and philosophy.

Not all reactions to the Industrial Revolution embraced progress. William Morris founded the Kelmscott Press in 1890 against what he regarded as the mass-produced, inferior, inhuman product of the machine. Styles of past eras were being copied in art schools and factories with an emphasis on quantity over quality. He and the writer/philosopher John Ruskin wished to renew an appreciation for hand-crafted, unique, labor-intensive products. Morris worked with every kind of design, including fabric, rugs, wallpaper, furniture, and typography. Thanks to Morris, the common person's home and furnishings became worthy of an artist's design. His highly stylized hand-printed books and tapestries are wonderful examples of English art nouveau. Morris was a key figure in the English Arts and Crafts movement. An intensely romantic idealist, he was deeply

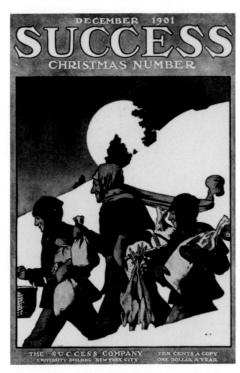

2-7
Maxfield Parrish.
Cover illustration for *Success* magazine. December 1901. Rare Book and Manuscript Library, Columbia University.

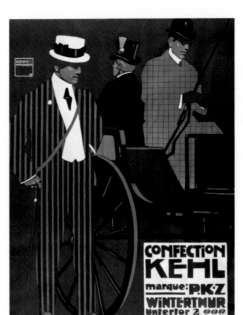

2-8
Ludwig Holwein.
Confection Kehl, Marque: PKZ, Winterthur Untertor 2. 1908. Lithograph, printed in color, 48½ × 36⅛" (123.2 × 91.7 cm). The Museum of Modern Art, New York. Gift of Peter Muller-Munk. Photograph © 2001 The Museum of Modern Art, New York.

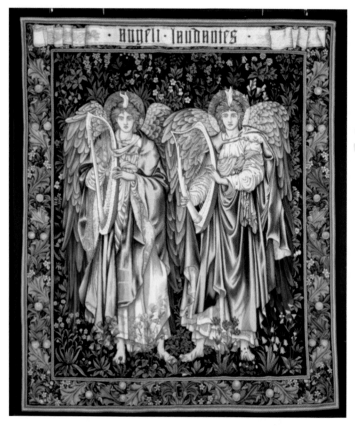

2-9
William Morris.
Tapestry 'Angeli Laudantes' 1894. H 240.7 cm × W 204.5 cm. This wool and silk tapestry was made from figures taken from Sir Edward Burne-Jones's cartoon for a stained glass window. Collection of the Victoria and Albert Museum.

concerned with the ethics of art. He believed bad design was equated with a faulty ethical system. He is credited, along with the Bauhaus, with bringing about a renewal of the standards of craftsmanship (Figure 2-9). His work inspired the European modernists.

THE TURN OF THE CENTURY

The turn of the century brought fundamental changes in our understanding of the world. In 1905 Albert Einstein made public his theory of relativity and altered our ideas of space and time. They became interrelated variables instead of isolated absolutes. After Sigmund Freud published *The Interpretation of Dreams* in 1909, dreams were no longer considered simply fantastic, clearly divided from reality. Sexuality also was no longer

safely reserved for the bedroom, but appeared in various symbols in everyday life. The accepted boundaries of reality began to shift.

Existentialism further undermined faith in absolutes by suggesting there is no single correct answer or moral action. Instead we are individually responsible for shaping meaning.

Meanwhile, travel and the growth of a communications network made it possible for us to hear of cultures with different lifestyles, beliefs, and perceptions. This communications explosion continues to be one of the most important influences on society today. As designers we are an important part of its development as we begin the new century. Design is a reflection of society and helps shape it.

In 1907 Pablo Picasso completed his painting *Les Demoiselles d'Avignon* (Figure 2-10). Pointing the way to cubism, it emphasized the flat surface of the canvas and resembled the symbolic, patterned figures of African art. The relationship between the figures and the picture plane itself was ambiguous. As cubism developed, shapes became increasingly abstracted, showing objects from multiple points of view, with transparent overlapping. They denied an absolute, inviolate place in space for any single object. In these respects cubism influenced the subsequent development of 20th-century design. Nature was no longer the only form of reality to depict. The human mind itself played a part in structuring reality. The cubist practice of integrating letterforms into paintings influenced the typography of subsequent movements.

In Germany, Friedrich Nietzsche and the nihilist rebellion contributed to the expressionist movement, which appeared around 1905. This movement aspired to show subjective emotions and responses rather than objective reality. The idea that art is primarily self-expression led to a dramatic

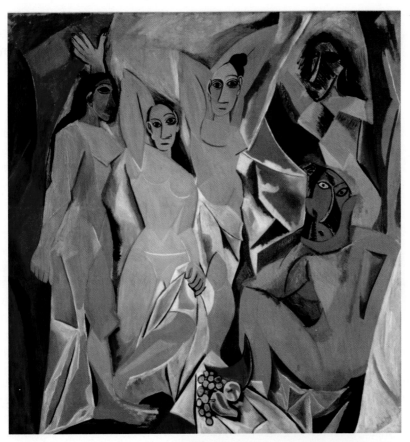

non-naturalistic art typified by Oskar Kokoschka and Ernst Kirchner (Figure 2-11). In Paris in 1905 the first exhibition of a group of artists who would be called "les fauves" ("the wild beasts") was held. Similar in look to expressionism, with its open disregard of the forms of nature, fauvism favored wild expressive colors. Expressionism ended around 1920. Neoexpressionism, influenced by the expressionists and the fauves, shows up today in contemporary illustration.

In 1890 the German psychologist Christian von Ehrenfels published an essay called "On Gestalt Qualities." Within this paper was the suggestion that the *Gestalt* (total entity) is larger than the sum of its parts. Ehrenfels suggested that the parts interact to form a new whole. Our perception of an object is influenced by the

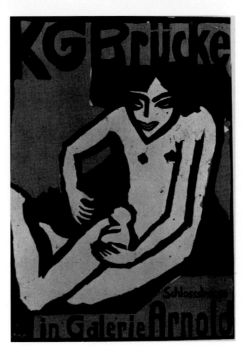

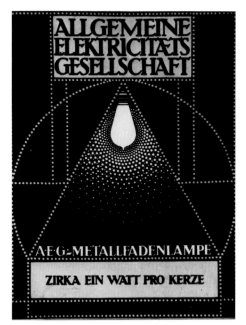

2-12
Peter Behrens.
Poster for AEG light bulbs.
1901.

arrangement of objects around it. This work pointed the way to another new idea. Reality could be seen as dependent on context rather than as absolute.

In 1910 at the Frankfurt Institute of Psychology, Max Wertheimer, an admirer of Ehrenfels, began research on apparent movement, which is the basis for the motion picture. He asked why we perceive some images as belonging together and others not. He arrived at the Gestalt principle of unit-forming, which describes how we organize and interpret patterns from our environment. Simply put, things that are similar will be perceptually grouped together. (For a more detailed description of unit-forming factors, see Chapter 5.) Wolfgang Köhler and Kurt Koffka carried on Wertheimer's investigations, and later Rudolf Arnheim applied these principles to art and visual perception through much of the 20th century.

Germany also gave birth to Peter Behrens, a pictorial and graphic artist who moved into architecture. He was an artist of the Deutscher Werkbund, founded in 1907. Inspired by William Morris and the English Arts and Crafts movement, the Werkbund artists believed in examining the moral questions inherent in art and in preventing commercial and industrial abuse. Behrens was given the first corporate identity job in the history of design. He was asked to design for AEG, a large German corporation, the architecture, advertising, products, and everything else (Figure 2-12). He taught Walter Gropius, who would later become famous as a leader of the Bauhaus.

MODERNISM

The European modernist era spans roughly 1908 to1933, from the early days of cubism until Hitler's rise. It encompassed fine art, graphic design, and architecture through various movements including cubism, futurism, Plakatstil, suprematism, dada, de Stijl, the Bauhaus, and constructivism. Many artists and designers fit into multiple categories.

The years before World War I brought new movements that continued to expand our notion of reality. *Futurism* showed time itself on canvas by capturing motion through multiple images. The movement was established around 1909 by the Italian poet Emilio Marinetti and developed by artists such as Giacomo Balla, Gino Severini, and artist/designer E. McKnight Kauffer. The futurist artists were so named for their optimistic belief that the machines of the industrial age would lead to a better future. Ironically and sadly, many artists of the movement were killed in World War I (Figure 2-13).

Futurism's influence, however, continued. Motion pictures were popular by 1910. They widened our visual reality, creating images that moved through time, as the futurists hoped their paintings would do.

A flat-color pictorial design that maintained a balance between 2-D design structure and imagery, *Plakatstil* emerged in Germany early in the 20th century. Lucian

Bernhard created a compelling series of advertising posters using imagery made from flat colors with an emphasis on shape, combined with the product name (Figure 2-14).

Around this same time, another movement surfaced that would strongly influence graphic design. *Dada* was founded in 1916 by a group of poets, the chief of whom was the Rumanian Tristan Tzara. Its name, like the movement itself, had no meaning, according to the dadaists. The following poem is by Tzara:

> *Colonial syllogism*
> *No one can escape from destiny*
> *No one can escape from DADA*
> *Only DADA can enable you to escape*
>   *from destiny.*
>   *You own me: 943-50 francs.*
> *No more drunkards!*
> *No more aeroplanes!*
> *No more vigor!*
> *No more urinary passages!*
> *No more enigmas!*

The dadaists were extremely important in 20th-century art and philosophy because they questioned meaning itself with an assault on all accepted values and conventional behavior. Marcel Duchamp exhibited such things as bicycle wheels, urinals, and bottle racks, challenging the criteria by which we define something as art. He stated, "I was interested in ideas—not merely in visual products. I wanted to put painting again at the service of the mind."

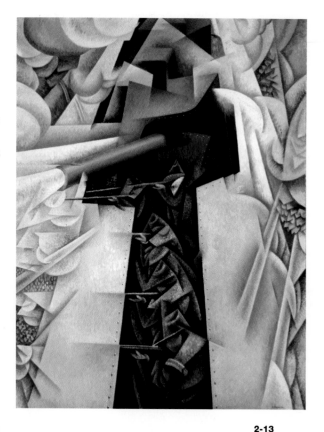

2-13
Gino Severini.

Armored Train in Action. (Train blindé en action). 1915. Oil on canvas. 45⅝ × 34⅞" (115.8 × 88.5 cm). The Museum of Modern Art, New York. Gift of Richard S. Zeisler. Photograph © 2001 The Museum of Modern Art, New York.

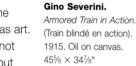
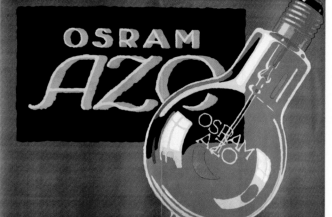

2-14
Lucian Bernhard (Emil Kahn).

Osram AZO. (c. 1910). Lithograph, printed in color, 17⅝ × 37⅜" (44.7 × 95.9 cm). The Museum of Modern Art, New York. Purchase Fund. Photograph © 2001 The Museum of Modern Art, New York.

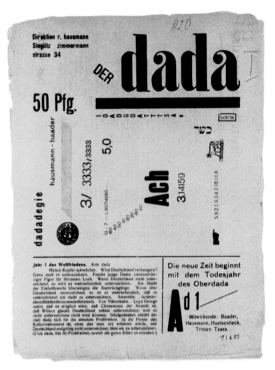

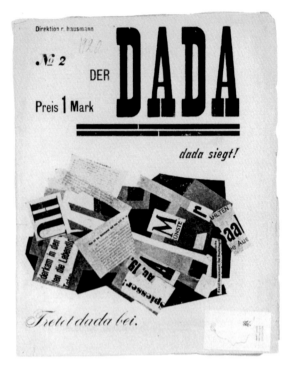

2-15, 2-16
Der Dada covers. 1920.
Collection, The Chicago
Art Institute. Mary
Reynolds Collection.

2-17
Kurt Schwitters.
*Merz Drawing 83. Drawing
F. (Merzzeichnung 83.
Zeichnung F).* 1920.
Collage of cut-and-pasted
paper wrappers,
announcements, tickets,
5¾ × 4½" (14.6 × 11.4
cm). The Museum of
Modern Art, New York.
Katherine S. Dreier
Bequest. Photograph ©
1998 The Museum of
Modern Art, New York.

The dadaist poet Guillaume Apollinaire
created a series of "Calligrammes" around
1918 that seemed to break every known
rule of typography. One of the many dada
publications, *Der Dada,* introduced photomontage. It was characterized by an inten-
tional disorder. Letters of all types and sizes,
various languages, and dictionary illustrations mingled (Figures 2-15 and 2-16).
Figurative photographic images were treated
with the same freedom from conventions.
With "rayographs" or photograms and techniques such as solarization, Man Ray made
an important contribution to graphic design
in the form of photomontage.

Hannah Hoch and John Heartfield (Figure
5-4) were also important photomontage
artists, creating rich, unexpected visual
effects. Both Hoch and Heartfield made
political anti-Hitler images that spoke without words about political realities. Kurt
Schwitters, another dada artist, combined
cubism with dada for a series of collages
that remain a rich visual resource for artists
today (Figure 2-17).

ABSTRACT MOVEMENTS

The first totally abstract poster is attributed to Henry van de Velde in 1897 (Figure 2-18). A Belgian art nouveau artist, he moved to Germany in 1906 to teach and became interested in architecture and a more structural approach to art. An architect, designer, educator, and painter, his ideas contributed to the later development of the Bauhaus movement. Van de Velde's work is regarded as a precursor to 20th-century abstract painting. His only poster was for Tropon, a concentrated food product. In his writing he called for a new contemporary art that would integrate the best of the decorative and the applied arts of the past.

The first abstract painting is attributed to Wassily Kandinsky. He and others were working in an abstract fashion by 1911 (Figure 2-19). Such paintings, in Kandinsky's

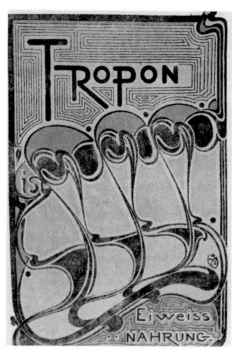

2-18
Henry van de Velde.
Tropon. 1897. Poster, 13¾ × 10⅝" (35 × 27 cm). Collection Kaiser Wilhelm Museum.

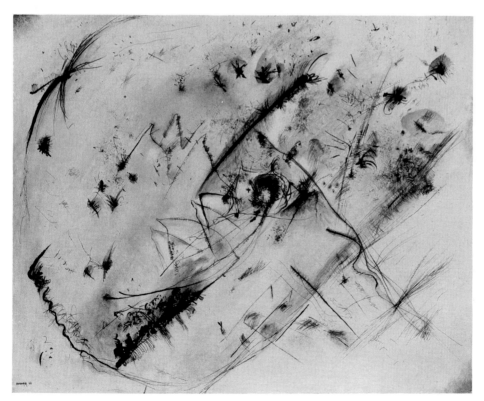

2-19
Wassily Kandinsky.
Light Picture. December 1913. Oil on canvas, 30⅝ × 39½" (77.7 × 100.3 cm). Collection, Solomon R. Guggenheim Museum, New York. Photo by Robert E. Mates.

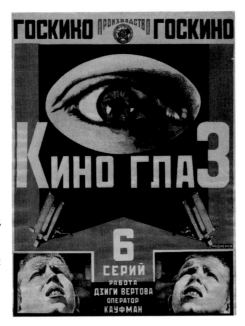

2-20
Aleksandr Rodchenko.
Kino Glaz (Film Eye). 1924. Lithograph, printed in color, 36½ × 27½" (92.5 × 70 cm). The Museum of Modern Art, New York. Gift of Jay Leyda. Photograph © 1998 The Museum of Modern Art, New York.

2-21
El Lissitzky.
USSR Russische Ausstellung (Russian Exhibition). 1929. Gravure, printed in color, 49 × 35¼" (124 × 89.5 cm). The Museum of Modern Art, New York. Gift of Philip Johnson, Jan Tschichold Collection. Photograph © 1998 The Museum of Modern Art, New York.

words, issue from "inner necessity." For Kandinsky, a painting was above all "spiritual," an attempt to render insights and awareness transcending obviously descriptive realism. Author of *On the Spiritual in Art,* he later joined the Weimar Bauhaus around 1920.

In 1913 the Russian Kazimir Malevich began painting abstract geometric compositions. Malevich formulated a theoretical basis for his paintings, which he called *suprematism.* He viewed them as the last chapter in easel painting that would point to a universal system of art headed by architecture. This architectonic approach led the way to constructivism, a movement that saw painting as a structurally driven construction, like architecture.

Constructivism began as a Soviet youth movement. The Russian Revolution of 1917 had many Russian artists combining propaganda and commerce in support of the new state enterprises and Revolutionary change. Civic-minded artists designed boxes, posters, and packaging intended to attract buyers to state products. Advertising became a means for artists, poets, and

others to advance the goals of Soviet society. Malevich, Aleksandr Rodchenko, and others were abstract painters whose goal to access the viewers' consciousness directly, adapted readily to advertising propaganda for the good of the Soviet society. The state enterprises flourished with the support of painters turned graphic designers (Figure 2-20). Rodchenko worked in a variety of mediums including filmmaking, and set and costume design for film and theater. He designed posters for several films using photocollage.

El Lissitzky is a Russian constructivist and designer who devoted a great deal of effort to propaganda work. He also developed the rules of typography and design that laid the groundwork for the development of grid systems. Designing a book of Vladimir Mayakovski's poetry, he wrote, "My pages relate to poetry in a way similar to a piano accompanying a violin. As thought and sound form a united imagination for the poet, namely poetry, so I have wanted to create a unity equivalent to poetry and typographical elements" (Figure 2-21). Lissitzky experimented with the photogram and fore-

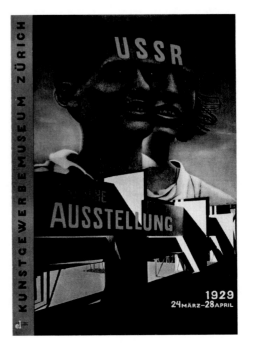

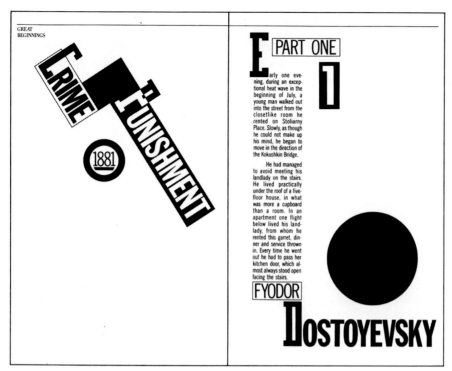

2-22
Paula Scher.
Two-page layout from
Great Beginnings. 1980.
Courtesy of the artist.

saw the importance photography would come to have in graphic design. This innovative thinking and design work spread its vision to other countries. In Germany, Lissitzky and the Bauhaus influenced advertising and packaging design. The contemporary designer Paula Scher uses the strong constructivist approach of Lissitzky's layouts to create a modern design (Figure 2-22).

Closely related to constructivism, *de Stijl* developed in Holland, where artists fled to avoid direct involvement in World War I (Figure 2-23). It flourished during the 1920s in Europe and strongly influenced the later

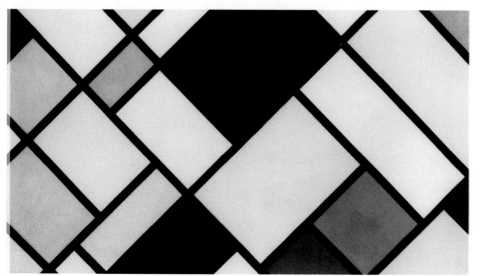

2-23
Theo van Doesburg.
Kontra-Komposition mit Dissonanzen XVI. 1925. Oil on canvas, 39½ × 71". (100 × 180 cm). Haags Gemeentemuseum, Den Haag. Copyright 1997 Artists Rights Society (ARS), New York/ Beeldrecht, Amsterdam.

Bauhaus work. De Stijl was anti-emotion and based on a utopian concept of style. At first glance, it may look similar to the Bauhaus movement described later, but de Stijl was more concerned with formal aesthetic problems than with function. The most widely known painters of the period are Piet Mondrian and Theo van Doesburg. Their style is the epitome of de Stijl, with straight black lines set at right angles to one another and a careful asymmetrical balancing of primary colors. Figure 2-24 shows an armchair by Rietveld, a leader of the movement. His design is reduced to its basic components of line, planes, and color. These de Stijl artists strongly influenced graphic design.

The School of Applied Arts and Crafts, founded by Henry van de Velde (Figure 2-18) in 1906 closed at the outbreak of war, and was reopened as the Bauhaus at Weimar in 1919. Walter Gropius, who worked with Peter Behrens at the German Werkbund, became the Bauhaus director. In 1922 the constructivist El Lissitzky met with Theo van Doesburg and Lazlo Moholy-Nagy in a congress of constructivists and dadaists in Germany. Their exchange of ideas formed a core for the Bauhaus after 1923. This German design school shaped 20th-century graphic design, product design, furniture, and architecture.

Expressionism, dada, constructivism and de Stijl influenced the Bauhaus in its early years. By the late 1920s, the Bauhaus was emphasizing functional graphic design. The Bauhaus trained artists in all areas. It attempted to bridge the gap between pure and applied art, to place equal importance on all areas of arts and crafts. It stressed

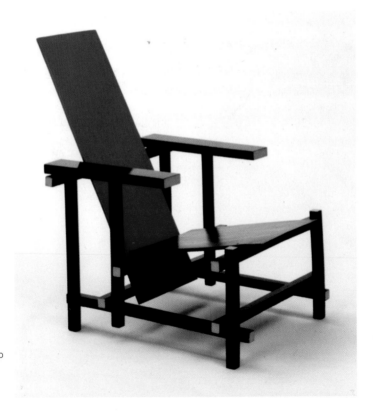

2-24
Rietveld, Gerrit.
Red and Blue Chair. (c. 1918). Wood, painted, height, 34⅛"; width, 26"; depth, 26½"
(86.5 × 66 × 83.8 cm); seat height: 13" (33 cm). The Museum of Modern Art, New York, Gift of Philip Johnson. Photograph © 2001 The Museum of Modern Art, New York.

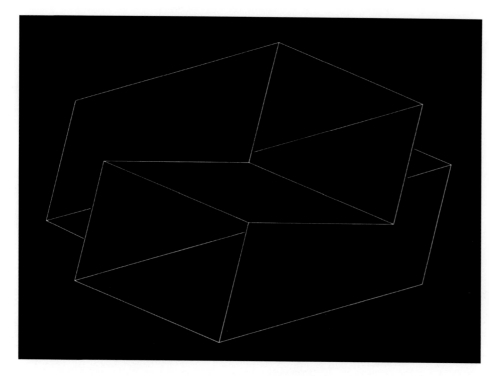

clean functional forms. The weavers, metalsmiths, and carpenters did not attempt to produce works of art, but rather good and useful designs in which form was tied to function. The industrial designer was born from this movement. Bauhaus publications featured asymmetry, a rectangular grid structure, and sans serif type.

The important contributions by artists of the Bauhaus are too numerous to mention in this brief overview. Here are a few who were influential in the development of graphic design. Josef Albers is known for his research into color and structural relationships (Figure 2-25). Anni Albers was a gifted fiber artist (Figure 2-26). Lazlo Moholy-Nagy developed photography as illustration. He saw the camera as a design tool that could be integrated with typography to create a new and better communication.

Herbert Bayer created several typeface designs, among them Futura and the

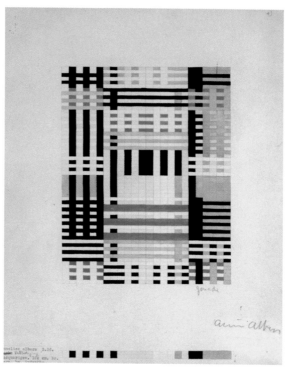

abcdefghi
jklmnopqr
stuvwxyz
a
dd

2-27
Herbert Bayer.
Studie zum
Universalalphabet. 1925.
Bauhaus-Archive.

"Universal" type (Figure 2-27). In keeping with the Bauhaus philosophy, he believed in removing personal values from the printed page, leaving it purely logical and functional in design (Figure 2-28). Bayer eliminated the capital letters from printed material and used extreme contrast of weight and size to establish a visual hierarchy. A looser design by Lyonel Feininger forms the title page for a portfolio, featuring the work of many famous Bauhaus artists (Figure 2-29).

Many of the Bauhaus artists immigrated to the United States after the Nazis forced

2-28
Herbert Bayer.
Kandinsky zum 60.
Geburstag. 1926. Offset lithograph, printed in color. 19 × 25" (48.2 × 63.5 cm). The Museum of Modern Art, New York. Gift of Mr. and Mrs. Alfred H. Barr, Jr. Photograph © 2001 The Museum of Modern Art, New York.

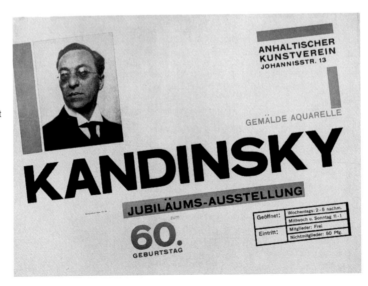

the closing of the Bauhaus in 1933. There they had a great influence on American architecture and graphic design. *The new typography* is a term used to describe Bauhaus-inspired new approaches to graphic design. Work from this period is also referred to as Swiss Design or the International Typographic Style. Jan Tschichold created typography with an emphasis on clarity. White space was used to create visual intervals in an asymmetrical layout. An underlying horizontal and vertical structure was used to unify the page. The Swiss also continued to develop the ideas of the Bauhaus in typography and layout design from the 1950s onward. Among those artists are Josef Muller-Brochmann, Emil Ruder, and Armin Hofmann. Their emphasis on visual unity and formal grid elements contributed greatly toward shaping the design field. Personal expressionism was rejected in favor of order and clarity.

FIGURATIVE MOVEMENTS

Art deco appeared as a definite style in Paris around 1925. It was especially influenced by art nouveau and also by African sculpture and cubism. Although it developed at the same time as the Bauhaus, art deco emphasized the figurative image with decorative appeal. It was applied to architecture, clothing, graphic design, advertising, packaging, crafts, and furniture. Artists associated with this movement include the Russian Erte and Georges Lepape (Figure 2-30), who contributed to *Vogue* magazine. Perhaps the best known and respected art deco artist, who exerts a strong influence today, is A. M. Cassandre. His posters and advertisements show the influence of cubism, but the forms retain a recognizable physical identity balanced with an intricate

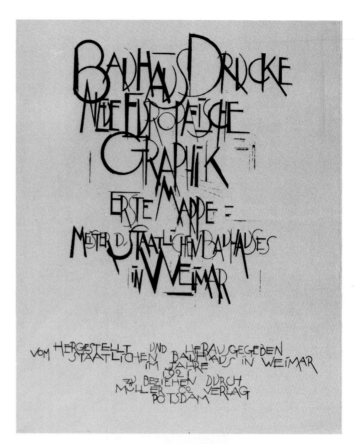

2-29
Lyonel Feininger.
Title page from *Nelle Europaeische Graphik I,* First Bauhaus Portfolio. 1921. Gift of Mrs. Henry C. Woods, Steuben Memorial Fund, Emil Eitel Fund, and Harold Joachine Purchase Fund. Collection, The Chicago Art Institute.

2-30
Georges Lepape.
Cover for *Vogue* magazine, 1930. Gouache. *Courtesy Vogue.* Copyright 1930 (renewed 1958, 1986) by the Condé Nast Publications Inc. *Photo courtesy UW-Whitewater Slide Library.*

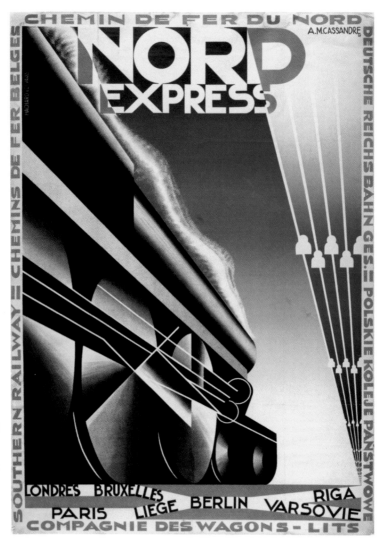

2-31
A. M. Cassandre.
Nord Express. 1927.
Lithograph, printed in color,
41 × 29½" (104.1 × 74.9
cm). The Museum of
Modern Art, New York. Gift
of French National
Railways. Photograph ©
2001 The Museum of
Modern Art, New York.

Gestalt unity (Figure 2-31). It is a very recognizable style, without the sometimes heady ideology of classical modernism. Art deco was out of favor for a time in the eyes of architects and designers because it followed none of the Bauhaus tenets of functional, nonornamental design. Now the style is often incorporated into the eclectic mix of contemporary design.

Surrealism also surfaced in the 1920s. Owing a philosophical debt to dada for its questioning attitude, it was joined by several dada artists. Andre Breton established it in 1924. He was another poet and writer start-ing a philosophical movement that would find visual expression. The surrealists drew inspiration from Freud's *Interpretation of Dreams.* Like the author James Joyce, who used stream-of-consciousness techniques rather than rational, linear development of characters, surrealists sought to reveal the subconscious.

Surrealism has exerted a strong influence on illustration. René Magritte is much imitated today, and in fact he created quite a lot of advertising illustration (Fig 2-32). Other surrealists, like Max Ernst and Man Ray, show the influence of dada in the unortho-

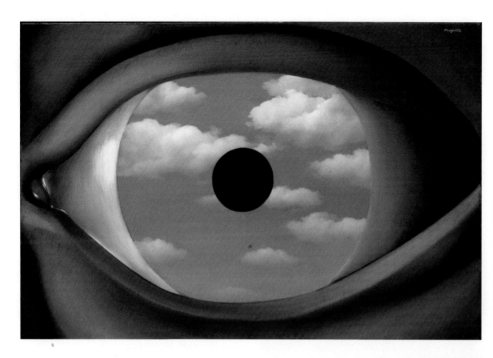

2-32
René Magritte.
The False Mirror (Le Faux Miroir). 1928. Oil on canvas. 21¼ × 31⅞". (54 × 80.9 cm). The Museum of Modern Art, New York. Purchase. Photograph © 2001 The Museum of Modern Art, New York.

dox and compelling arrangement of elements. Surrealism's search for unconscious motivation and innovative combinations continues to interest today's designer/advertiser. In the 1930s many surrealist artists were putting found objects in strange combinations that evoked poetic and unconscious associations. Figure 2-33 is an advertising photo created by a team of women designer/photographers that shows the interest of the time in surrealism. Upon close examination, we realize the attractive woman is a mannequin, although her hand is real. This forces the potential buyer to look again, a major aim of an advertisement.

AMERICAN DESIGN

Modernism greatly influenced American design. Lazlo Moholy-Nagy came to Chicago in 1937 to direct the New Bauhaus. It closed after one year, and Moholy operated his own Institute of Design from 1938 to 1946. This school offered the first complete modern design curriculum in America. The Illinois Institute of Technology is a

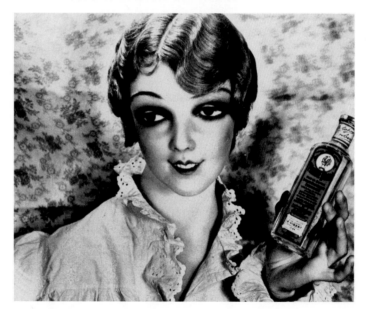

2-33
Studio Ringl & Pit (Grete Stern and Ellen Rosenberg Auerbach).
Pétrole Hahn. 1931. Gelatin silver print. 9⅜ × 11⅛" (23.8 × 28.3 cm).

descendant of the New Bauhaus. Many samples of modernist American graphics are shown throughout this text.

Lester Beall, an American-born Chicago artist, embraced modern design and European influences from cubism, constructivism, and dada. Working in New York in the

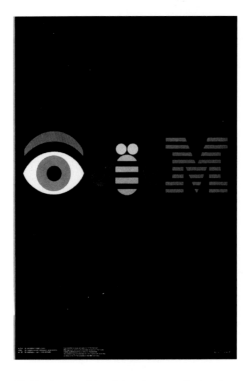

1940s, he combined drawing, symbols, photography, and mixed typefaces into a coher-
ent, eclectic design. Many young American
designers of the time drew inspiration from
European modern art and design, including
Paul Rand. Rand realized his role as a
designer involved reinventing the problem
presented by the client (Figures 2-34, 3-18,
9-4, 9-7, 9-8, and 9-10). He focused on
restating the problem, and he drew inspiration from painters such as Klee and Miró. His
books on design and his life's work are
extremely important contributions to the
field. Cipe Pineles, art director for *Seventeen,*
was one of the few women designers to gain

recognition during this period. After achieving national prominence as art director for
Glamour, British Vogue, and *Seventeen,*
Pineles became the first female member of
the New York Art Directors Club. Designers
from this period synthesized the influences of
European avant-garde and design movements to create new designs for magazines,
posters, advertisements, and corporate
communications.

By the 1950s, marketing research was an
important influence in business decisions.
Advertising designers dealt with the proliferation of national television and radio networks,
the emergence of large chain stores, and the
importance of public perception and corporate identity. The International Design
Conference in Aspen was founded in 1951 to
assess and discuss the role of design in the
commercial environment. This conference
continues to meet in Aspen every summer.

The 1950s saw the emergence of design
curriculums in universities and art schools
and the articulation of an important concept.
Leo Lionni (art director for *Fortune* magazine) stated that "Whatever . . . [the
designer's] activities, they involve, to some,
and various, extent, the shaping, interpretation and transmission of values." This issue
of values and the role of design in society is
an important current topic.

Push Pin Studios was founded in 1955 in
opposition to the spirit of Swiss design. The
founders included Seymour Chwast,
Reynold Ruffins, Ed Sorel, and Milton Glaser.
Glaser stated that, "We frequently find corruption more interesting than purity" (see
Figures 4-7 and 4-9). This studio revived art
nouveau, art deco, and narrative illustration,
turning to visual history for inspiration. This
attitude heralded postmodernism with its
historical references. Its founders continue
to contribute to the shape and direction of
design into the 21st century.

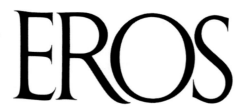

Marshall McLuhan noted the influence of television on communication and wrote about the potential for a global village united by a shared vision. McLuhan saw print media as an isolationist influence, giving rise to categorization, linear sequencing, and dogmatism. Television, according to McLuhan, has the potential to reunite society into a new global village. It certainly exerts a major influence on advertising and communication and, thus, on society. McLuhan's writings remain thought provoking today as media continues to evolve and influence our societal structures.

Magazine design was a creative area in the 1960s. In 1964 Ruth Ansel and Bea Feitler took charge of *Harper's Bazaar* as co–art directors. Drawing inspiration from pop art and underground images, *Harper's Bazaar* represented the glamour and glitter of the 1960s. Herb Lubalin, a major figure in the field, was art director for the counterculture magazines *Avant Garde* and *Eros* (Figures 2-35, 5-13, 5-17, and 5-27). Alternative publications with political and cultural commentary flourished during the 1960s.

Postmodernism

In the 1970s the term *postmodernism* was first applied to architecture, and a questioning of rational "Swiss design" led to "New Wave" or "postmodern" graphic design. Contradictory and coexistent trends make this a rich period for study. April Greiman's work is an example of New Wave design, mixing formal experiments with popular imagery (Figure 2-36). The remainder of the 20th century saw history as a shopping mall of styles. Art deco and art nouveau are among the styles that were revived and revised as decorative and figurative work regained respect.

Women had an important impact on design during this time and afterward.

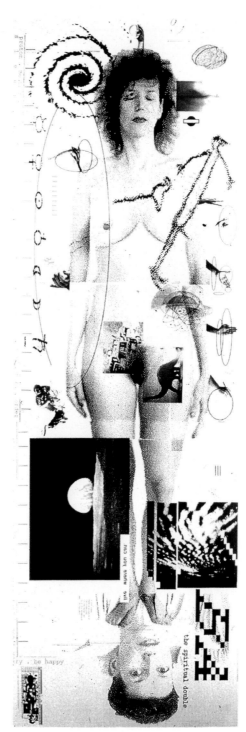

2-36
April Greiman.
Art director/designer. *Design Quarterly #133. Does It Make Sense?* Publication insert, Walker Art Center, 1986. MIT Press Publisher. *Courtesy of the artist.*

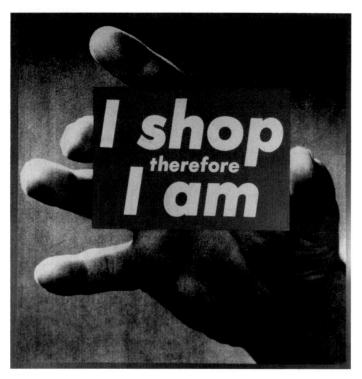

2-37
Barbara Kruger.
"Untitled" (I shop therefore I am). 1987. Photographic silkscreen/vinyl, 111 × 113" (289 × 286.8 cm).

2-38
Yokoo, Tadanori.
Japanese Society for the Rights of Authors, Composers, and Publishers. 1988. Silkscreen, printed in color, 40½ × 28⅝" (102.8 × 72.5 cm). The Museum of Modern Art, New York. Gift of the artist Photograph © 2001. The Museum of Modern Art, New York.

During the 1980s the question of "style over substance" became an important issue. Theorists such as Stuart Ewen questioned the role and impact of advertising design on society. Fine arts artist Barbara Kruger worked for a time as a layout artist and used those skills to develop an "advertising campaign" that is anti-advertising. Her mock ads and billboards used typographical devices and images to expose the persuasion/consumption cycle of commercial advertising (Figure 2-37). Figure 2-38 is also a good example of the visual complexity of Japanese postmodernism. This design combines visual motifs from a variety of cultures and periods, including Edouard Manet's painting *The Fifger,* and Michelangelo's Medici tombs.

A concern for the intellectual and historical foundations of design led to the publication of Philip Megg's *A History of Graphic Design,* a comprehensive and thoughtful

Designer and educator Katherine McCoy joined in questioning the modernist ideal of a permanent, universally valid aesthetic. She encouraged the production of visually rich and complex designs, believing there is more to design than the clear, impartial transmission of information. McCoy believes designers interpret and communicate cultural values through the forms they create.

Technology became an increasingly important issue during this time. Murial Cooper and others at Massachusetts Institute of Technology (MIT) developed the Visible Language Workshop, a multidisciplinary, multimedia program that brings together artists, designers, computer scientists, sociologists, and others to study communication in the electronic age. Electronic media could be used to explore and invent eclectic, personal art and design work.

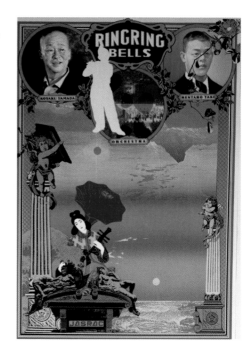

text that provides a foundation for many design history classes.

NEW TECHNOLOGIES

New technologies always influence the course of graphic design. We can trace our history and development from medieval manuscripts to Gutenberg's printing press to hot type, to cold type, to computer-generated type and image. Later chapters discuss this development in greater detail. In the opening years of the 21st century, the use of electronic technology in the United States and internationally has revolutionized design. Style and content are affected by the technology used in their creation. This chapter's brief history of design has shown that relationship, citing the invention of the printing press and of stone lithography as examples of earlier technologies that affected design and societal patterns of communication. The mid–20th century's emphasis on clarity and structural integrity is currently replaced by an interest in rich textural layers of information. Graphics are now generated with software programs that encourage stylistic complexity.

The Development of Computer Graphics

The use of computers to draw images dates back to 1953 when a simple visual display of a bouncing ball was used to calculate and show military targets. Funding for the development of computers and computer graphics in the United States originally came from the Defense Department. In 1962 at MIT Ivan Sutherland created the first interactive computer graphics display. A light pen touched to the video screen could draw a line stretched from the previous point. Although its early development was tied to defense and aerospace, computer graphics has a wide variety of applications, from engineering, medicine, and geology, to graphic design, animation, the film industry, and the Internet. (Figures 2-39, 2-40, and 2-41).

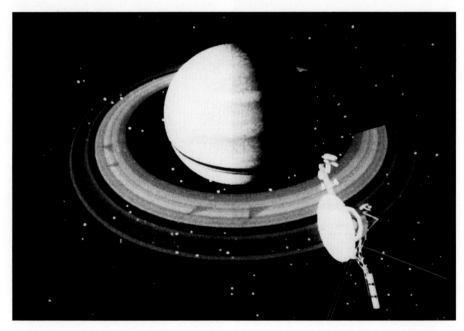

2-39
Don Davis.
Voyager 2 at Saturn Minus 3 Hours. Painting over computer-generated image. Painted for NASA and JPL.

2-40
A CAT scan cross section of the brain. Different densities appear in different colors. *Courtesy of Judson Rosebush Co.*

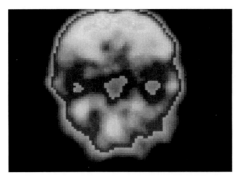

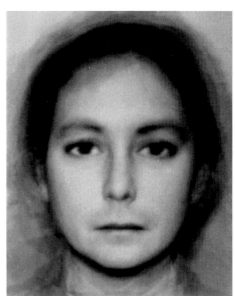

2-41
Nancy Burson with **Richard Carling** and **David Kramlich.**
Androgyny. 1982. The photograph is a composite image of twelve faces (six men and six women). *Courtesy of the artist.*

The Internet and Interactivity

Text, photography, animation, illustration, sound, and video can now be combined and linked. Figure 2-42 shows a multimedia fine art installation by artist educator Coleen Deck. Unlike books, film, or video that present linear information, the new media is truly interactive and presents nonlinear browsing opportunities.

2-42
Coleen Deck.
Search Twice, first and second diptych. 2001. This diptych installation uses Adobe After Effects to integrate image and motion. *Courtesy of the artist.*

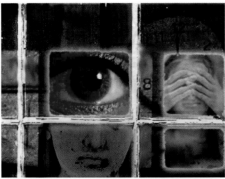

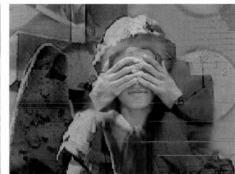

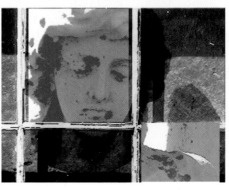

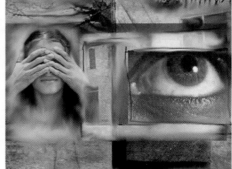

The Internet offers not only interactivity, but also freedom from the physical restraints of traditional media. CD-ROM storage, and DVD disks offer interactivity, but only the Internet travels through time and space with no physical barrier. This new media promises to transform the nature of communication as well as geographic and national boundaries.

THE FUTURE

During the 20th century we have progressed along a visual escalation from photography to film to video to computers to the World Wide Web. Computer graphics has come a long way since the Macintosh was introduced in the mid-1980s. The Internet is rapidly becoming a vehicle for marketing products and disseminating information of all kinds. Producing Web sites is a growing market for graphic designers, and the complexity of these sites is increasing rapidly. Our ability to communicate with interactive visuals and to create desktop video and 3-D animation are also developing a new market for graphic designers.

Virtual reality is another new and developing technology. It extends our senses by allowing a person to move through and interact with a computer-simulated environment by wearing special glasses and clothing or other sensors (Figure 2-43). These monitor our movements and gestures in the alternate virtual world. Psychologist R. L. Gregory stated in his book *Eye and Brain,* "The seeing of objects involves many sources of information beyond those meeting the eye when we look at an object. It involves knowledge of objects from previous experience and not only sight but touch, taste, smell, hearing, and perhaps also temperature or pain." What might be the future impact of virtual reality on design and communication?

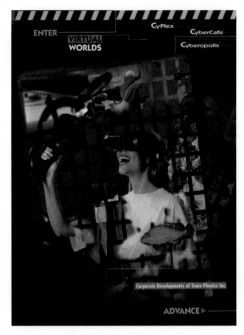

2-43
Denis A. Dale.
Marketing, copywriting, and design for a chromatic 3-D promotional folder and inserts for Transphonics, Inc. View with Chromatek 3-D glasses for VR effect. This four-color piece with two varnishes was printed from an electronic file directly to a digital press. *Courtesy of the artist.*

As we continue into the 21st century, it is interesting to remember the important developments at the turn of the last century. It will be an exciting and challenging future for designers who are intent on maintaining an emphasis on issues of values and content while learning and using a proliferation of new media.

Project

In consultation with your instructor, select and research a contemporary designer mentioned here or elsewhere in the text. Prepare a paper and classroom presentation based on your research. Describe the designer's work, philosophy, and background. Shoot slides of the work, or prepare to present visual materials in another fashion.

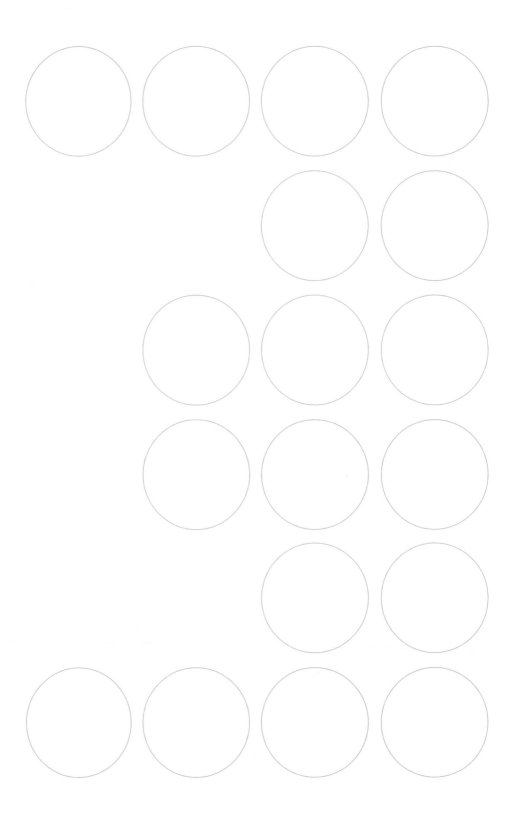

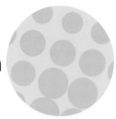

Chapter 3 ⸬ perception

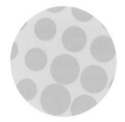

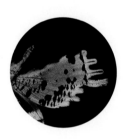

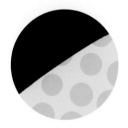

SEEING AND BELIEVING

Graphic designers do more than decorate a surface. They work with the fundamental principles of perception. When we look at a printed page, whether it is covered with type, illustrations, or a photograph, there is more than meets the eye. The brain is sifting and cataloging the images. We carry a load of experiences, innate responses, and physiological considerations that interact with those images. Designs that effectively use that process have the creative strength of sight itself on their side.

As soon as the first mark is made on a blank sheet of paper, it is altered by the eye. We cannot see only a flat mark on a flat piece of paper. Our past experience, our expectations, and the structure of the brain itself filter the information. The visual illusions created through this process are a real part of perception. *Realism in art and design is not an absolute but a convention that our culture and personal background create from visual data.*

Search for Simplicity

The Gestalt psychologists have investigated the way humans process information from a two-dimensional surface. There is an interplay of tensions among shapes on a flat surface because the appearance of any one element or shape depends on its surroundings. These elements and surroundings are interpreted by an active eye that seeks the simplest satisfactory explanation for what it sees. Any mark drawn on paper stimulates this active, interpretive response from eye and brain: We finish uncompleted shapes, group similar shapes, and see foreground and background on a flat surface. Their experiments led Gestalt psychologists to describe a basic law of visual perception: Any stimulus pattern tends to be seen as a structure as simple as conditions permit. This law is similar to the principle of parsi-

mony known to scientists, which states that when several hypotheses fit the facts, the simplest one should be accepted.

In science, elegance and success result from explaining a phenomenon with the minimum number of steps. A similar elegance can be achieved on the printed page. A great deal may be happening on a page although few marks exist. In fact, adding *more* marks without understanding their effect can often make *less* happen. That is poor design.

We discuss the manner in which the Gestalt psychologists believe our brain interprets and groups the images on a flat surface in the following chapters. It is generally recognized as a useful tool for designing visual images so they will be comprehended as we want. No single theory, however, explains all there is to visual perception. Most of what there is to know has yet to be discovered.

Interpretations

The lines in Figure 3-1 demonstrate our busy interaction with simple marks drawn on a page. These interpretations are influenced by the culture in which we live. We accept the black mark in *a* as nearer than the white field it occupies, although they both exist on the same physical plane on the surface of the page. Adding a second mark of a larger size (*b*) causes another interpretation involving depth. The larger mark seems closer in space than the smaller one. A line placed vertically that divides the space (*c*) will not disturb the two-dimensional quality. Add an angled line (*d*), and a sense of space begins to develop. With the addition of two angled lines (*e*), suddenly the eye may see the perspective of a road or railroad tracks running at an angle into the distance. The addition of size and value changes enrich our possible interpretations.

Perception, and thus communication, is always colored by interpretation. Context,

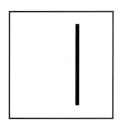
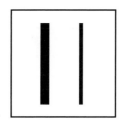
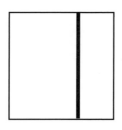
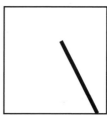
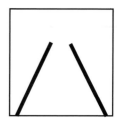

3-1a   **3-1b**   **3-1c**   **3-1d**   **3-1e**

personal experience, and culturally incul-cated systems of signs and symbols play a strong role in perception. Later chapters discuss this phenomenon from varying perspectives. *Semiotics* is the study of influ-ences on our perception. It goes beyond lin-guistics to incorporate the visual language of sign and symbol. The field of semiotics often breaks down visuals into the categories of icon, symbol, and index. The *icon* looks like the thing. A road sign with an image of a car is an icon. A road sign with a circle and slash, meaning "forbidden," is an example of a *symbol* that has a culturally accepted meaning. Words are also considered sym-bols of the thing they reference. An *index* is a visual we have learned to associate with a particular meaning. For example, a ther-mometer is an index of temperature. A foot-print can indicate a deer. The study of semi-otics crosses between the field of linguistics and the field of visual language.

FIGURE/GROUND

If we are aware of how the eye and brain organize marks on a flat surface to give them meaning, we will be much more suc-cessful in creating designs that do what we intend. The most fundamental organiza-tional principle of sight for an artist working on a flat, two-dimensional surface is figure/ground. It is sometimes called posi-tive/negative space. An ability to see and structure both areas is crucial to the designer.

Whenever we look at a mark on a page we see it as an object distinct from its back-ground. This distinction is the fundamental, first step in perception. A thing (figure) is only visible to the extent that it is seen as sepa-rate from its background (ground). This the-ory has application in every area of percep-tion. A tree, for example, can only be seen in relation to the space around it, the "not-treeness." We are able to look at the shapes and lines of a photograph and recognize a "picture" because of figure/ground grouping. Figure 3-2 shows a contemporary illustration with a dynamic figure/ground relationship

3-2
David McLimans.
Freelance illustrator, Madison, WI. An intricate play of figure/ground and repetition of shape make up this beautifully designed illustration. *Courtesy of the artist.*

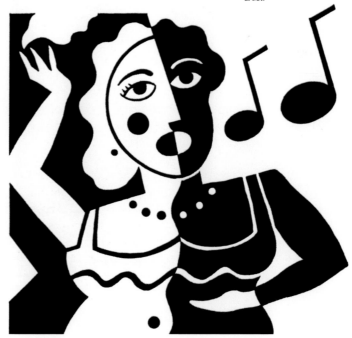

figure/ground = positive/negative space.

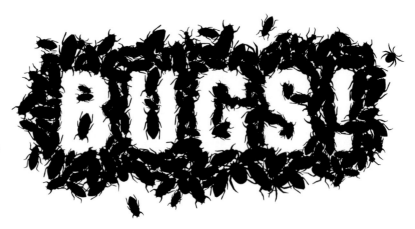

3-3

Bugs! logo created for a campaign for the Minnesota Zoo by Rapp Collins Communications. Designer **Bruce Edwards** has won numerous national awards for this design, including awards from Print, Communication Arts, and Adobe Design.

3-4

Emile Preetorius.

Licht und Schatten (Light and Shadow). 1910. Lithograph, printed in color, 11¾ × 8¾" (29.8 × 22.2 cm). The Museum of Modern Art, New York. Gift of The Lauder Foundation, Leonard and Evelyn Lauder Fund. Photograph © 1998 The Museum of Modern Art, New York.

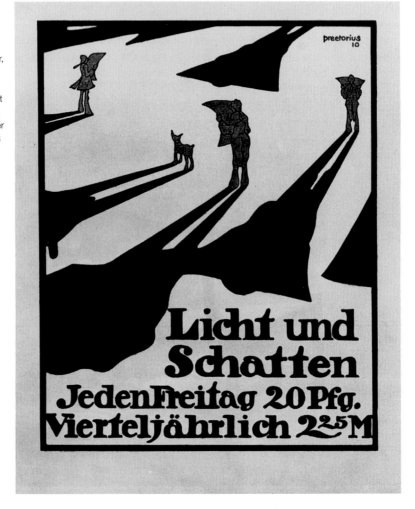

that encourages varied readings. Is the white figure in profile, or do the white and black combine into a single figure? This design is both very abstract and very figurative.

Figure 3-3 makes a playful and effective use of this grouping. We are able to recognize and read words because we organize the letters into a figure lying against a ground. We can change our focus from the insects to the white space and back again. *At its best, design becomes inseparable from communication. Form becomes content.*

Categories

Every figure seems to lie at some location in front of the ground. Designing well depends on handling both areas. Many beginning artists concentrate only on the mark they make and are not aware of the white space surrounding it. Remember, this space, or ground, is as integral a part of the page as the figure placed on it. The three main categories in figure/ground shaping are stable, reversible, and ambiguous.

Stable Figure/Ground

Each two-dimensional mark or shape is perceived in an unchanging relationship of object against background. Toulouse-Lautrec (see Figure 2-2) played deliberately with the tension of a stable figure/ground relationship on the verge of breaking down, as did the illustrator Aubrey Beardsley (see Figure 2-6). The poster by Emile Preetorius also has a great deal of compelling figure/ground tension (Figure 3-4).

Reversible Figure/Ground

Figure and ground can be focused on equally. What was initially ground becomes figure (see Figure 3-3). Because we cannot simultaneously perceive both images as figure, we keep switching. Many logo designs use reversible figure/ground, as you will discover in Chapter 5. Figure 3-5 is a personal logo by a young designer that makes good use of figure/ground.

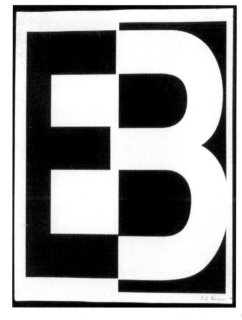

3-5
Personal logo designed by Eric Borreson.

Ambiguous Figure/Ground

In some puzzle pictures, one figure may turn out to be made up of another, or of several different pictures (Figure 3-6, 3-23).

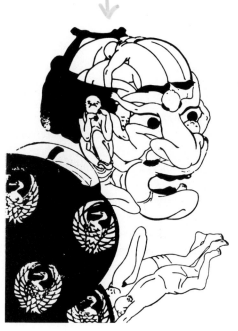

3-6
Japanese symbolic picture. Nineteenth century. An example of ambiguous figure/ground.

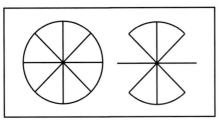

3-7a

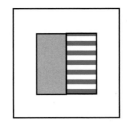

3-7b

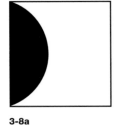

3-8a

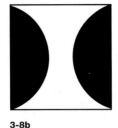

3-8b

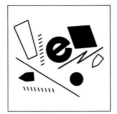

3-8c

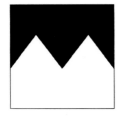

3-9

3
- Convex shapes are more easily seen as figure than concave (Figure 3-8a).

4
- Simplicity (especially symmetry) predisposes area to be seen as figure (Figure 3-8b).

5
- Familiarity causes a shape to pull out from its surroundings. As we focus on it, it becomes figure, while the surroundings become ground (Figure 3-8c).

6
- The lower half of a horizontally divided area reads as the solid figure to which gravity anchors us (Figure 3-9).

7
- There is a tendency for black to be viewed as the predominant figure more readily than white. Rotating Figure 3-9 will help demonstrate this effect.

Letterforms

How does this figure/ground phenomenon affect letterforms, the basic ingredient of the printed page? Stop now and do Exercise 1. As you do the exercise you will realize that figure/ground affects letterforms the same as any mark on the page. Using type effectively depends on seeing both the black shapes of the letters and the white shapes between, within, and around them. You must pay close attention to the shape of the ground areas, called *counters* (Figure 3-10). This has direct application in logo and layout design (Chapters 5 and 7).

Because we tend to read for verbal information and not for visual information, we are rarely aware of the appearance of the type itself. We read it, but do not "see" it, unless we are dealing with designers who deliberately treat typography as a design element to be manipulated.

For the first several chapters, we will be concerned with type as a pure design element while you learn to "see" it. Only display, or headline-size, letterforms are used. Look closely at the letter *A*'s shown in this chapter and study all the parts of their structure, paying close attention to the

Conditions

Once mastered, figure/ground grouping is an invaluable tool. It is complex and deserves study. Here are some conditions under which one area appears as figure and another as ground. Use these principles when completing the first exercise at the end of this chapter.

1
- The enclosed or surrounded area tends to be seen as figure; the surrounding, unbounded one as ground (Figure 3-7a).

2
- Visual texture makes for figure perception. The eye will be drawn to a textured area before it is drawn to a non-textured area (Figure 3-7b).

counters. Renaissance artist Albrecht Dürer constructed his own type style. His structural diagrams demonstrate the careful shaping and measurements necessary when hand-constructing letterforms (Figure 3-11). Computer software has simplified the creation of new type styles, but a discerning eye is still the most important ingredient.

SHAPE

Design is the arrangement of shapes. They underlie every drawing, painting, or graphic design. It is possible for an artist to become

3-10

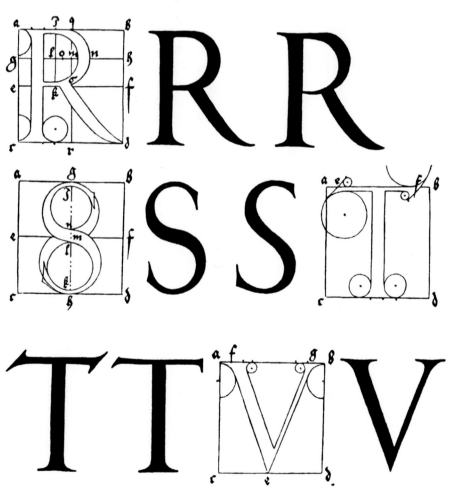

3-11
Albrecht Dürer.
On the Just Shaping of Letters. 1525

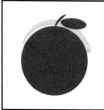

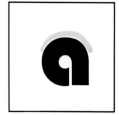

3-12
Look for similarity of shape in type and image.

dimensional work such as a ceramic piece or a sculpture. A rectangle and a circle are 2-D shapes, whereas a box and a sphere are 3-D volumes. Just as a 2-D surface can give the illustration of volume (Figure 3-13), a 3-D metal sculpture can use 2-D shape to enrich its surface design. Figure 3-14 shows a beautiful repetition of rectangles in the surface treatment and basic structure of a contemporary teapot design.

Grouping Shapes

Every visual experience is seen in the context of space and time. As every shape is affected by surrounding shapes, so it is influenced by preceding sights.

The normal sense of sight grasps shape immediately by seizing on an overall pattern. Research has demonstrated that grouping letters into words makes it possible to recall the letters more accurately than when they are presented alone. If it is possible to group marks into a recognizable or repeating shape, the eye will do so, because it is the simplest way to perceive and remember them.

Shape Versus Subject

For the graphic designer, the shape of a circle may represent the letter *O*, a diagram of a courtyard, a drawing of a wheel, or a photograph of a musical instrument. These objects are not linked by subject matter to any common theme. They are linked by shape. Through basic shape you can bring unity to a group of seemingly

enamored with the subject matter and forget about basic shapes. Develop the ability to see and think in terms of shapes even though those shapes look like apples or oranges or letterforms. Shape occurs both in figure and in ground (Figure 3-12).

Shape Versus Volume

A shape is an area created by an enclosing boundary that defines the outer edges. The boundary can be a line, a color, or a value change. *Shape* describes a two-dimensional artwork; *volume* describes a three-

3-13
This rectangle can be made to resemble a camera, but it is still made up of only two-dimensional shapes.

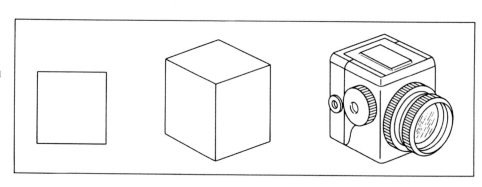

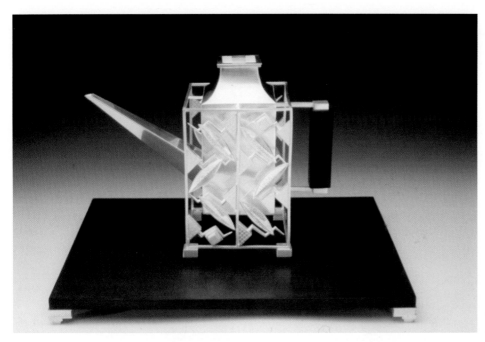

3-14
Linda Threadgill.
2000. Teapot, sterling silver. Photo credit: James Threadgill. *Courtesy of the artist.*

disparate objects. (As you will see, the designer works with so many disparate objects that to be blind to their shapes would result in utter chaos on the page.) Repeating similar shapes in different objects is an excellent way to bring visual unity to a design.

The Form of Shapes

An artist may choose to represent an object or person *realistically,* by an image similar to an unaltered photograph. Actually, reality is a little more difficult to define than that. Philosophers have been working on it for centuries. We know that visual reality is a combination of the shapes on the page and the viewer's interaction with them.

An artist/designer may also represent the subject in a purposeful *distortion* or *stylization* that can bring extra emphasis to an emotional quality, as in Figure 3-15, a beautiful example of shape finding from the 18th century.

Abstraction is another approach. It implies a simplification of existing shapes.

Details are ignored, but the subject is often still recognizable. Often the pure design shapes of the subject are emphasized, as in

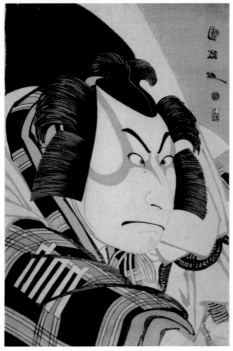

3-15
Utagawa Kunimasa.
Japanese, 1773–1810. Bust Portrayal of Nakamura Nakazo II as Matsuomaru, 1796. Color woodcut (right panel of an oban triptych), 15⅛ × 10¼" (38.5 × 26 cm). Achenbach Foundation for Graphic Arts purchase, 1970. Photo © Legion of Honor, Fine Arts Museums of San Francisco.

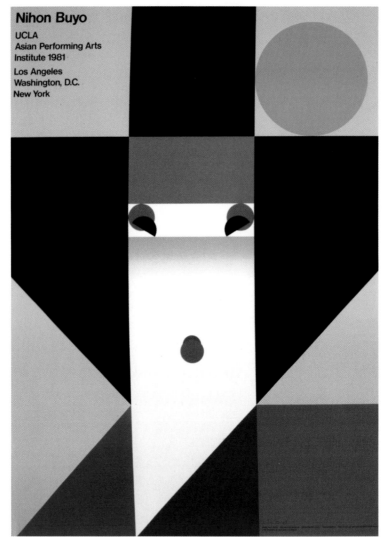

Nihon Buyo

UCLA
Asian Performing Arts
Institute 1981

Los Angeles
Washington, D.C.
New York

3-16
Ikko Tanaka.
Nihon Buyo. 1981. Offset lithograph. 40½ × 28¾" (102.2 × 73 cm). The Museum of Modern Art, New York. Gift of the College of Fine Arts, UCLA. Photograph © 2001 The Museum of Modern Art, New York.

Figure 3-16, a portrait from the late 20th century.

Purely *nonobjective* shapes are abstractions that have no recognizable realistic shapes. The constructivists worked with nonobjective shapes to give structure and character to their designs. Nonobjective shapes are the basis of the invisible, underlying structure of layout design.

Letterform Shapes

The ability to see shapes is especially important with letterforms. True, they are a symbol of something, but first and foremost they are pure shape, a fundamental design element. Successful layout and logo design depend on creating unity through the play of similarity and variety of letterform shapes.

The distinction is often made between geometric shapes and curvilinear, organic shapes. Jasper Johns utilizes a free, expressive, curvilinear line. Our eye alternates among numerals as we recognize the multiple overlap in Figure 3-17. Figure 3-18 shows the logo for ABC designed by Paul Rand, using a skillful repetition of basic shapes.

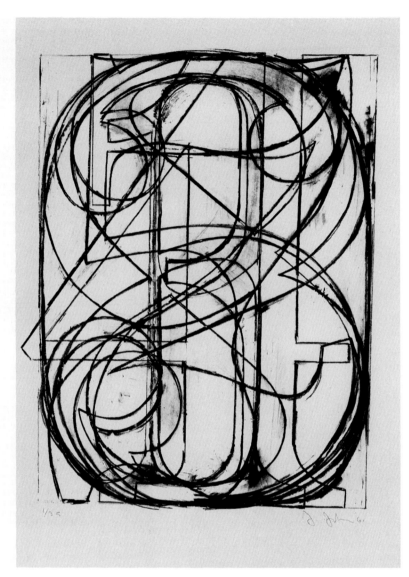

3-17
Jasper Johns.
0–9. 1960. Lithograph, printed in black, composition: 24 × 8⅞" (61 × 47.9 cm). The Museum of Modern Art, New York. Gift of Mr. and Mrs. Armand P. Bartos. Photograph © 1998 The Museum of Modern Art, New York. © 1998 Jasper Johns/Licensed by VAGA, New York, NY.

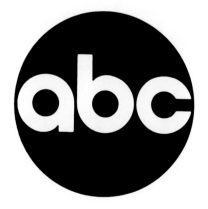

3-18
Paul Rand.
Trademark, the American Broadcasting Corporation, 1962. *Courtesy of Mrs. Marion Rand.*

(right)
3-19
Parts of a letterform.

(bottom)
3-20
These five varied but highly legible typestyles are, from top to bottom, Garamond, Baskerville, Helvetica, Stone Sans, and Rockwell.

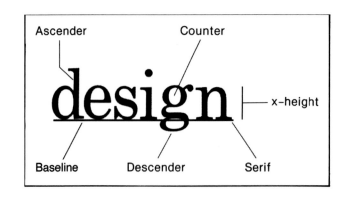

abcdefghijklmn

abcdefghijklmn

abcdefghijklmn

abcdefghijklmn

abcdefghijklmn

Type styles often have different expressive qualities depending on their shapes. Those with hard, straight edges and angular corners have a colder, more reserved feeling than typestyles with graceful curves, which have a relaxed, sensual feeling. To become sensitive to the shapes in a letterform, look carefully at its anatomy (Figure 3-19). Then learn the differences among type styles. Chapter 6 discusses the history and classification of type styles. Right now, however, concentrate on making comparisons among a few classic type styles (Figure 3-20).

Terminology

The following list of definitions will help you know what to look for when comparing shapes in letterforms.

Counter

The white shapes inside the letter. Duplicating a letterform accurately calls for close attention to both the white and the black shapes (the figure and the ground). When drawing a letterform or designing with one, think of yourself as drawing the white shapes.

Serif

The stroke that projects off the main stroke of the letter at the bottom or the top. Letters without serifs are called sans serif.

Type Size

Type size is measured by points. A 72-point type is 1 inch high, for example, as measured from the top of the ascender to the bottom of the descender.

x-Height

The height of the body of a lowercase letter like *x* or *a*. It does not include ascender or descender. The x-height will vary in typefaces even though the point size is identical. This makes different typestyles of the same point size appear larger or smaller. Type size is measured from the top of the ascender to

the bottom of the descender. Thus 10-point Garamond has a small x-height and long ascenders and descenders; 10-point Univers has a larger x-height and smaller ascenders and descenders.

The Swiss designer Adrian Frutiger developed Univers in 1954. It was the first typestyle available in many fonts, with a consistent x-height throughout (Figure 3-21).

Ascender

The part of the lowercase letter that rises above the body of the letter. The letter *a* has no ascender, but the letter *b* does.

Descender

The part of the lowercase letter that falls below the body of the letter. The letters *a b c d e* have no descenders, but the letter *g* does.

Typeface

Style of lettering. Most typefaces vary a great deal, when you develop an eye for the differences. Each family of typefaces may contain variations like *italic* and *bold* in addition to regular, or *roman*.

Font

A font is a specific size and variation on a typeface. (Bold Baskerville is a different font from Italic Baskerville, for example.)

Baseline

The line that the typography sits on is called a baseline.

Stress

The distribution of weight through the thinnest part of a letterform. It can be easily seen by drawing a line through the thinnest part of an *o* and observing the slant of the line (Figure 3-22).

Using this terminology, look at each style and ask yourself the following questions:

How much variation is there between thick and thin strokes?

Which style has a short x-height?

Which style has a tall x-height?

abcde fgkl*hij* **mnopq** **stuvw** *xyz*

3-21
Univers has a consistent x-height in all its font variations.

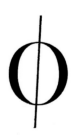

3-22

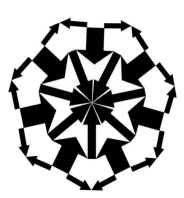

3-23a Eric Weubben

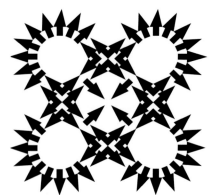

3-23b Melissa Wirth

3-23c Nicole Allen

3-23

Student solutions to Exercise 1.

Which has the longest ascenders and descenders?

What are the differences in the serifs?

Which type has the most vertical stress?

What are the similarities among letters that belong to one style?

Exercises

1. **a.** Group several copies of an arrow to form an interesting and symmetrical pattern. Stress the creation of shapes in figure and in ground (Figure 3-23).

   b. Place the letter *H* inside a rectangular format. Use a Helvetica type style (see Figure 3-24). Place the letter and its values so the *H* becomes ground instead of figure. Familiarity makes this exercise difficult.

   c. Choose one of the type styles shown in this chapter. Repeat a letterform in a symmetrical pattern.

What do you see as figure? Why? Can you change the figure into ground? Figure 3.25.

2. The letter *A* has been shown to you in five different typefaces (Figure 3-20). To help you recognize the shapes of different faces and learn to handle your tools, trace each of these letters and transfer them to drawing paper or illustration board. Reproduce them in ink or pencil so they are "letter perfect." Hand skills continue to be valuable to the graphic designer in the planning, conceptual, and sketching stages. When you have finished and your work has been critiqued, you will be ready to proceed with the first main project. You may choose to work with pencil and

3-24

(far right)
3-25
Lindsay Riesop

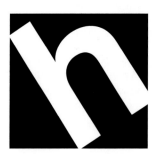

ink throughout this next assignment or to finish executing your design sketches on the computer in a vector graphics program.

Project

1. Figure/Ground and Letterforms

Applying figure/ground to letterform shapes is the best way to really see typography. Choose two letterforms from the type styles shown in this chapter. If they are your initials, you might choose to use this design for a business card and letterhead later. Create a design that uses one letter as the figure and another as the ground. This relationship can be stable, reversible, or ambiguous as long as it remains possible to read both letterforms. Remember the importance of thumbnails. Explore a minimum of 15 possibilities.

Fit your design within an 8 × 10" (20 × 25 cm) format. Keep your letters "true to form" and "letter perfect." Use solid black or white shapes without outlining, crosshatching, or screening. You can (1) extend the edge of a shape, (2) overlap a form, or (3) hide an edge by placing a black letter against a black background or white against white. Do not, however, distort their basic shapes. Bring out the beauty, variety, and personality of those shapes. Figures 3-26 (a), (b), (c) are student designs based on this project. Once this problem is solved successfully, do your own experiments with figure/ground and letterforms.

Objectives

Learn to see the shapes in typography and to begin to recognize fonts.
Use thumbnails to explore and evaluate alternative solutions.
Experiment with creating figure/ground relationships.
Learn to manipulate tools and software.

3-26
Student solutions to Exercise 1.

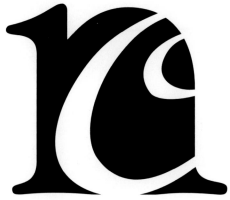

3-26a Christy Niewolny

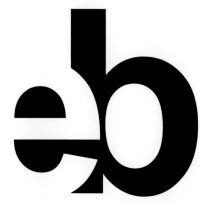

3-26b Erin Bartelson

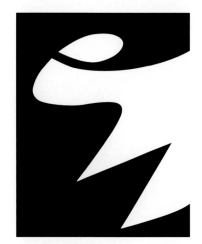

3-26c Eric Weubben

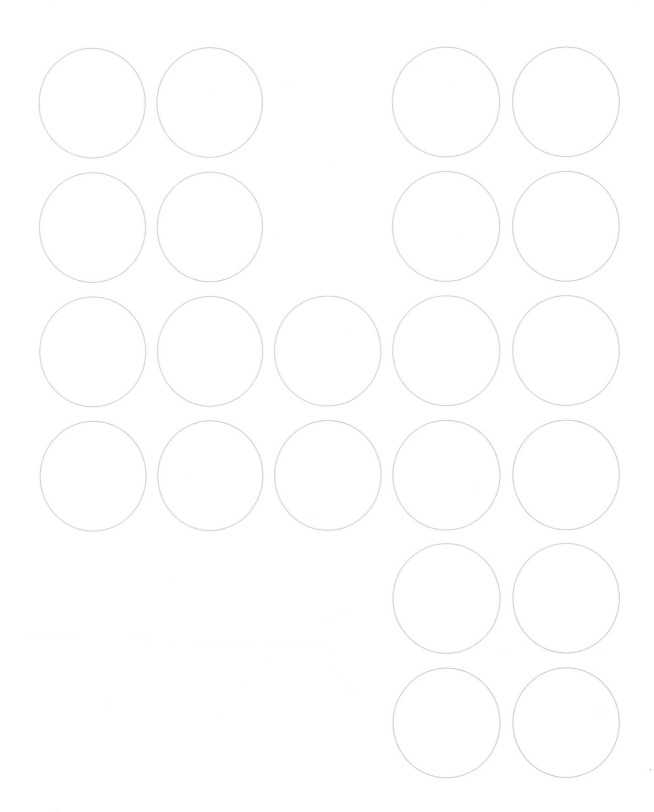

Chapter 4 ⦂⦂⦂ toward a dynamic balance

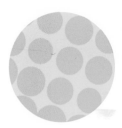

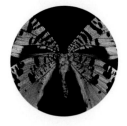

VISUAL AND INTELLECTUAL UNITY

Two kinds of unified communication occur in graphic design. Intellectual unity is idea generated and word dominated. The mind, not the eye, makes the grouping. Visual unity, in contrast, is created by placement of design elements visible to the eye.

The poster in Figure 4-1 by the famous early-20th-century designer A. M. Cassandre is unified both intellectually and visually. It is a poster for an optician, so it is intellectually unified by the slogan, the emphasis on the eyeglasses, and the bright, clear area of vision through which the eyes peer at us. It is visually unified through a complex series of events as the small type "frames the eyes" and leads our eye down and into the O of

4-1
A. M. Cassandre.
Poster for an optician.

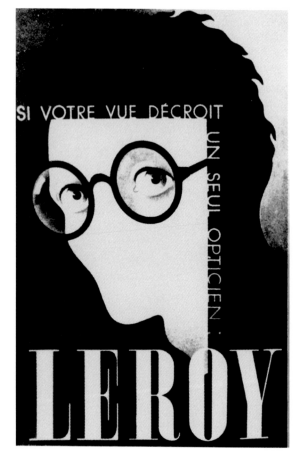

"Leroy." The size of this small type echoes the serif on the larger word. The verticality of the typography in "Leroy" is echoed by the bright rectangle surrounding the face.

Imagine that a designer and a writer are hanging a gallery show of a photojournalist's work. The designer is hanging photographs together that have similar value and shapes. The writer is following behind, rehanging the photos together according to subject matter: a picture of a burning building next to one of firefighters. One is *thinking* of subject matter (intellectual unity); the other is *looking* at design (visual unity).

As a design student, you are learning to see the visual unity in a composition and to create with an eye for it. Few people have this skill. Study the form of your design. Once you have mastered the visual "language," you will be able to use it to strengthen both visual and intellectual communication. Both are important and should work together.

Design as Abstraction

Abstract art drew attention to pure visual design. It was "about" color, value, shape, texture, and direction, although often incorporating recognizable imagery. In a purely nonobjective painting by Piet Mondrian (Figure 4-2), we are intrigued by the breakup of space and the distribution of value and color. There is no "picture" to distract us from the visual information. Theo van Doesburg, Mondrian, and the de Stijl movement had a tremendous influence on graphic design as layout artists began arranging their shapes and blocks of type into asymmetrically balanced compositions.

A good graphic artist must be a good abstract artist, using both pictorial and nonobjective elements. Figure 4-3 shows an International Style layout by Swiss designer J. Müller-Brockmann that demonstrates a strong eye for pure design shapes reminiscent of Mondrian's surface divisions and strong horizontal/vertical orientation.

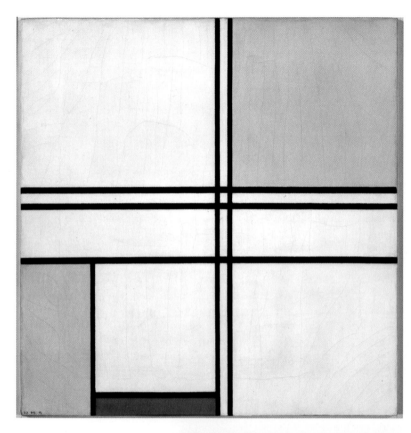

4-2
Piet Mondrian.
Composition Gray-Red.
1935. Oil on canvas,
57.5×55.6 cm. Gift of
Mrs. Gilbert W. Chapman,
1949. 518. ©1987 the Art
Institute of Chicago. All
rights reserved.

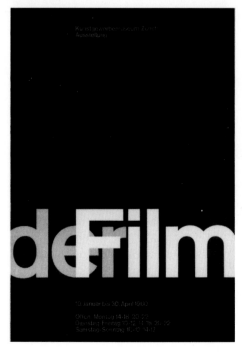

4-3
J. Müller-Brockmann.
Poster for
Kunstgewerbemuseum,
Zurich. 1960.

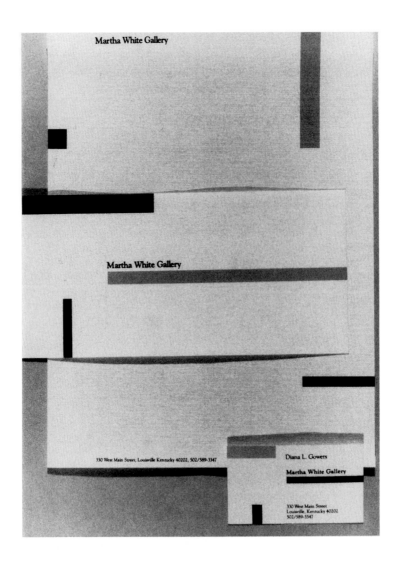

4-4
Julius Friedman.
Art director, designer.
Images design firm.
Louisville, KY.

Figure 4-4 by contemporary Louisville designer Julius Friedman shows a de Stijl influence on letterhead design.

Graphic design is essentially an abstract art that combines a greatly varied array of elements into a formal 2-D structure. A work should be balanced and visually compelling in its own right as well as supportive of an idea. *Design is a visual language.* The 20th-century movements in art and design contributed greatly to our current understanding of that language. The fields of Gestalt psychology and semiotics have also helped us understand how meaning is formed.

Working Together

In a design firm, the visual design of a project is given full consideration. Copywriters, however, often dominate the ad agency. Many other places that employ designers also have word people in key positions. These people tend to be sensitive primarily to words and ideas (intellectual unity). They are not trained in visual communication. For this angle they will rely on you. Together you can assure, as the Bauhaus would say, that the *form* of a design matches its *function.*

Constructivist El Lissitzky said, "The words on the printed page are meant to be looked at, not listened to." How do we *look* at designs, and how do we *create* visually unified ones? The answer has a great deal to do with balance.

VISUAL DYNAMICS

A ladder leaning precariously against a wall will make us tense with a sense of impending collapse. A diver poised at the top of the high dive fills us with suspense. We are not passive viewers. We project our experience into all that we see, including the printed page.

How do we project our physical experience into that flat rectangular surface? Kinesthetic projection (sensory experience stimulated by bodily movements and tensions) is operating, whether we deal with pictures of people or the abstract shapes of type design. Figure 4-5 by Don Egensteiner demonstrates the attraction of gravity on

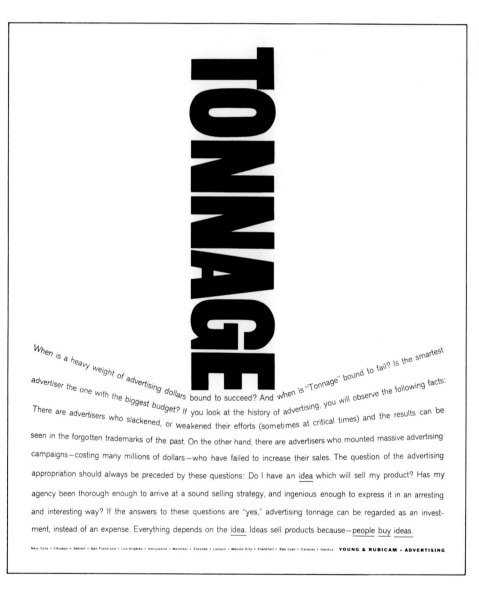

4-5
Don Egensteiner.
(Young & Rubicam, Inc.)
Ad in *Fortune* magazine.
1960.

When is a heavy weight of advertising dollars bound to succeed? And when is "Tonnage" bound to fail? Is the smartest advertiser the one with the biggest budget? If you look at the history of advertising, you will observe the following facts: There are advertisers who slackened, or weakened their efforts (sometimes at critical times) and the results can be seen in the forgotten trademarks of the past. On the other hand, there are advertisers who mounted massive advertising campaigns—costing many millions of dollars—who have failed to increase their sales. The question of the advertising appropriation should always be preceded by these questions: Do I have an idea which will sell my product? Has my agency been thorough enough to arrive at a sound selling strategy, and ingenious enough to express it in an arresting and interesting way? If the answers to these questions are "yes," advertising tonnage can be regarded as an investment, instead of an expense. Everything depends on the idea. Ideas sell products because—people buy ideas.

New York • Chicago • Detroit • San Francisco • Los Angeles • Hollywood • Montreal • Toronto • London • Mexico City • Frankfurt • San Juan • Caracas • Geneva YOUNG & RUBICAM • ADVERTISING

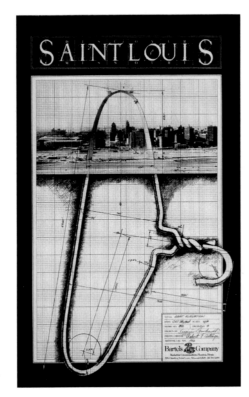

4-6
Self-Promotional Ad.
Bartels and Company, St.
Louis, MO.

organizes the space around the mark. *This dynamic tension is not contained in the paper itself, nor in the graphite, ink, or computers we use. It is created by our interaction with the image.*

Top to Bottom

We are uncomfortable with shapes clustered at the top of a page with open space beneath them. We have observed in the world around us that many more things are at rest on the ground than in the sky. There is a sense of suspense as we wait for the fall if they are not "standing" on anything. We experience a design as "top heavy" much more quickly than as "bottom heavy."

Milton Glaser is a contemporary designer, illustrator, and one of the founders of Push Pin Studios. He has been a major force in graphic design for over 45 years. He deliberately plays with this top-to-bottom tension in his double portrait of dancer Nijinsky (Figure 4-7). All that anchors the dancing gravity-defying feet is the line of the baseboard under the left foot and the vertical line at the corner.

Type designers have long believed in the importance of putting extra weight at the bottom of a letterform to make it look firm and stable. The *8* and *3* in Figure 4-8 look top heavy when viewed upside down, as here. Book designers customarily leave more space at the bottom than at the top of a page. They understand that a sense of balance cannot be achieved by placing identical margins at the top and bottom of a composition. This is the same principle used when matting artwork. The bottom measurement is slightly greater than the top, allowing for an optical center that is slightly different than the mathematical center.

Vertical and Horizontal

We find horizontal and vertical lines stable, probably because they remind us of our vertical bodies on the horizontal earth. Milton

type. Our culture reads a page from top to bottom, a movement that matches our experience with gravity. It is harder for us to read a design of words or images that asks the eye to go from bottom to top.

We project emotional as well as physical experience onto the page. An illustration of a man stabbed causes discomfort due to such projection. Visual form stirs up memories and expectations. That is why visual perception is so dynamic.

Loose strokes that allow the process of construction to show through also arouse this dynamic tension. The visible brush stroke or "mark of the maker" pulls viewers into the process of creation. Many interesting and appealing printed pieces are created by allowing the tension of the creative process to show through as in this delightful pun (Figure 4-6).

As you saw in Chapter 3, any mark made on a sheet of paper upsets the surface and

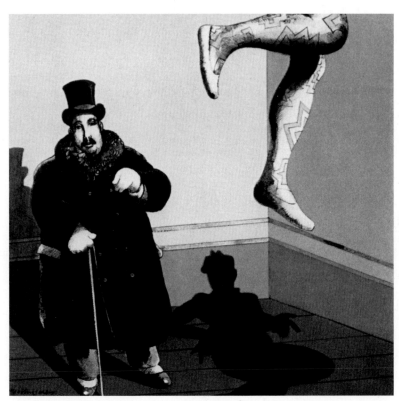

4-7
Milton Glaser.
*Portrait of Nijinsky &
Diaghilev* designed and
illustrated for *Audience*
magazine. *Courtesy of the
artist.*

Glaser again deliberately violates this sense
of stability in Figure 4-9. As he comments,
"The diagonal of this figure gives the illustration its surreal perversity."

We find diagonal lines dynamic because
they seem in a state of flux, poised for
movement toward the more stable horizontal or vertical. The de Stijl artist Theo van
Doesburg deviated from Mondrian's horizontal and vertical compositions, stating that
the modern human spirit felt a need to
express a sharp contrast to those right
angles found in architecture and landscape.
An oblique angle is one of the quickest,
most effective means of showing tension.
This tension can be created by placing a
single shape at an oblique angle or by placing the entire composition at an angle. Part
of the delight in Figure 4-9 is the unusual
and unanticipated angled figure. This kind
of design solution can surprise and interest
the viewer.

Left to Right

In Western cultures we read from the left to
the right side of the page, and this experience may influence the way we look for balance between those two sides of a design.
The left side is the more important, emphasized by the fact that our attention goes
there first. Pictorial movement from the left
toward the right seems to require less effort
than movement in the opposite direction. An
animal speeding from the right to the left, for
example, seems to be overcoming more

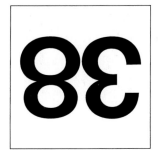

4-8
Type turned upside down
looks top heavy.

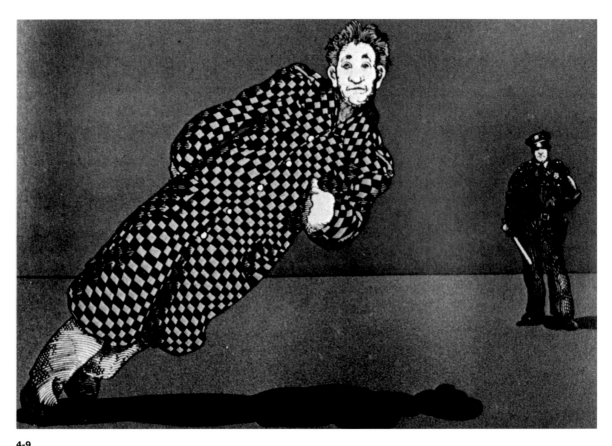

4-9
Milton Glaser.
A drawing created to illustrate a story in *Audience* magazine about a man with a crooked head. *Courtesy of the artist.*

resistance than one shown moving from left to right. You can explore this left-to-right balance by holding your designs up to a mirror. They may now appear unbalanced.

Overall

Every two-dimensional shape, line, figure/ground relationship, value, color, and so on, possesses visual dynamics. We have seen the dynamic value of a kinesthetic reaction, or empathy with the image. There is more to the dynamic of perception, however. We have all seen images of a supposedly moving figure that appears in awkward, static immobility. The objects of dancer or automobile can lead us to expect movement, but only skillful control of visual language can evoke it. Successful communication requires balance, the directing and conducting of visual tensions.

BALANCE

Every healthy person has a sense of balance. It allows us to remain upright and walk, run, or ride a bicycle. Our eye is pleased with a balanced composition, just as we are pleased with our ability to ride a bicycle and not wobble (Figure 4-10). Lack of balance in a design will irritate viewers and impair the communication. In isomorphic terms, we identify our physical structure with the physical layout/structure of the page and can feel in danger of "falling off the bicycle." How do we create a unified, "ridable," and well-balanced design?

When the dynamic tension between elements is balanced, we are most likely to communicate our intended message. Otherwise, the eye is confused. It shifts from element to element, wanting to move things so they sit

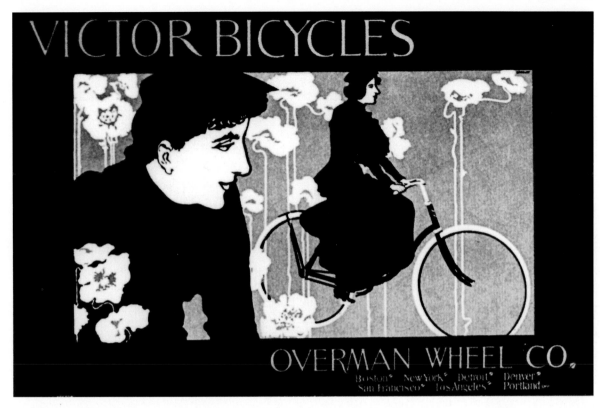

4-10
Will Bradley.
Poster for Victor Bicycles.
1899. *Courtesy of the
UW–Whitewater Slide
Library.*

right on the page, as we want to straighten a picture hanging crooked on a wall. The viewer so bothered will pay less attention to the quality or content of the picture.

Balance is achieved by two forces of equal strength that pull in opposite directions or by multiple forces pulling in different directions whose strengths offset one another. Think of visual balance as a multiple rope pull where, for the moment, all teams are exerting the same strength on the rope. It is not a state of rest, but a state of equal tension (Figure 4-11).

If the simplest and quietest form of balance were always desirable, we would see dull art. However, too much predictability and unity disturbs us just as too much chaos. We are animals of change and tension. We strive for growth and life. A simple decrease in visual tension resulting in a quiet balance will not satisfy us for long. An

interplay between tension-heightening and tension-reducing visual devices seems to satisfy us and match our kinesthetic and emotional experience. *We yearn for diversity as well as unity*.

Symmetry

The two basic types of balance are symmetry and asymmetry. In symmetrical balance, identical shapes are repeated from left to right in mirrored positions on either side of a

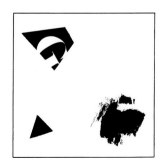

4-11
Elements in balance.

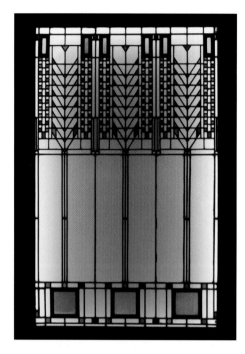

4-12
Tree of Life Window, 1904
by Frank Lloyd Wright.
Photo © Legion of Honor,
Fine Arts Museums of San
Francisco.

central vertical axis. Figure 4-12 is a symmetrical stained glass window design by architect Frank Lloyd Wright. Figure 4-13 is a symmetrical logo design. Some symmetrical designs also repeat from top to bottom, often in a radial pattern. Symmetrical balance dominated painting and architecture until the Renaissance. It dominated graphic design throughout the first centuries of the printing trade, when type was carefully set in centered, formally ordered pages. The traditional book form is a classic example of symmetry (Figure 4-14).

Symmetrical design with its quiet sense of order is useful whenever stability and a sense of tradition are important. It uses contrasts of value, texture, and shape to relieve boredom and introduce variety. Figure 4-15 by pop artist Andy Warhol deliberately introduces boredom through repetition of shape and placement. In doing so he also examines the nature and blurs the boundaries between fine art and applied design.

There are various ways to achieve symmetry. The most common has a similarity of form on either side of a central dividing line. Symmetrical balance can happen even when images are not precisely identical on either side of this axis. Some differences may occur in shape, color, or value. The important consideration is whether the overall balance of shape, value, and color remains primarily symmetrical. That symmetry may be vertical, horizontal, radial (the elements radiate from a central point), or overall.

Asymmetry

Asymmetrical design has a greater sense of movement and change, of possible instability and relative weights. It is like taking your bicycle through an obstacle course. It is a contemporary balance that reflects the changing times. Symmetrical design has a logical certainty that is lacking in asymmetrical design. In symmetrical design a 2" (5 cm) square in the upper left dictates another such square in the upper right. In asymmetrical design that square could be balanced by a vast number of shapes, values, colors, or textures. The effects can be difficult, challenging, and visually exciting.

Asymmetrical designs are balanced through contrast to achieve equal visual weight among elements. To be effective, contrast must be definitive. Shapes that are almost but not definitely different are irritating to the eye. Figure 4-16 is an asymmetrical design that uses several forms of contrast in both figures and letterforms to achieve a balanced, intriguing design.

4-13
Margo Chase.
Logo design for a
recording company.
Courtesy of the artist.

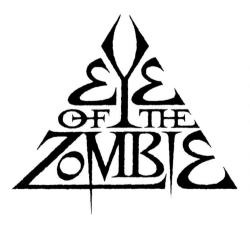

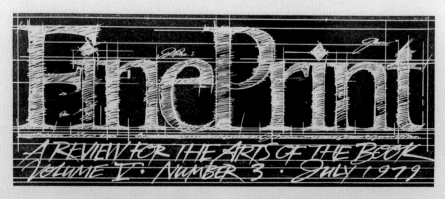

The Five Books of J.G. Lubbock

BY COLIN FRANKLIN

Mr. J.G. Lubbock, book artist, printmaker and author, lives in an obscure corner of Suffolk well protected by a confusing maze of lanes; thus there need be no fear of mass intrusion if I suggest that to know his books one should visit him. Since 1966 his surprising productions have grown among us, bearing his varied and splendid prints and his own struggling cosmic prose printed with the Cambridge taste of Will and Sebastian Carter of The Rampant Lions Press, and nobody has known quite what to make of it all. "Prints are okay," people say, "so long as you don't have to read the books." The sea comes into his writing, and he lives near an estuary. Thinking of another member of his family, Basil Lubbock, whose book *The Last of the Wind-jammers* I desired as a boy, I had imagined a blustery beard-ed sailor, talented as seamen often are with their hobbies but greatly out of depth in prose. Mostly it was rather high-flying stuff, like this from his first book:

> The process of production of the work of art is of more inter-est than the results even to the spectator, because the work must always, by virtue of the artist's imperfection as a transmitter, be inferior to the transcendent reality sensed by him.

He seemed to range rather casually over the universe, tak-ing in science or the sea as a car needs to pause at the garage. Was it all rather peculiar and pretentious?

It was not. Mr. Lubbock looks a little like portraits of James Joyce, and keeps the Cambridge diffidence of his youth. Few men preserve themselves without worldly corruption through a full span of professional life and re-turn to complete their proper artistic purpose, but he ap-pears to be achieving just that. "Art in books" had appealed to him since undergraduate years at Trinity, where varied Books of Hours and the Trinity College Apocalypse had

provided an enduring wish. As an engineer and living at the edge of London, there had simply been no time for all that; the vanity and indulgence of art waited, and at his retirement burst with energy upon a sudden summer.

He works in mixed method – etching, aquatint, engrav-ing – but always with color and using one plate only. In his studio by the sloping field he was coloring a large chrome-surfaced plate which went through the etching press as he heaved spokes of the old wheel like a sailor at his helm. And out came one of the astonishing religious land-scapes, everything looking easy apart from the effort. Hand-coloring of sky and forest background occupied less than two minutes. Later, the laying of a resin-dust ground for aquatint looked simple, the brushing of acid-resist any-one's job. But the vision and energy of these prints. . . . (See illustrations, page 89.)

It has all happened fast for J.G. Lubbock, at an unusual phase of life. Raymond Lister in his book on *British Ro-mantic Art* wrote that "the fuller development and com-plete synthesis of the aesthetic possibilities of form in Na-ture have, even now, only just begun to be realized, in the work of artists like Graham Sutherland, Paul Nash, and Ivon Hitchens; but most of all in such works as some little known, but extremely beautiful engravings by J.G. Lub-bock, and Morris Cox." The link with Morris Cox and the Gogmagog Press, with comparable and complex examples of color printing, is apt, of course, and I find it entirely sympathetic, though deep differences suggest themselves if one thinks of the two together. Morris Cox has spent his life as an artist, humbly and with a single mind; Lubbock's religious art has survived a conventional career in one of the professions, showing its strength in release. The Gog-magog Press of Morris Cox makes everything, prints, binds, adapts to a table-press and by laborious improvisa-tion produces "form in Nature," as Mr. Lister phrases it.

4-14
Scott Walker and **Tim Girvin.** Page design for Fine Print. 1979.

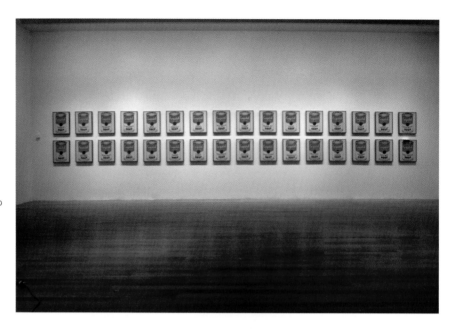

4-15
Andy Warhol.
Campbell's Soup Cans.
1962. Synthetic polymer
paint on canvas, thirty-two
works, each 20 × 16"
(50.8 × 40.6 cm). The
Museum of Modern Art,
New York. Purchase and
partial gift of Irving Blum.
Photograph © 2001 The
Museum of Modern Art,
New York.

4-16
Michael David Brown.
Death in the Afternoon
from *Creativity Illustrated.*
1983. An example of
asymmetrical balance.

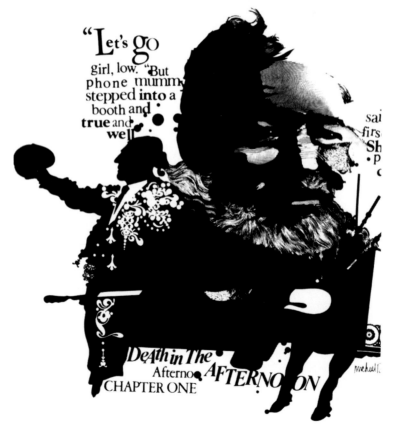

Balance Through Contrast

Symmetry achieves balance through likeness; asymmetry achieves balance through contrast. The easiest way to achieve visual unity would be to make one shape into an overall symmetrical pattern on the page. A full book page with nothing on it but a solid block of type is visually unified, no matter what the words say. It is also visually dull. In the case of novels, this visual dullness is deliberate. The reader is directed to the content of the words without distraction. In most publications and advertising design, however, this unity must be tempered with contrast if it is to attract and hold the viewer. The designer is usually working with many different elements. Most successful designs rely on a carefully juggled balance of similarities and contrasts.

There are two considerations in setting up balance through contrast: weight and direction. *Weight* is the strength or dominance of the visual object. *Direction* is the way the eye is drawn between elements over the flat surface. Balance is determined by the natural weight of an element and by the directional forces in the composition. Weight and direction are influenced by several forces listed below.

Location

The center of a composition will support more weight than the edges. Although a shape is most stable when in the center, it also is visually "light." Small shapes at the edges of a composition can balance large ones in the middle (Figure 4-17a).

Spatial Depth

Vistas that lead the eye into the page have great visual strength. We project ourselves into the spatial illusion, so it seems to have greater presence of size (Figure 4-17b).

Size

Visual weight also depends on size (Figure 4-17c)—the larger the heavier. Size is the most basic and often used form of contrast in graphic design. The contrast between large and small should be sharp and definite without overpowering the smaller elements so they cannot contribute their share. Most successful designs benefit greatly from size contrast in type or in image. In layout design the contrast is often between large and small photographs and between headline

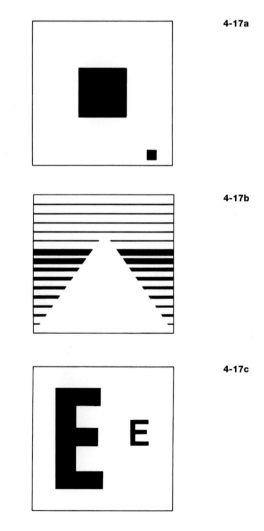

4-17a

4-17b

4-17c

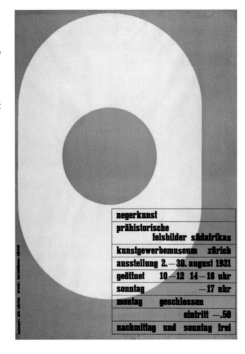

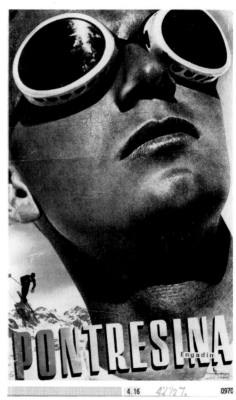

and text type as in this 1931 poster design by Max Bill (Figure 4-18).

An interesting sort of size contrast is contrast in expected size. The large element is played small and vice versa, resulting in a visual double take, as in this 1935 poster depicting skiing and ski goggles (Figure 4-19).

Texture

A small, highly textured area will contrast with and balance a larger area of simple texture (Figure 4-20a). This rule refers to visual, not tactile texture. Contrast of texture is especially useful with text type (type smaller than 14 point, used to set the body of copy).

Isolation

A shape that appears isolated from its surroundings will draw attention to itself more quickly and have greater visual weight than one surrounded by other shapes (Figure 4-20b).

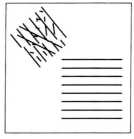

4-20a

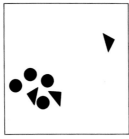

4-20b

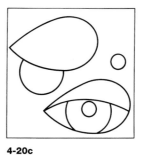

4-20c

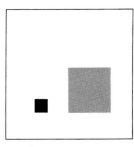

4-20d

Subject Matter

The natural interest of a subject matter will draw the viewer's eye and increase visual weight. It also can create directional movement as we move our eyes between lovers or follow the eye direction of a figure. Our eyes are drawn to the realistic representation of something that interests us (Figure 4-20c). The design in Figure 4-21 is an important American designer from the last half of the 20th century, Herb Lubalin. The subject is playfully suggested with placement.

Value

Areas of high contrast have strong visual weight. A small area of deep black will contrast with and balance a larger area of gray when both are placed against a white background (Figure 4-20d). The creation of light and dark areas in a drawing, painting, photograph, or illustration produces a dramatic play of values that delights the eye. Alexey Brodovitch designed these pages for a visual arts magazine in the 1950s (Figure 4-22). The high contrast of texture, size,

MARЯIAGE

4-21
Herb Lubalin.
1965. Photo © Herb Lubalin Design Center, Cooper Union, NY

and cropping of images create an extremely well-balanced and very dynamic layout.

Typography also uses value contrast. The contrast of a black, heavy type against a light one helps relieve boredom and makes the page more readable. Contrasts between headings and text matter and the white areas of paper can create three distinct weights: the black bar of the heading is played against the gray, textured rectangle of the text type, both of which contrast with the white areas of the background page. Designers will sometimes alternate boldface and regular weight type for a visual pattern.

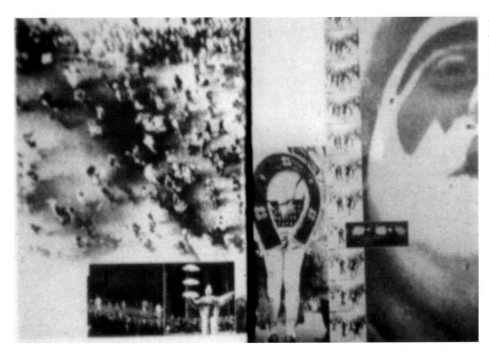

4-22
Alexey Brodovitch.
Pages from Portfolio, 1951. *Photo courtesy of the Whitewater slide library.*

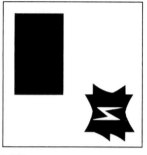

4-23a

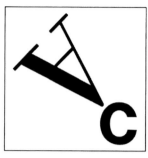

4-23b

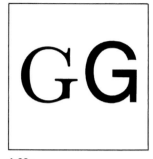

4-23c

Shape

The shape of objects generates a directional pull along the main structural lines. Complicated contours also have a greater visual weight than simple ones. Therefore a small complex shape will contrast with and balance a larger simple shape (Figure 4-23a). One block of type might be set in a long, thin ragged rectangle while another is set in a large, square block form. Contrast in shape also works with single letterforms. You might play the round openness of an *O* against the pointed complexities of a *W* or the shape of an uppercase *A* against a lowercase *c* (Figure 4-23b).

Structure

In type design, structure refers to the contrasting characteristics of type families. It is a kind of contrast of shape. Compare the *G* in Helvetica with the *G* in Baskerville (Figure 4-23c). They are the same basic shape, but their differences are important in typography. Their structures—thick/thin, serif/sans serif—are different. The logo design in Figure 4-24 plays with both contrast and similarity, as well as a clever visual pun equating the *V* with facial structure.

Color

The brighter and more intense the color, the heavier it will be visually. A large grey blue shape will be balanced by a small bright red shape. A small bright intense green will contrast with and balance a large toned-down, low-intensity green. In graphic design, each additional color costs money, so it must be used wisely. A second color can be used to enliven a magazine from cover to cover or only on those pages that are cut from the same printed signature. Remember, in one-color design, that color need not be black. It can be a rich gray, a deep green, or any color you can envision working with your combination of type and image.

4-24
Margo Chase.
Margo Chase Design, Los Angeles. Logo design for Virgin Records. *Courtesy of the artist.*

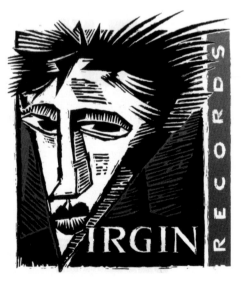

Exercises

1. Do some thumbnail sketches to experiment with the statements a–d. Start with letterforms for these sketches in

order to become better acquainted with them before you try images. The principles of balance function the same, whether applied to type or image. It is easier to understand the fundamentals of an abstract visual language if you begin with simple shapes and letterforms and progress to pictorial designs. What design dynamics are influencing each of these situations?

a. A shape placed in a corner is protected by the two sides of the rectangle. Place the same shape farther out into the space around it, and it seems more vulnerable.

b. Two shapes placed side by side will look less lonely than one.

c. Two shapes (an *e* or an *a* work well) placed back to back will appear uncommunicative, unfriendly.

d. A point placed against a soft curve will cause a sensation of discomfort. (An *A* and an *e* again work well.)

2. Using traditional collage and/or computer software such as Freehand or Illustrator, select letterforms or simple shapes to demonstrate the following principles. It can be fun to use a font like Webdings for clip art shapes.

a. A single shape can balance several shapes.

b. A large shape can be balanced by a group of smaller shapes.

c. Shapes can be balanced by negative space.

d. A dark shape can be balanced by a larger, lighter shape.

e. A large flat shape can be balanced by a smaller, textured shape.

3. Prepare a classroom presentation based on a critique of a poster, advertisement, or illustration. Describe how it achieves or fails to achieve visual and intellectual unity.

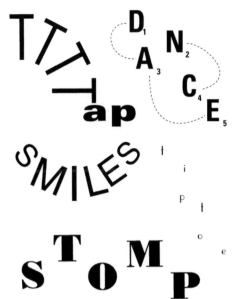

4-25
Becky Kliese.
Word illustration, "Movement."

Assignment 1: Word Illustration

This project asks you to concentrate on placement, contrast, and kinesthetic projection to create a balanced and interesting design. Figure 4-25 shows student designs based on this project.

Choose a word to illustrate. Practice on those listed below. Then find your own word from class discussion or your own research. A dictionary can be useful. Do a minimum of 15 thumbnails. Base these thumbnails and your project on existing type styles. Search for an appropriate one. Do not use pictures or distort your letterforms into pictures to tell your story. Let the letterforms communicate their message *visually* through size, color, value, shape, structure, texture, placement, and kinesthetic projection. Tell visually what the word says intellectually. Be able to describe the tensions and balancing forces.

Execute your design so it fits with an 11 × 14" (28 × 36 cm) format. Use black and one shade of gray if it will strengthen your design. If you use a computer-generated solution, stay within the same design limitations of size and color. Do not

4-26
Solutions by
a. Michelle Storrm,
b. Miguel Villarreal,
c. Melissa Wirth,
d. Jeremy Weber.

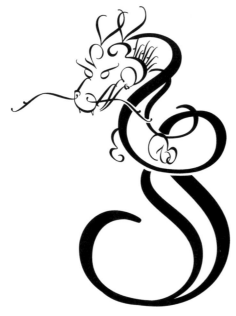

a

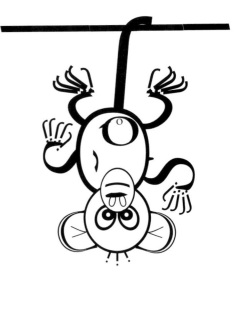

b

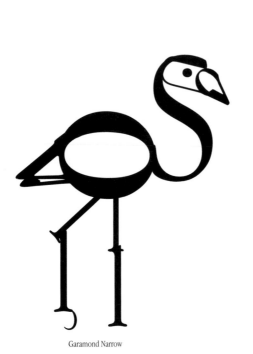

Garamond Narrow

c

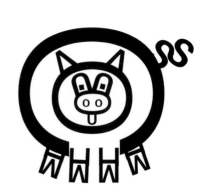

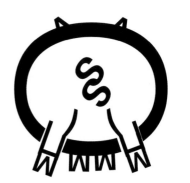

d

allow the seductive nature of the software to lure you into distorting the basic shape of the letterform. Enjoy it for its clarity and beauty of design. Retain its integrity.

Practice Words

Rain
Elephant
Reflection
Divide
Direction
Invisible
Allover
Black and Blue
Wrong Font
Alone
Repeat
Swiss Cheese

Assignment 2: Elephonts

Create an animal out of typographic forms. Choose a typestyle, and stay with its family of fonts, resizing and rotating as desired. Choose the typography carefully, looking for both shapes and the feeling the typestyle communicates. Feel free to reverse values, overlap, and cut and paste to create your animal, but again, avoid stretching and distorting the proportions of the type. Place your animal somewhere within the rectangle of an 8½ × 11" (21.5 × 28 cm) page, in either a vertical or a horizontal format. Be sensitive to the edges of the overall composition and the open spaces. Figure 4-26 shows several playful and creative student solutions.

Objectives

Practice creating a visually balanced design.
Explore the personalities of varying type styles.
Increase your control of media, tools, and software, as well as your respect for precision.

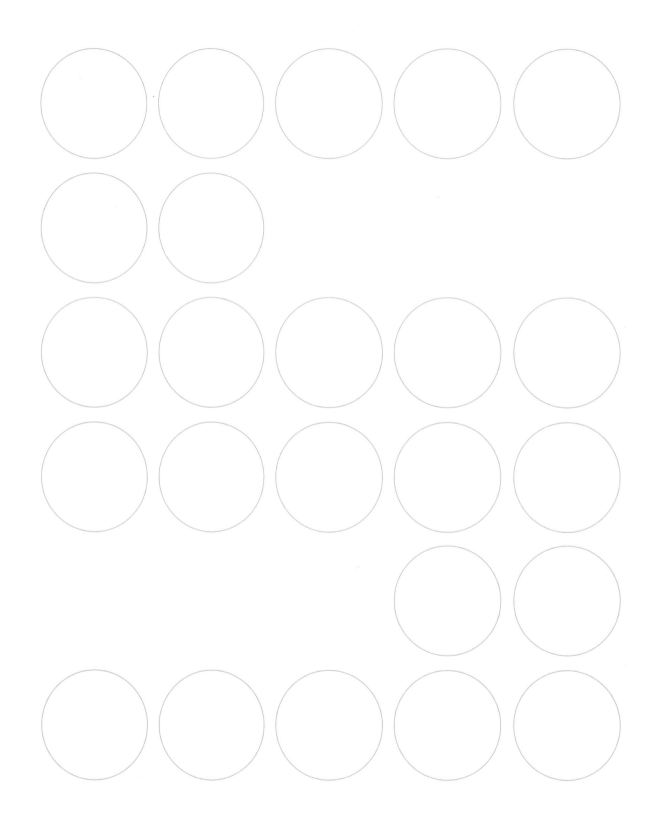

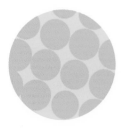

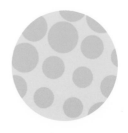

Chapter 5 ⋮⋮⋮ good gestalt

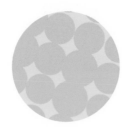

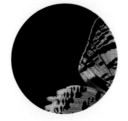

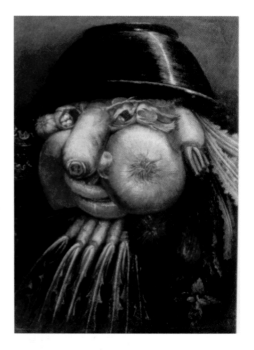

5-1

THE WHOLE AND THE PARTS

The Gestalt school of psychology, which began in Germany around 1912, investigated how we see and organize visual information into a meaningful whole. The conviction developed that the whole is more than the sum of its parts. This whole cannot be perceived by a simple addition of isolated parts. Each part is influenced by those around it.

WHOLE

As you read the word above, you are perceiving the whole word, not the individual letterforms that make it up. You can still examine each letter individually, but however you add it up, the *word* is more than the sum of those separate letterforms (Figure 5-1).

When you sew a shirt, you begin with pieces of fabric cut into parts. When the parts have been assembled, a new thing has been created. The collar, the facing, and the sleeve still exist, but they have a new "whole" identity called a shirt.

Giuseppe Arcimboldo, a painter from the 16th century, demonstrates the principle clearly in the portrait in Figure 5-2. A close examination reveals the separate parts that make up this head. A similar example is the contemporary alphabet made up of objects in Figure 5-3.

(right)
5-2
Guiseppe Arcimboldo.
Sixteenth century.

5-3
Julius Friedman and
Walter McCord.
Co-designers. Logo for
Images design firm.

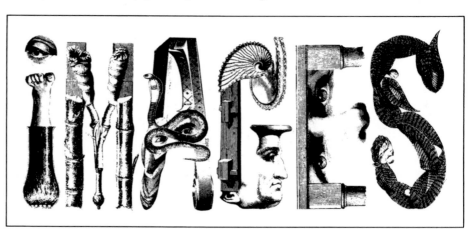

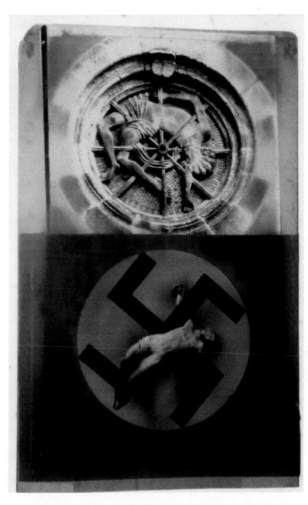

5-4
"As in the Middle Ages . . . so in the Third Reich."
Photomontage by **John Heartfield,** 1934. This powerful comment on Hitler's regime makes beautiful and effective use of the gestalt principle of similarity that evokes a gestalt conceptual closure.

The early Gestalt psychologists and many other researchers into visual perception have discovered that the eye seeks a unified whole, or *gestalt.* Knowing how the eye seeks a gestalt can help you analyze and create successful designs. By knowing what connections the eye will draw for itself, you eliminate clutter and produce a clearly articulated design.

GESTALT PRINCIPLES

A designer works not simply with lines on paper, but with perceptual structure. Learn these gestalt perceptual principles and you can take advantage of the way object, eye, and graphic creation interweave. A powerful and beautiful example can be found in the editorial illustration by John Heartfield (Figure 5-4). Many of the images in this chapter combine a variety of gestalt principles.

Similarity

When we see things that are similar, we naturally group them. Grouping by similarity occurs when we see similar shape, size, color, spatial location (proximity), angle, or value. All things are similar in some respects and different in others. In a group of similar shapes and angles, we will notice a dissimilar shape or angle (Figure 5-5).

similarity

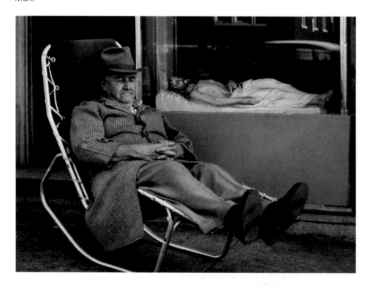

Similarity is necessary before we can compare differences. In the photograph by Gordon Baer (Figure 5-6), we are attracted by a similarity of sleeping forms and then begin an internal dialogue about their message. It is useful for the designer to know that the eye will notice and group similarities while separating differences. The symbol and logotype created for Alcoa by Saul Bass, a renowned American designer, relies on similarity of shape. Count the triangles in Figure 5-7. In Figure 5-8, contemporary designer Margo Chase uses a similarity of line quality to create a dynamic, unified logo for Esprit.

Proximity

Grouping by similarity in spatial location is called *proximity,* or nearness. The closer two visual elements are, the more likely we will see them as a group (Figure 5-9). The proximity of lines or edges makes it easier for the eye to group them to form a figure (Figure 5-10).

(right)
5-5

5-6
Gordon Baer.
Freelance photographer, Cincinnati, OH. *Two Old Men.*

(right)
5-7
Saul Bass.
Trademark for Alcoa. *Courtesy, Aluminum Company of America.*

(right)
5-8
Margo Chase.
Logo for Esprit woman, a romantic line, made up of figures and hearts.

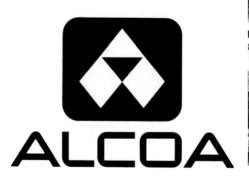

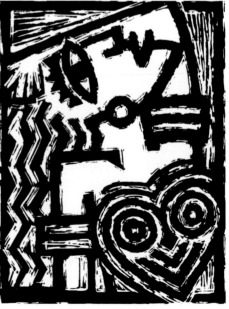

prox imity

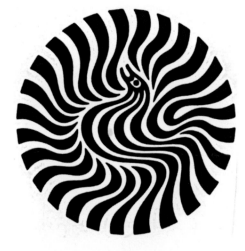

Continuation

The viewer's eye will follow a line or curve. Continuation occurs when the eye is carried smoothly into the line or curve of an adjoining object (Figure 5-11).

The eye is pleased by shapes that are not interrupted, but form a harmonious relationship with adjoining shapes. The symbol of the U.S. Energy Extension Service (Figure 5-12) uses continuation to emphasize the moving, dynamic nature of energy.

(left)
5-9

(right)
5-10
Stephan Kantscheff, Bulgarian designer, created this beautiful example of rhythm and repetition in symbol design. *Courtesy of the artist.*

continuation

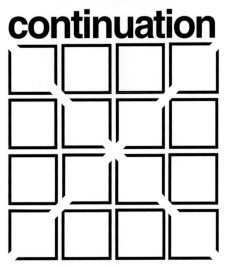

5-11

5-12
George Jadowski, designer, **Danny C. Jones,** art director. Symbol for the U.S. Energy Extension Service.

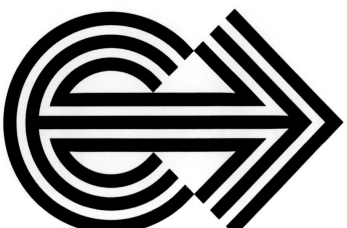

(top left)
5-13
Herb Lubalin (art director) and **Alan Peckolick** (designer) created this magazine logo in 1967. It makes a quiet but elegant usage of placement and continuation.

(top right)
5-14

(left)
5-15
Pat Hughes and **Steve Quinn.**
This symbol for 1 + 1 Design Firm uses reversible figure/ground and closure.

(bottom right)
5-16
Stephan Kantscheff.
Symbol for the Staatliches Operettentheater in Sofia, Bulgaria.

(bottom left)
5-17
Herb Lubalin.
1965. This creation by an important 20th-century designer relies on an anthropomorphic identification with the shape of letterforms to bring closure.

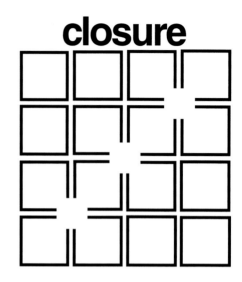

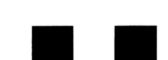

Continuation can also be achieved through implied directional lines (Figure 5-13).

Closure

Familiar shapes are more readily seen as complete than incomplete. When the eye completes a line or curve in order to form a familiar shape, closure has occurred (Figure 5-14). This step is sometimes accompanied by a reaction, "Oh, now I see!" Figure 5-15 is a symbol created by the 1 + 1 Design Firm. Do you see the plus sign created by the figure/ground relationship? Part of the closure in this example includes a sudden connection with the name of the firm. This sort of connection is especially useful in trademark design. An elegant editorial statement is made in Figure 5-16.

Figure 5-17 by Herb Lubalin calls for active conceptual participation by the viewer.

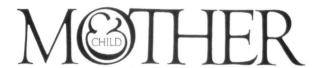

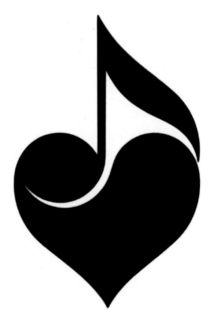

figure ground

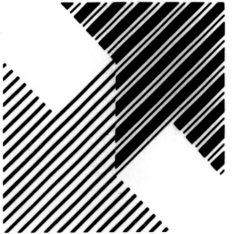

Figure/Ground

The fundamental law of perception that
makes it possible to discern objects is the
figure/ground relationship. The eye and mind
separate an object (figure) from its surroundings (ground). As you read this page, your
eye is separating out words (figure) from
ground (paper). Many times the relationship
between figure and ground is dynamic and
ambiguous, offering more than one solution
to the searching eye, as we discussed in
Chapter 3 (Figure 5-18). Remember that
these gestalt relationships in graphic design
are always intended to help structure an
appropriate communication. The most lovely
design is not successful if it fails to present
the subject appropriately. Figure 5-19 presents a fairly abstract symbolic notion of the
delivery and exchange of information.

Sometimes referred to as positive and
negative space relationship, this principle is
crucial to shaping a strong design. You must
be aware of creating shapes in the "leftover"
ground every time you create a figure.
Figure 5-20 uses this fact in an entertaining
way, similar to the work of M. C. Escher.

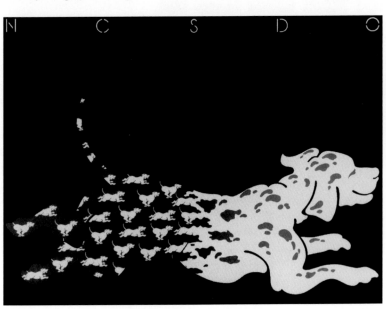

5-20
Whitney Sherman,
illustrator; **Martin
Bennett** and **Mary Pat
Andrea,** designers.
North Charles Street
Design Organization. This
poster announces an
upcoming move to a new
location.

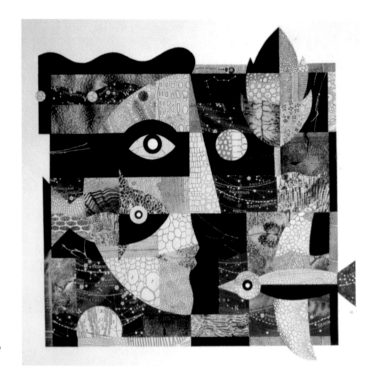

5-21
David McLimans.
Illustration courtesy of the artist.

5-22
Lippincott and Margulies, Inc. Trademark for Case Corporation. The company recently adopted a new logo design.

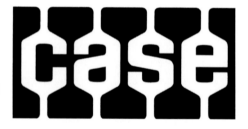

Figure 5-21 is a contemporary illustration that also uses the figure/ground relationship as an inherent part of its rich structure.

In Figure 5-22, the logo for Case Equipment Company, the figure/ground relationship is remarkably strong.

TRADEMARKS

The interplay of gestalt principles occurs in all areas of design but is clearest in the creation of logo and symbol trademarks. Here, form and function are closely related. We have examined form. Next we consider function. The project in this chapter will ask you to relate these two considerations.

FUNCTIONS

Symbols and trademarks have served many functions in history. The early Christians relied on the symbol of the fish to identify themselves to one another secretly. In the Dark Ages, family trademarks were used. No nobleman in the same region could wear the same coat of arms. These "arms" came to mark the owner's possessions. Peasants used simpler "housemarks," which were especially useful because few people could read (Figure 5-23). Also, each medieval craftsman inscribed a personal mark on his products and hung out a sign showing his calling. During the Renaissance, the three golden balls of the Medici family symbolized moneylending. The Medici mark can still be seen today, pirated by modern pawnbrokers. More recently, in the western United States, each cattle rancher had a brand or mark. Many still do (Figure 5-24).

Today, trademarks are widely used by corporations. The trademark is any unique name or symbol used to identify a product and to distinguish it from others. These unique marks can be registered and protected by law. Their primary use is to increase brand recognition and advertise products and services. The use of trademarks, or logos, is growing as individuals identify themselves on letterheads, résumés, and home pages. Consumers come to rely on the quality associated with a trademark and are willing to try new products identified with that recognized trademark.

Making "Marks"

Unlike other forms of advertising, the modern trademark is a often long-term design. It may appear on letterhead, company trucks, packaging, employee uniforms, newsletters, and so on. Designers can spend months developing and testing one trademark. Only a strong design with a simple, unified gestalt will stand the test of repeated exposure.

Keep several other points in mind when developing a mark:

1. You are not just "making your mark on the world"; you are making a mark to symbolize your client and your client's product. It must reflect the nature and quality of that product to an audience. Research the company, product, and audience. As designer Paul Rand said, "A trademark is created by a designer, but *made* by a corporation. A trademark is a picture, an image . . . of a corporation."
2. The mark is often reproduced in many different sizes, from the company vehicle to a business card. Your design must remain legible and strong in all circumstances.
3. Because this mark may be reproduced in newspaper advertising or with severely limited in-house duplicating facilities, it must reproduce well in one color.
4. Many trademarks are seen in adverse viewing conditions, such as short exposure, poor lighting, competitive

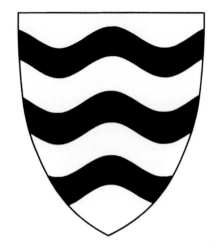

5-23

5-24

surroundings, and lack of viewer interest. Under such conditions, simplicity is a virtue. A simple, interesting shape with a good gestalt is easier to remember than a more complex design.

Some designers refer to all trademarks as *logos,* whereas others have a complex system of subtle categories. The two most common categories of trademarks, however, are symbol and logo.

Symbols

Webster's Tenth New Collegiate Dictionary says a symbol is "something that stands for or suggests something else by reason of relationship, association, convention, or accidental resemblance; especially: a visual sign of something invisible. . . . An arbitrary or conventional sign used in writing or printing operations, quantities, elements, relationships, or qualities." Historically important symbols include national flags, the cross, and the swastika.

The symbol is a type of trademark used to represent a company or product. It can be abstract or pictorial, but it does not usually include letterforms. It represents invisible qualities of a product, such as reliability, durability, strength, or warmth.

A symbol has several advantages, including:

1. Original construction
2. Simple gestalt resulting in quick recognition
3. A strong association that "colors" the symbol's interpretation.

Figure 5-25, a symbol proposed for the California Conservation Corps, demonstrates all three qualities.

A pictogram is a symbol used to cross language barriers for international signage. It is found in bilingual cities, such as Montreal, for traffic signs. It is also found in airports

and on safety instructions inside airplanes. It is pictorial rather than abstract (Figure 5-26).

Symbols can also be examined in the light of semiotics, where an image takes on a culturally accepted meaning that goes beyond its merely recognizable shape, as just discussed. An *icon* is a sign that bears a direct relationship to the object described. Realistic drawings and photographs are examples. Semiotics goes on to define an *index* as a sign that bears a direct relationship to the object, without simply showing that object. For example, the shadow of a building indicates its presence. This can be a useful way to approach the creation of a mark. Symbol, icon, and index all are considered good approaches in the creation of a trademark symbol.

Logos

The second category of trademark is called *logo* or *logotype.* The logo is a unique type or lettering that spells out the name of the company or product. It may be hand lettered, but is usually constructed out of variations on an existing typeface. Historically, it developed after the symbol, because it requires a literate audience.

When you create a logo, choose type that suits the nature of your client and audience. A successful, unique logo is often more difficult to design than a symbol, because it entails both visual and verbal communication. Figure 5-27 was created for *Reader's Digest* by one of the most respected and influential logo designers, Herb Lubalin. The clean, bold type style makes it easy to see the play on similar shapes that creates the "family connection" hidden in the word. Figure 5-28 was created for Ditto Company, a duplication products manufacturer. Compare this type style with the one before. Each is distinctively suited to its use.

The advantages of a logotype include (1) original construction and (2) easy identification with company or product.

5-25
Michael Vanderbyl.
Symbol proposed but not adopted for the California Conservation Corps.
Courtesy of the artist.

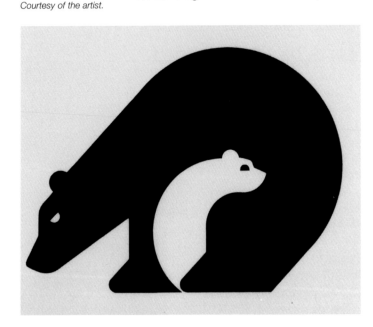

A *combination mark* is a symbol and logo used together. These marks can be more difficult to construct with a good gestalt because of their complexity. They are often used, however, because they combine the advantages of symbol and logo.

In all these marks, gestalt principles help create a unified and striking design. With good gestalt, form and function interweave in a powerful whole.

Exercises

This assignment is best done with graph paper, or you may want to use a vector graphics program with the grid turned on, utilizing guides and rulers (Figure 5-29).

1. Select a circle 1½" (4 cm) in diameter (or slightly more), and practice overlapping two of them to create new and varied shapes. Then try three circles. Do not use line, only shape and black and white values. Reverse one out of another for more interesting effects.

2. Place a circle in various positions within a square. Do not use line. Use black and white shapes. Experiment with size and border violations.

3. Set up a series of vertical lines so the white lines gradually grow small while the black lines expand. Start by making a series of vertical lines ¼"(5 mm) apart. Each line can then be thickened.

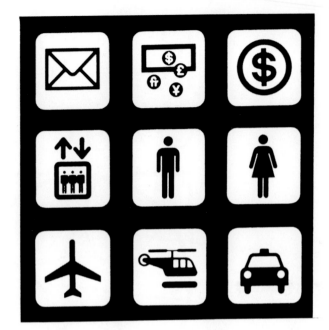

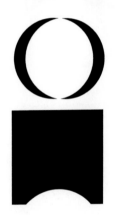

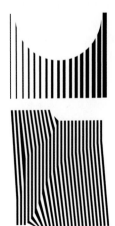

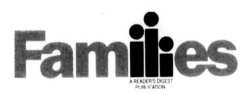

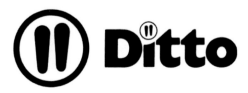

5-26
Roger Cook and **Don Shanosky.**
(Cook and Shanosky Associates). Department of Transportation pictograms prepared by the American Institute of Graphic Arts (AIGA).

(far left, top)
5-27
Herb Lubalin.
Trademark created for *Reader's Digest.* Assigned to Military Family Communication, publisher of *Families* magazine.

(far left, bottom)
5-28
Logotype for Ditto Corporation. The Ditto trademark is a federally registered trademark of Starkey Chemical Process Co. of LaGrange, IL.

((bottom right)
5-29
Eric Weubben.
Line variations using an anomaly, or change, in an expected pattern.

RIVE GAUCHE

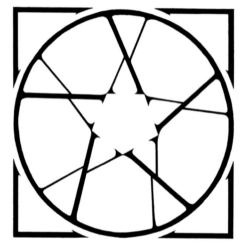

5-30
Lynette Schwartz.
This combination mark for a men's clothing store is unified by similarity of shape in type and image.

4. Create a break or anomaly in a series of vertical lines.
5. Examine the illustrations in this chapter and identify the unifying gestalt features in each mark.
6. Use one or more of these exercises to develop an appropriate symbol for a company of your choice. Figures 5-30 is a student design created for a related project.

Project

Combination Mark

Design a combination mark for a company described here. You may combine logo and symbol into one image or present them as two images, carefully placed together. Experiment with many alternatives in your thumbnail sketches. Incorporate each of the gestalt principles discussed in this chapter into your thumbnail investigation.

Begin with an existing type style and make careful alterations. Spend time looking through typebooks. Experiment with fonts, finding which are appropriate for the company you have selected. List the name of the font next to your pencil sketch.

After consultation with the instructor, select two thumbnails to create as full-size roughs for final review. Fine-tune and execute the strongest within an 8 × 10" (19 × 25 cm) format. Use only one color. Execute in either paint, ink, cut paper, or a vector graphics computer program.

Keep your design visually strong and uncluttered. Be prepared to discuss the gestalt principles involved during the critique. Use at least two of them in your final trademark. Also consider the audience your trademark will be reaching. What will appeal to them? Consider the company. What will be an accurate and positive image? Be prepared to discuss the function of your trademark and why the design suits it.

Trademark design

1. The Museum of Transportation Logo

The Museum of Transportation is a new museum located in your state, needing a logo. It has a permanent collection that includes all forms of personal and mass transport vehicles in the state from the history of transportation. Consider things as diverse as the first wheel, children's scooters, boats, and Lear jets. Consider the places people go and things people use transportation for. Include the name of the institution along with an image to create a combination mark. You will have an opportunity later to design a poster for this exhibition.

2. Narnia Zoo

This is a large, well-funded, but new zoo. It hosts everything from aardvarks to insects to zebras and emphasizes preservation of endangered species and habitats. It is planning a special exhibition for which you will create a name and design a poster in a later

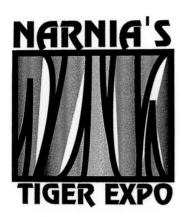

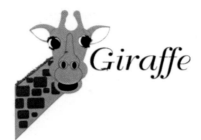

(left)
5-31
Russ Jacobs.
Continuation unites type
and image in this
combination mark for a
special exhibition at the
zoo.

assignment. Design a symbol or combination mark for this zoo. Consider creating signage for different areas of the zoo.

Second optional assignment: Design a logo, symbol, or combination mark for the special exhibition (see Figures 5-31 and 5-32).

Process
Begin this assignment with a series of at least twenty thumbnails. You may want to experiment with trademarks for both institutions. Refine the best into two or three roughs, doing all necessary visual research. Proceed with the final trademark design after class discussion.

Objective
- Communicate the nature of an institution with a design that appeals to the public.
- Apply gestalt principles to develop a trademark that is more than the sum of its parts.
- Research for appropriate images in periodicals, the library, original photos, or the Internet.

Variations
Ask your instructor to assign existing corporations that need a new trademark design.

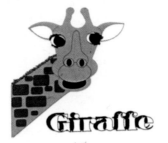

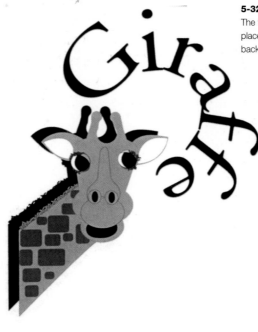

5-32a
Experimentation with type placement enriches this zoo signage by Dawn Kast.

5-32b
The final design uses type placement to bring the eye back to the symbol.

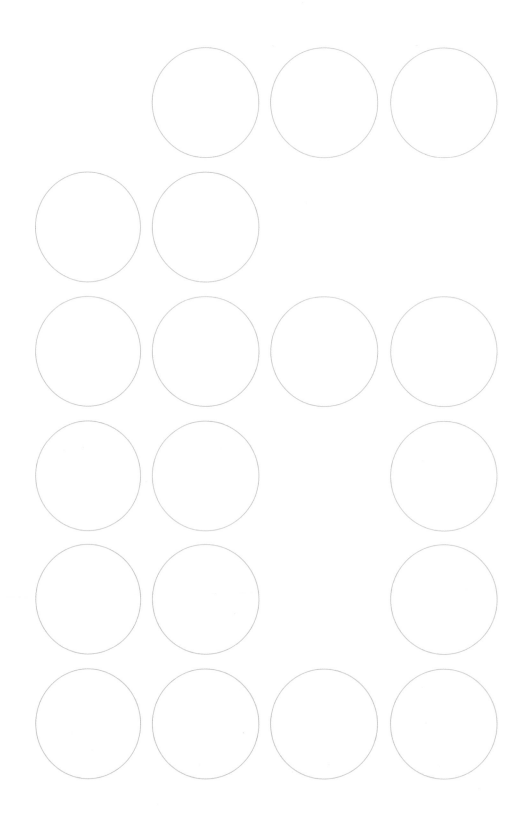

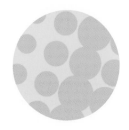

Chapter 6 ::::: using text type

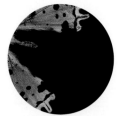

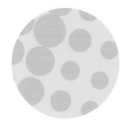

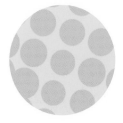

THE DEVELOPMENT OF WRITTEN COMMUNICATION

Since the first person made a mark in the sand for another to find, we have been communicating with a visual language. The earliest forms of visual communication were pictorial drawings of everyday objects, such as weapons and animals. As the desire to communicate grew, these pictures were combined to convey thoughts and ideas.

With visual language, it became possible to conquer time. An individual's mark could be seen and understood after the maker had moved on or even died. *Civilization developed along with our visual record of the spoken language. So did the importance of the individual.*

Alphabets

The first systematized alphabet was created by the Egyptians. It was partly abstract symbols and partly pictures. The Phoenicians added consonants around 1600 B.C. A nation of merchants, they needed an efficient, condensed language for business transactions. This need led to a significant breakthrough: Symbols were used to represent not objects, but the sounds of speech. A different symbol stood for each recognizable spoken sound. It was a much shorter and more efficient system of written language.

The Greeks adapted the Phoenician system, and around 1000 B.C. the Romans modified the Greek alphabet. Our alphabet is derived from the Roman version. The Romans devised a total of twenty-three letters. The letter *J* was added to our alphabet just over five hundred years ago (Figure 6-1).

As designers working with the letters of the alphabet, we have thousands of years of history behind us. The shape of letters has been largely determined by the tools used to create them. The Egyptians used reeds for writing on papyrus. This method created a pattern of thick and thin strokes. The Greeks used a stylus on tablets, whereas important Roman inscriptions were chiseled into stone. These forms developed with few curved lines, because curves were difficult to carve. The Greek and Egyptian alphabets had no serifs. They evolved with the Roman alphabet, perhaps to make inscriptions seem to sit better optically when chiseled in stone. Medieval handwritten scrolls kept the alphabet alive during the Middle Ages. These scrolls gradually evolved into folded manuscript books, produced by religious orders. Our most common typefaces are imitations of early handwriting or modifications of early typefaces modeled after the lettering in manuscript books. From the invention of the first printing press in 1440 until the 18th century, type designs were based on handwriting.

Influence of Technology

Innovation in printing technology during the Industrial Revolution contributed to the

6-1
The Phoenician, Greek, and Roman alphabets.

1. Phoenician alphabet

2. Greek alphabet

3. Roman alphabet

development of new type styles. Advances in mechanical design and cast-iron parts were applied to the printing press in the early 1800s, allowing for a much larger printed sheet. The *London Times* was the first to replace the hand press with a steam-powered printing press that could print over a thousand impressions an hour. Another important innovation of the 1800s was the invention of the Linotype machine in 1886 by Ottmar Mergenthaler. It replaced setting type by hand with a keyboard-operated machine that generated lines of type cast in melted lead. These lines of type were locked into slim wooden "cases" before printing. The invention of photo typography in the 1960s heralded the Age of Information as it became increasingly easy and important to disseminate information by word and image. Computers now make it possible to develop variations on existing typestyles quickly. Specialized software makes the creation of new styles simpler and more accessible than ever before, and digital presses continue to speed print production. Whatever technology is used, in whatever century, the eye and mind of the designer remains a vital factor.

TYPE CATEGORIES

Like the alphabet, typography has undergone a long development. A brief look at its history will help you assemble and recognize types with similar attributes. History provides a key to proper use.

The type category we refer to as *old style,* with gently blended serifs leading into thick and thin strokes, was created in 1470 by Nicholas Jenson, a Venetian printer. The French typographer Claude Garamond built his type style Garamond on Jenson's design. This classic remains in use today. A modern revival of 15th-century Italian types occurred in Europe and the United States around 1890. Englishman William Morris produced a type called Golden that recalled the spirit of the 15th century (see Figure 6-2).

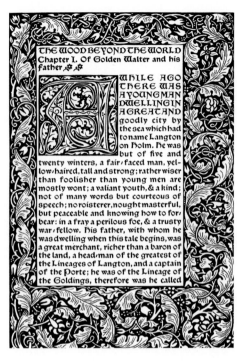

6-2
William Morris.
Page from *The Wood Beyond the World.* 1894. 9½ x 6¾" (24 × 17 cm). Kelmscott Press.

Most roman types have variations available called *italics.* They are a slanted form that relates to the original type style but does not duplicate it. Venetian printer Aldus Manutius is credited with developing italics in 1501 as a method of fitting more characters on a line to save space. For about forty years, italic was simply another style of type, until an italic was consciously developed from an upright roman mold. Today most roman types have matching italics as well as several other variations such as bold and condensed.

Roman faces with strong contrast between thick and thin strokes and with thin serifs were developed in the 18th century. These faces are generally classified as *transitional.* They were more precise because they were designed for the printing industry. A widespread interest in copperplate engraving at that time helped the development of types that incorporate a very fine line.

Bodoni and Didot imitated the engraver's tool with precise hairline strokes. The term *modern* is used to describe this 18th-century type.

In the 19th century, many new faces were developed, with a wide variety of looks. The sans serifs and the Egyptians are among them. A revival of the old classic typefaces, such as Jenson, occurred. Printers such as William Morris contributed to the history of typography during this time, creating some handsome typefaces.

Since the early 19th century, serif and sans serif types have alternated in popularity. A great interest surrounded sans serif in the mid–20th century. Bauhaus designers in Germany during the 1920s began designing sans serif faces such as Futura. In the 1950s Univers and Helvetica became the dominant typeface used by design professionals. The sans serif dominance lasted throughout the 1960s and 1970s. Newer versions of the Helvetica typeface show more consistency among font variations. Large x-height and beautiful positive and negative shapes accompany a clean precision and understated elegance of line. The horizontals are cut along a common line.

Figure 6-3 is a layout by contemporary designer Paula Scher that uses sans serif type to evoke an earlier era. Today's designers choose from a rich array of old and new type styles. In fact, such an extensive array of fonts is available on computer that selecting one can be quite difficult. A basic familiarity with typography will help you develop a discerning eye.

Historic Type Families
Old Style

Characteristics of old style faces (Figure 6-4) include thick and thin stroke serifs that seem to merge into the main strokes. This feature is called *bracketing.* Garamond and Caslon are examples. Created in 1617, Garamond was the first typeface designed to appear uniformly printed rather than hand lettered. It remained the principal typeface for over two hundred years, with many derivatives.

Transitional

A blending of old style and modern, the transitional has emphasis on thicks and thins and gracefully bracketed serifs (Figure 6-5). It is lighter than old style and has a more precise, controlled character. It is less

6-3
Paula Scher.
Layout design for *The Magic Mountain* in "Great Beginnings" brochure. *Courtesy of the artist.*

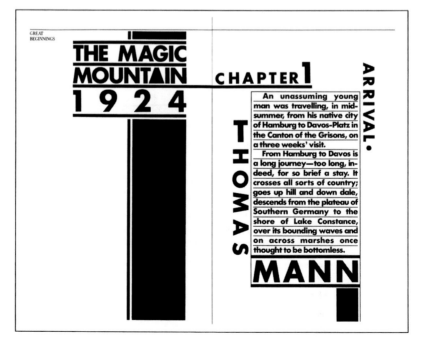

abcdefghijklmn
opqrstuvwxyz
ABCDEFGHIJK
LMNOPQRSTU
VWXYZ$12344
567890(.,""''-;:!)?&

abcdefghijklmnop
qrstuvwxyzAB
CDEFGHIJKLM
NOPQRSTUV
WXYZ$1234567
890(.,""''-;:!)?&

Garamond Book

Since the first person made a mark in the sand for another to find, we have been communicating with a visual language. The earliest forms of visual communication were pictorial drawings of everyday objects such as weapons and animals. As the desire to communicate grew, these pictures were combined to convey thoughts and ideas. With visual language, it became possible to "conquer" time. An individual's mark could be seen and understood after the maker had moved or even died. Civilization developed along with our visual record of the spoken language. So did the importance of the individual.

8/9

Since the first person made a mark in the sand for another to find, we have been communicating with a visual language. The earliest forms of visual communication were pictorial drawings of everyday objects such as weapons and animals. As the desire to communicate grew, these pictures were combined to convey thoughts and ideas. With visual language, it became possible to "conquer" time. An individual's mark could be seen and understood after the maker had moved or even died. Civilization developed along with our visual record of the spoken language. So

8/10

Since the first person made a mark in the sand for another to find, we have been communicating with a visual language. The earliest forms of visual communication were pictorial drawings of everyday objects such as weapons and animals. As the desire to communicate grew, these pictures were combined to convey thoughts and ideas. With visual language, it became possible to "conquer" time. An individual's mark could be seen and understood after the maker had moved or even died. Civilization de-

8/11

Since the first person made a mark in the sand for another to find, we have been communicating with a visual language. The earliest forms of visual communication were pictorial drawings of everyday objects such as weapons and animals. As the desire to communicate grew, these pictures were combined to convey thoughts and ideas. With visual language, it became possible to "conquer" time. An individual's mark could be seen and understood after the maker had moved or even died. Civilization de-

9/10

Since the first person made a mark in the sand for another to find, we have been communicating with a visual language. The earliest forms of visual communication were pictorial drawings of everyday objects such as weapons and animals. As the desire to communicate grew, these pictures were combined to convey thoughts and ideas. With visual language, it became possible to "conquer" time. An individual's mark could be seen and understood

9/11

Baskerville

Since the first person made a mark in the sand for another to find, we have been communicating with a visual language. The earliest forms of visual communication were pictorial drawings of everyday objects such as weapons and animals. As the desire to communicate grew, these pictures were combined to convey thoughts and ideas. With visual language, it became possible to "conquer" time. An individual's mark could be seen and understood after the maker had moved or even died. Civilization developed along with our visual record of the spoken language. So did the importance of the individual.

8/9

Since the first person made a mark in the sand for another to find, we have been communicating with a visual language. The earliest forms of visual communication were pictorial drawings of everyday objects such as weapons and animals. As the desire to communicate grew, these pictures were combined to convey thoughts and ideas. With visual language, it became possible to "conquer" time. An individual's mark could be seen and understood after the maker had moved or even died. Civilization developed along with our visual record of the spoken

8/10

Since the first person made a mark in the sand for another to find, we have been communicating with a visual language. The earliest forms of visual communication were pictorial drawings of everyday objects such as weapons and animals. As the desire to communicate grew, these pictures were combined to convey thoughts and ideas. With visual language, it became possible to "conquer" time. An individual's mark could be seen and understood after the maker had moved or even died. Civili-

8/11

Since the first person made a mark in the sand for another to find, we have been communicating with a visual language. The earliest forms of visual communication were pictorial drawings of everyday objects such as weapons and animals. As the desire to communicate grew, these pictures were combined to convey thoughts and ideas. With visual language, it became possible to "conquer" time. An individual's mark could be seen and understood after the maker had moved or even died.

9/10

Since the first person made a mark in the sand for another to find, we have been communicating with a visual language. The earliest forms of visual communication were pictorial drawings of everyday objects such as weapons and animals. As the desire to communicate grew, these pictures were combined to convey thoughts and ideas. With visual language, it became possible to "conquer" time. An individual's mark could be seen and

9/11

6-6

Point size and leading affect one another.

mechanical and upright, however, than the modern faces.

Baskerville was designed in 1757 by John Baskerville, an amateur printer. The transitional Baskerville has straighter and more mechanical lines than the old style typefaces, with flatter serifs that come to a fine tip. Increased contrast between the thick and thin strokes of the letterforms and the rounded brackets give it more delicacy than old style faces such as Caslon.

John Baskerville introduced several technical innovations that affected the appearance of his type. He passed printed sheets through heated copper cylinders to smooth out the rough texture of the paper then in use. This smooth surface made it possible to reproduce delicate serifs clearly. Figure 6-6 shows text-size Garamond and Baskerville fonts in various combinations of point size and leading.

Modern

The modern styles evolved from transitional types. They have still greater variation between thicks and thins. Modern typefaces are characterized by thin serifs that join the body with a stiff unbracketed corner. There is strong vertical stress to the letters. The serifs are hairline thin.

Bodoni (Figure 6-7) fits this category. It was created in the late 1700s by Firmin Didot, a Frenchman who also gave Europe a fully developed type measurement system.

Egyptian

The first slab-serif type style was introduced around 1815. The category was dubbed "Egyptian" because Egyptian artifacts and Egyptian travel were in vogue. Napoleon's conquest of Egypt aroused great enthusiasm for that country. During this period, type

abcdefghijklmnopq
rstuvwxyzABCDEFG
HIJKLMNOPQRST
UVWXYZ$12345678
90(.,""''-;:!)?&

6-7
Bodoni, a modern face.

6-8
Lubalin Graph, an
"Egyptian" slab-serif face.

abcdeefghijkl
mnopqrstuvwx
yzABCDEFGHI
JKLMNOPQRST
UVWXYZ$123
4567890(.,'""-;:!)?&

6-9
Helvetica, a sans serif face.

ABCDEFGHIJKL
MNOPQRSTUV
WXYZ&abcdefg
hijklmnopqrstuvw
xyz1234567890
$.," -:;!?

design became less predictable and more eclectic. The characteristics were mixed and recombined, producing many variations. The heavy square serifs in this category often match the strokes in thickness. There is less difference between thicks and thins than in the modern and transitional periods. Clarendon and Century are examples of this group.

The popularity of square slab-serif type decreased greatly in the early 20th century, but then revived somewhat in its latter decades. Lubalin Graph (Figure 6-8), designed in 1974 by Herb Lubalin, Tony Di Spigna, and Joe Sundwall, has the characteristics of Egyptian type styles, as does Rockwell, shown in Chapter 3.

Sans Serif

William Caslon created the original sans serif in the early 1800s. The 1920s saw the development of sans serif type families including Gill Sans, created by Eric Gill, as well as Herbert Bayer's Universal Alphabet. In the 1950s designers of the International School examined available typefaces and found them lacking. Weight changes were not subtle enough, and the various weights and widths in a type family often lacked coherency. This disorder was natural, because they were often designed by different people. A young Swiss type designer named Adrian Frutiger developed a sans serif style called Univers. He created a completely consistent family of types in all possible weights and widths.

Several classic sans serif typefaces were designed at the German Bauhaus (see Chapter 2). Influenced by the Bauhaus, the Swiss firm Haas worked with the German Stempel foundry to produce Helvetica (Figure 6-9). It is still considered by many designers to be the perfect type— versatile, legible, and elegant (Figure 6-10).

Helvetica

Since the first person made a mark in the sand for another to find, we have been communicating with a visual language. The earliest forms of visual communication were pictorial drawings of everyday objects such as weapons and animals. As the desire to communicate grew, these pictures were combined to convey thoughts and ideas. With visual language, it became possible to "conquer" time. An individual's mark could be seen and understood after the maker had moved or even died. Civilization developed along with our visual record of the spoken language. So did the importance of the individual.

8/9

Since the first person made a mark in the sand for another to find, we have been communicating with a visual language. The earliest forms of visual communication were pictorial drawings of everyday objects such as weapons and animals. As the desire to communicate grew, these pictures were combined to convey thoughts and ideas. With visual language, it became possible to "conquer" time. An individual's mark could be seen and understood after the maker had moved or even died. Civilization developed along with our visual record of the spoken

8/10

Since the first person made a mark in the sand for another to find, we have been communicating with a visual language. The earliest forms of visual communication were pictorial drawings of everyday objects such as weapons and animals. As the desire to communicate grew, these pictures were combined to convey thoughts and ideas. With visual language, it became possible to "conquer" time. An individual's mark could be seen and understood after the maker had moved or even died. Civi-

8/11

Since the first person made a mark in the sand for another to find, we have been communicating with a visual language. The earliest forms of visual communication were pictorial drawings of everyday objects such as weapons and animals. As the desire to communicate grew, these pictures were combined to convey thoughts and ideas. With visual language, it became possible to "conquer" time. An individual's mark could be seen and understood after the maker had moved or even died.

9/10

Since the first person made a mark in the sand for another to find, we have been communicating with a visual language. The earliest forms of visual communication were pictorial drawings of everyday objects such as weapons and animals. As the desire to communicate grew, these pictures were combined to convey thoughts and ideas. With visual language, it became possible to "conquer" time. An individual's mark could be seen and

9/11

6-10

6-11
El Lissitzky.
Table of Contents from Plastic Figures of the Electro-Mechanical Show: Victory over the Sun. 1923. Collection, The Chicago Art Institute. Gift of the Print and Drawing Club. Gaylord Donnelley and Wm. McCallin Mckee Fund, 1966.

6-12
Diane Fenster.
Book cover for *Ecology.* This appropriate use of an unusual typestyle fits well with the illustration. *Courtesy of the artist.*

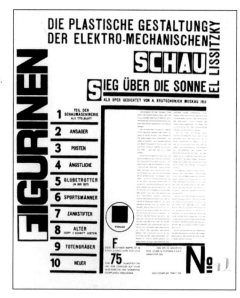

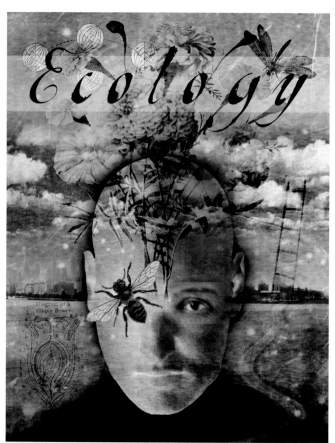

Figure 6-11 shows a design from 1923 using a grid layout and sans serif type by El Lissitzky. A leading Russian Constructivist, Lissitzky believed in the power of graphic design to influence social order. He helped export Constructivist theory and style to Europe through his printed work and lectures.

Miscellaneous Faces
Many fonts do not seem to belong to any category. They are often experimental, ornamental styles of limited application, sometimes created by hand. These eccentric types are rarely suitable for text type, but do find appropriate usage in display headings such as the book cover in Figure 6-12 where type and image are delicately integrated.

It is possible to use specialized, ornate styles in display headlines and not hamper readability too greatly. In large amounts of body copy, however, every subtle variation has a cumulative effect that can seriously hinder readability. A classic, all-purpose type style will remain legible and unobtrusive as body type. Selecting an appropriate, legible, and beautiful text type calls for a sensitive, educated eye. Figures 6-13 and Figure 6-14 show a few of the all-purpose styles.

TYPE FAMILIES

The five categories of type we have discussed are filled with type families, such as Bodoni and Baskerville. Each family comes in a variety of weights and sizes. A family is all the variations of a particular typeface. Helvetica, for example, now comes in a series of variations described as light condensed, medium condensed, bold condensed, ultra light, ultra light condensed, ultra light italic, light, medium, regular, medium light, bold, bold italic, and bold

American typewriter light	Benguiat medium cond	Beton light	ITC Bookman light italic
ABCDEFGHIJ KLMNOPQRR STUVWXYZØ abcdeefghijkl mnopqrstuv?! wxyzæœø12 34567890£¢$	ABCDEFGHIJKL" MNOPQRSTUVW XYZÆŒÇØabcd efghijklmnopqrs tuvwxyzæœçø1 234567890ß£$¢ ?!&%§()/«~-~^~»″*;:	ABCDEFGHIJKL MNOPQRSTUV WXYZabcdefghi jklmnopqrstuvwx yz 1234567890 Æ ŒÇØæœçøß £$ ¢&%?!()«»/*;॰^·~	ABCDEFGHIJKLMNO PQRSTUVWXYZ·AB ·ABCDEFGHIJK LMNOPQRR·STU VV·WWW·XYZ·ÇTh ÆŒØabcdefghijklm nopqrstuvwxyze·fifiç fihk·mnopqr·ræœø ß123456789012345 890£$¢&%?!S@#[(«»:;*«,/)]
American typewriter med	Benguiat medium cond	Beton bold	Bookman
ABCDEFGHIJ! KLMNOPQRŒ STUVWXYZØ ÆÇabcdefghij klmnopqrstu? vwxyzæœçøß 1234567890£ $¢&%§(«»:;·*/)	ABCDEFGHIJKL MNOPQRSTUV WXYZÆŒÇØab cdefghijklmnop» qrstuvwxyzæœ çø1234567890ß £$¢?!&%§()/«~-~^~»	ABCDEFGHIJK LMNOPQRST() UVWXYZabcd efghijklmnopq, rstuvwxyz1234! 567890ÆŒÇØ? æœçøß£$¢&%.	AA·ABBCDDEF ·EFGHIIJJK·KL ·LMM·NNO·PQR PRSTU·UVVWX ·WXY·YZÆabcde fghijklmnopqr·stu vwxyy·zæœøç1234 567890ÆŒØÇß&! ?G&$(·/·:.:)
American typewriter bold	Benguiat bold cond	Beton extra bold	Bookman italic
ABCDEFGHI JKLMNOPQ RSTUVWX? YZ!abcdeefg hijklmnopq rstuvwxyz1 234567890ॐ*	ABCDEFGHIJKL" MNOPQRSTUVW XYZÆŒÇØabcd efghijklmnopqr stuvwxyzæœçø* 1234567890 ß£$ ¢?!&%§()/«~-~^~»;:	**ABCDEFGHIJ KLMNOPQR STUVWXYZ? abcdefghijkm lnopqrstuvwx yzæœçø:1234 567890ÆŒØ! £$¢%&ß(ã»+;)**	*A·A·ABBCCD ·DE·EF·FGG·HII HJJKK·KL·LMM MN·N·NO·PQR PRRR·SSTTU! UV·VW·WXYZa bcdefghhijkklmnn opqrr·Stuvwwxy·z 1234567890&·Th&·:.:*

6-13

Some good type styles for body copy as well as display type.

Caslon antiqua medium	Cheltenham book	Futura light	Futura extra bold
ABCDEFGHI JKLMNOPQ RSTUVWX YZabcdefghijk lmnopqrstuvw xyz123456789 0&ß?!%$£(≈⁝«»+)	ABCDEFGHIJ KLMNOPQRS TUVWXYZ a bcdefghijklmn opqrstuvwxy zæ1234567890 ŒØ&ß$£¢%⌢	ABCDEFGHIJKL! MNOPQRSTUV WXYZÆŒÇØ abcdefghijklmno pqrstuvwxyzæ? œçø 12345678 90ß£$¢&%()«»;,	ABCDEFGHIJK LMNOPQRST¢ UVWXYZ ÆŒ ÇØabcdefghij! klmnopqrstuv wxyzæœçøß1 234567890£ $&%?(«».;,≈⁝)
Caslon italic	Cheltenham book italic	Futura medium	Futura extra bold italic
ABCDEFGHI JKLMNOPQR STUVWXYZ Œabcdefghijkln mopqrstuvwxyz 1234567890Æ? &%ß$£¢!Ø(≈⁝)	ABCDEFGHIJ KLMNOPQRS TUVWXYZŒ abcdefghijklm nopqrstuvwxy zæ1234567890 ØÆ&ß$£¢%?!	ABCDEFGHIJK LMNOPQRSTU VWXYZ abcde fghijklmnopqrst uvwxyzø12345 67890ŒÆØ& %ß?!¢$(≈⁝)	ABCDEFGHIJK LMNOPQRSÆ TUVWXYZŒÇ Øabcdefghijk lmnopqrstuv? wxyzæœçøß1 234567890$ £&%!(«».;,≈⁝)
Caslon modern	Cheltenham ultra	Futura demi bold	Futura extra
ABCDEFGH IJKLMNOPQ RSTUVWXZ Yabcdefghijkl mnopqrstuvw xyzœæøç1234 567890ÆŒß &%$£?!Ø(⁝⁝)	ABCDEFGHI JKLMNOPQ RSTUVWXY Zabcdefghij klmnopqrst uvwxyz1234 567890ŒØ&	ABCDEFGHIJK LMNOPQRSTU VWXYZabcde fghijklmnopqrs tuvwxyz-1234 567890ŒÆ£ $Ø&%ß?!(≈⁝)	ABCDEFGHIJK LMNOPQRSTU VWXYZÆŒØÇ abcdefghijkln mopqrstuvwx yzæ12345678 90!?&£$ß(«»⁝)

6-14

extended. Figure 6-15 illustrates the Helvetica family.

A specific variation in a specific size is called a font. For example, 18-point Helvetica italic is a font. A great variety of shapes exist in a single font. There are 26 capitals, 26 lowercase letter forms, and assorted numerals and punctuation marks. These various shapes can be successfully combined into a unified design because of the similarities in width, brackets, serifs, and x-height. A well-designed type font is an excellent example of the interplay of repetition and variety that makes for good design.

Computerized layout gives the designer the ability to make a wide variety of changes in these carefully designed fonts. Vector programs allow type to be mirrored, scaled with varying horizontal and vertical values, and otherwise manipulated for effect. The pre-computer hot type technology was based on actual physical pieces of metal shaped into letterforms. These could not be stretched or set to overlap unless the sheet was printed twice and the font recast. Now that everything is possible, an enthusiasm for exploration needs to be tempered by respect for the subtle and complex beauty of a font.

Selection

How do you select which style of type to use? What factors are involved in designing with text type? Selecting the type for a given layout means making decisions in six interrelated areas: type size, line length, type style, leading, spacing, and format.

Designers sometimes set their own type as they develop a layout design. But whether you set the type yourself or someone else prepares it, the six characteristics mentioned earlier need to be specified. It is important to develop a fine, critical eye for type quality, watching for problems such as uneven letterspacing and low resolution. Oftentimes the type printed on a desktop laser printer inkjet is unsuitable for reproduction, especially if the type is reversed and in a small serif font (Figure 6-16).

Helvetica LIGHT CONDENSED
Helvetica MEDIUM CONDENSED
Helvetica BOLD CONDENSED
Helvetica ULTRA LIGHT
Helvetica ULTRA LIGHT ITALIC
Helvetica LIGHT
Helvetica MEDIUM
Helvetica REGULAR
Helvetica MEDIUM ITALIC
Helvetica BOLD
Helvetica BOLD ITALIC
Helvetica BOLD EXTENDED
HELVETICA OUTLINE

6-15
The Helvetica family.

6-16

This is an example of a reversed 9 point serif font. Often such delicate lines will be overwhelmed by a reversal.

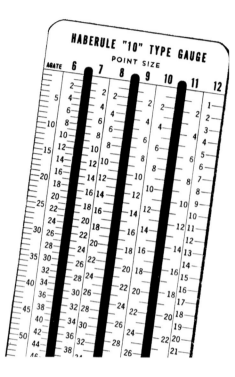

6-17
This pica rule gives measurements in points, picas, and inches.

Size

Text type is any type that is under 14 points in size. A point is a unit of measurement based on the pica. There are 12 points in a pica and approximately 6 picas in an inch, so there are 72 points in an inch (Figure 6-18). The point system of measurement was introduced in the 18th century because the small sizes of text type called for a measuring system with extremely fine increments (Figure 6-17).

Type size is measured in points until it reaches about 2" (5 cm) high. It is available

6-18
Type is measured in points until it reaches about 2" (5 cm) high.

from 5 points to 72 points on desktop computer menus, or larger sizes can be specified (Figure 6-18). When measuring type size by hand, include the ascender and descender in the measurement. The easiest way to measure type without a computer is by comparing it with a type specimen book and matching the size visually. It can also be measured with a point and pica ruler. Remember to measure from top to ascender to bottom of descender.

When choosing a type size, keep the audience in mind. Type smaller than 10 points is often difficult for older people to read.

Type size can be difficult to judge on the computer monitor, because the screen image may not be the same size as your final printed page. Also, the vertical, backlit quality of a monitor is a very different medium than the printed page, and we interact with it differently. Student designers have a tendency to choose sizes that are too large when they first begin designing with type on the computer. It is easier to judge the effect of typography accurately in a printed proof than on line. If the final format will be a Web page, however, this changes.

Line Length

Line length also is measured by the pica system. It is the length in picas of a line of text type. When laying out a page and marking copy for the typesetter, use pica measurements. The dimensions of the page

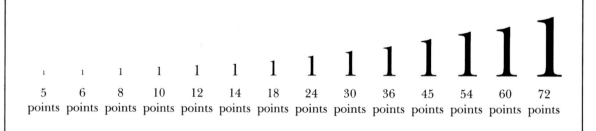

itself, however, are usually expressed in inches (or centimeters). For example, an 8-point type may be set in a 22-pica line length on an 8½ × 11" (22 × 28 cm) page format.

The length of a line is closely related to the size of type. A small point size such as 6 point or 8 point on a line 44 picas long is difficult to read. The type seems to jump around along the midsection of the line, and the eye must search for the beginning of each new line. This trouble is worse when there is insufficient space between lines. Usually you want the reader's eye to move smoothly, never being forced to slow down or lose its place. The standard line length and point size ratio for optimal legibility is a line of 50 to 70 characters long. To remember this ratio, keep in mind that line length should be approximately double the point size. An 8-point type sits well on a 16-pica line. Variations on this theme can be used purposely to slow the reader down.

Style

When you choose text type, legibility is a prime consideration. Although there are many beautiful, elegant, and accessible styles, stay away from styles with an excess of ornamentation when selecting text type.

Next, seek a type appropriate to the audience, the publication, and your own sense of aesthetics. Sans serif has a modern feel and is highly legible in the limited amounts of copy used in most annual reports, newsletters, and so on. The serif types are generally more traditional and classical in feeling. They are easier to read in large amounts. Many of the newer styles strive to combine the virtues of serif and sans serif type.

Trends arise in type, just as in music, clothes, and lifestyles. Notice how they change from year to year. Use the ones that seem both appropriate and aesthetically pleasing.

The printing process can help determine type style selection. Delicate, hairline serifs are not appropriate when a heavy ink coverage is required, because the ink will block up the serifs and result in a blotchy look. Heavily textured paper will also make a delicate serif unadvisable. The texture of the paper will cause the finely inked serifs to break up.

Beginning designers often combine several type styles in a typographical layout. They choose each for its own beauty and interest but forget the effect of the whole design. Diverse styles usually refuse to combine into an organized whole and have an undisciplined and chaotic look. Many experienced designers prefer to work within one type family, drawing on its bold, italic, and roman faces (Figure 6-19). They achieve a look of variety without risking going outside one family. This course is certainly the safest for a new designer.

Exciting layouts, however, often do mix distinctively different typefaces. Mixing takes sensitivity to how the styles affect one another and contribute to the whole. A good rule of thumb when mixing type families is to make certain they are very different. The composition will work if there is either deliberate similarity or definite variety. It can confuse and displease the eye if the distinctions are muddy. Figure 6-20 is a highly successful design that combines type styles to make a point. The MacPros layout in Figure 6-21 uses typography to achieve an overlapping visual texture. Contemporary designers have many more choices of typefaces and design effects than ever before.

Leading

Leading (pronounced like the metal lead) describes the vertical spacing between lines of type. The historical origin of the term goes back to hot-metal typesetting, when a thin strip of lead was inserted as a spacer between lines of metal type. This type and

Helvetica ultra light	Helvetica medium	Helvetica bold	Helvetica medium outline
ABCDEFGHIJ KLMNOPQRS TUVWXYZØa bcdefghijklmno pqrstuvwxyzæ 1234567890&! ?$£%ßŒÆ	ABCDEFGHI JKLMNOPQ RSTUVWXY Zabcdefghijk lmnopqrstuv wxyz123456 7890ß&?!(	ABCDEFGHIJ KLMNOPQRS TUVWXYZab cdefghijklmn opqrstuvwxy zæœç12345 67890ÆŒØ? !£$¢%ß&(	ABCDEFGH IJKLMNOP QRSTUVW XYZ123456 7890ÆŒ&! %?£$¢Ø(

Helvetica ultra light italic	Helvetica bold italic	Helvetica light	Helvetica light cond
ABCDEFGHIJ KLMNOPQRS TUVWXYZabc defghijklmnopq rstuvwxyzæœ 1234567890$ £&%?!ßÆŒØ	***ABCDEFGHIJ KLMNOPQRS TUVWXYZab cdefghijklmn opqrstuvwxy zæœç:12345 67890ÆŒØ! ?&%£$¢ß(***	ABCDEFGHIJ KLMNOPQRS TUVWXYZab cdefghijklmno pqrstuvwxyz 1 234567890?! %$£&ßØ(	ABCDEFGHIJKL MNOPQRSTUVW XYZÆŒØabcde fghijklmnopqrstu vwxyzæœç1234 567890ŒÇØÆ¢ £$ß%?!&/(

Helvetica medium italic	Helvetica bold extended	Helvetica regular	Helvetica medium cond
ABCDEFGHIJ KLMNOPQRS TUVWXYZØa bcdefghijklmn opqrstuvwxyz 1234567890?! ß&£$%Œ	**ABCDEFGH IJKLMNOP QRSTUVXY WZÆŒÇØ abcdefghik jlmnopqrst uvwxyzç12 34567890 ß$£&?!%(**	ABCDEFGHI· JKLMNOPQ? RSTUVWXY- ZÆØabcdef! ghijklmnopqr stuvwxyzæø 1234567890 £$&%(	ABCDEFGHIJKL MNOPQRSTUVW XYZabcdefghijkl mnopqrstuvwxy zæ1234567890! ?&%£$ßÆŒ(

6-19
One type family can offer a great deal of variety.

leading were locked together into a galley, inked, and printed. Leading strongly affects the look and readability of the layout. Type is considered to be set solid when no space is inserted between the descender of the top line and the ascender of the bottom line. A 10-point type set on a 10-point leading is an example of solid leading. Herb Lubalin's design for *Avant Garde* magazine in 1967 uses very tight leading (see Figure 7-10). How much leading you use is important. Several factors affect that decision. Among those factors are type size, line length, and type style (see Figures 6-6, 6-10).

Type Size

Leading must be proportionate to the size of the type. Although there is no standard, correct leading for any certain type size, we often find 10-point type set on 12-point leading. An extra 2 points of space have been inserted between the lines of type. A larger or smaller type size will require less extra leading. A 14-point type might need

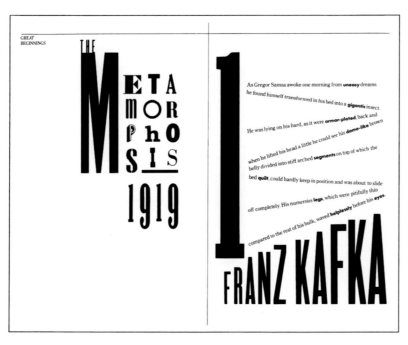

6-20
Paula Scher.
Layout design for *The Metamorphosis* in "Great Beginnings" brochure. *Courtesy of the artist.*

only 14- or 15-point leading, for instance. It is rare to find minus leading, or a 10-point type set on a 9-point leading. Current typesetting technology makes it possible to set one line of type on top of another and to weave entire paragraphs over each other for visual texture. The important criteria is always "is it appropriate" and "is it good design"? Does the form follow and enhance the function?

Line Length

Line length is an important factor in determining leading. The longer the line, the more leading is appropriate. With longer line lengths, the eye has a tendency to wander.

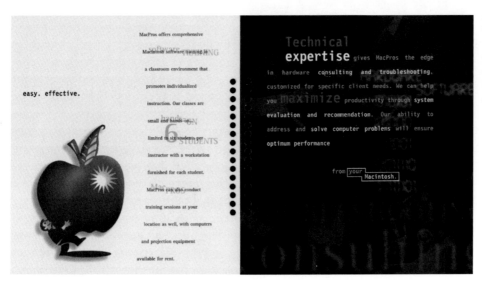

6-21
This brochure for MacPros plays with overlapping typography, as well as changes in size and style in order to get a point across.

If there is insufficient space between lines, you will find yourself reading the line above or beneath and having difficulty finding the beginning of each line.

Type Style

Three aspects of the type style also affect leading: x-height, vertical stress, and serif versus sans serif. The x-height, as you know, refers to the size of the body of the letter, without its ascender and descender. The x-height of Helvetica is much greater than the x-height of an older type such as Garamond. Consequently the Helvetica would probably require more leading. It does not have lots of extra white space packed around its body because it has relatively short ascenders and descenders, so the lines of type appear closer together.

The vertical stress of a type style also affects leading because the stronger the vertical emphasis, the more the eye is drawn up and down instead of along the line of type. Hence the greater the vertical stress, the more leading required. A type style such as Baskerville has a strong vertical stress and requires more leading than Garamond.

A serif helps draw the eye along in a horizontal direction, so serif type is generally considered easier to read than sans serif type. Sans serif type usually requires more leading than the serif style to keep the eye moving smoothly along.

Spacing

Letterspacing is the amount of space between letters of a word (Figure 6-22). A good figure/ground relationship between letterforms is as important with text type as with display type. If the letters are spaced too far apart, the eye must jump

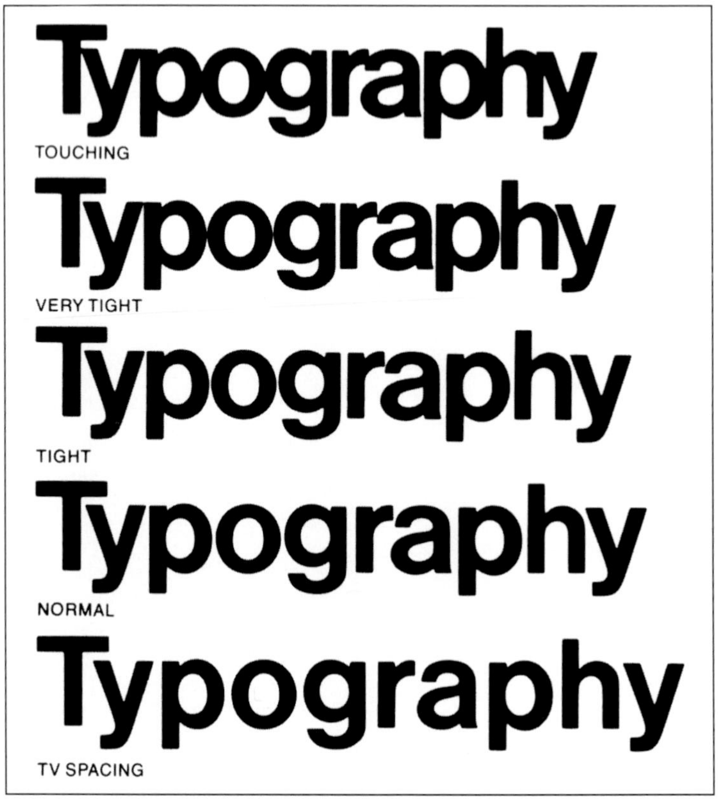

6-22

There is a great deal of difference between tight and loose letterspacing.

Typography
TOUCHING

Typography
VERY TIGHT

Typography
TIGHT

Typography
NORMAL

Typography
TV SPACING

between letters, and reading becomes strained.

Whether designing with text type or display type, keep an eye out for the creation of equal volumes of white space between individual letterforms. *Kerning* is a term that describes the specific adjustment of space between individual letterforms. An "IH," for example, will require a different spacing than an "MN" (Figure 6-23). Again, examine Lubalin's design.

The amount of space between words is called *word spacing.* If it is too great, it is difficult for the eye to move quickly along the line of type. There is a tendency to pause between individual words. The reader should be unaware of the space between words, and aware instead of their content.

Word spacing usually is not a problem with text type, unless the type is being set in a justified format (flush left and flush right edges). To make the lines come out even, the computer will insert extra space between words. If the line length is long, with many words, this addition is not noticeable. However, if the line length is short, great white holes seem to appear in the copy (Figure 6-24). Look at your local newspaper, and squint. Often rivers of white will appear in the columns of text type as a result of poor word spacing.

Format

Format design refers to the arrangement of lines of type on the page (Figure 6-25). There are two basic categories: justified and unjustified. In *justified* type the lines are all the same length, so that the left and right edges of the column of type are straight. This format is commonly used in newspaper layout and text and trade books. It is appropriate when speed and ease of reading are the primary considerations. Justified copy is considered by many to be slightly easier to read than unjustified copy. The straight, squared-off

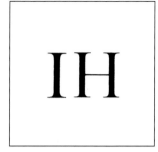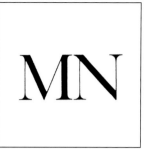

6-23
Spacing between letterforms must vary to please the eye.

columns of type give an orderly, classical feeling to the page.

Unjustified copy can be arranged in a variety of ways: flush left, flush right, centered, and asymmetrical. The "New Typography" of the 1920s believed ragged right type was more readable than a justified format. Unequal line length was also an important part of the International Style.

Flush Left

The flush left format calls for a straight left edge and a ragged right edge. Typewritten copy is usually flush left. This format is commonly used in annual reports, brochures, identification lines under photographs, and any time when a slightly more informal look is desired than can be achieved with justified type. One of the benefits of this format is that it is possible to avoid hyphenated words. Page layout software programs usually allow the user to set parameters for

The head of the nation's military, Gen. Fidel Ramos, warned Thursday of a possible plot by disaffected officers. His office said he had "warned any military adventurers against embarking on such a rash course of action because it could be bloody and destabilizing."

6-24
Justifying copy in a short line length will cause white holes to appear.

The design principles of proximity, similarity grouping, and focal point are all important considerations in layout design. Variations in point size and font style function like a code to guide a reader.

The headings and subheadings in this text, for example, are carefully chosen to visually group information topics and to separate out new topics.

These headings should be physically grouped in closer proximity to the information they introduce than to the unrelated paragraph above.

These headings should be physically grouped in closer proximity to the information they introduce than to the unrelated paragraph above.

6-25
Variations in format.

hyphenation. A designer can specify how many can happen in succession and just how ragged the right or left edge can become.

Flush Right

The flush right format is unusual and consequently difficult to read. It has a ragged left edge and is used for design effect in special situations. It is difficult for the eye to search out the beginning of each new line without a common starting point.

Centered

Centered copy is often found in headlines or invitations, but rarely in standard copy. It is a slow-reading, classical format that encourages the reader to pause after each line. It is important to make logical breaks at the end of each line. This format has a pronounced irregular shape and packs a lot of space

around itself. The white space and irregular outline can draw the eye strongly. Consider the content of your material, how rapidly it should be read, and the overall look of the page before deciding on a centered format.

Asymmetrical

Asymmetrically arranged type can put across the point of a poem or an important statement. Asymmetry is also used in display type to achieve better balance among letterforms. Contour type is a form of asymmetry that fits the shape of an illustration, following its contour. Type that is set around the squared edge of a photo is called a *runaround.* Occasionally type will be set in the shape of a contour itself.

The ancient Egyptians and Greeks originally experimented with this format. It was used early in the 20th century by the poet Apollinaire and more recently by contemporary designers. Figure 6-26 is a typographic illustration created by a recent design graduate.

Style and Content

Typography sets a visual tone depending on the variables we have just examined. The style, the leading, and the format all contribute to a nonverbal communication that has a great deal to say. This visual communication, or visual language, affects the image of the client. It is a function of the choices the designer has made partly as a personal preference, partly in response to the client's needs, and partly in response to contemporary design trends.

Specific type styles and layout designs are associated with historical periods. Type styles can evoke the mood of an era just through careful type selection and usage. The 20th century in the United States has seen many styles come into vogue and then fade out. Typestyles reflect their era's philosophical and technological status.

Wood display type was widely used in the 1800s. By the latter part of the century, these wooden type styles became elaborate, beautifully decorative designs. Type styles and trends continued to change, reflecting the sensibilities and technology of the time. Broadway type style was popular in the 1930s; the sans serif styles of Helvetica and Univers were widely used in the 1950s and 1960s. Today's styles show an appreciation for classic style as well as an eclectic willingness to experiment with unusual graphic effects, as digital typesetting encourages stylistic innovation.

With the advent of digital typography, special effects with type and layout design are easier to achieve than ever before. Experimentation is good, especially when tempered by a firm knowledge of traditional typographic design principles.

Some Problems

Once the format for the layout is selected and the type is set, some awkward accidents may occur. If you are aware of these problems, you can avoid them.

Widows and orphans are romantic names designating isolated line endings and dangling words. A *widow* is a short line that ends a paragraph and appears at the top or bottom of a printed column. An *orphan* is a single word that also appears in the isolated position and is most distressing when it appears at the top of a new page.

Hyphenation can also become a problem, especially if the line length is short and the format is justified. Too many hyphenated words will interfere with legibility. Hyphens should always fall at syllables, and they should not chop the word into unrecognizable segments.

A DESIGN SUMMARY

Good design using typography is a delicate thing. It relies on so many interrelated variables that it cannot be reduced to a simple formula. Here, however, are a few summary comments:

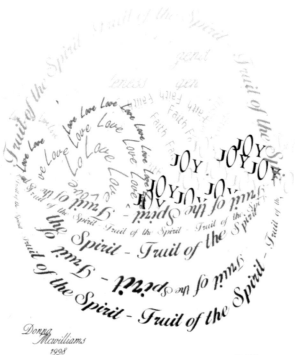

6-26
An asymmetrical typographic illustration by illustrator **D. McWilliams** for her student portfolio.

- When choosing type styles, remember that it is wise to either mix very different fonts or to stay within the same type family. For example, two fairly similar serif fonts will be more difficult to use together than a serif and a sans serif. Staying within a family gives a wide but unified choice.
- A combination of multiple fonts with strong personalities and highly distinctive styles are difficult to use together because they all call for attention. Thus it becomes difficult to establish a visual hierarchy.
- The design principles of proximity, similarity grouping, and focal point are all important considerations in layout design. Variations in point size and font style function like a code to guide a

reader. The headings and subheadings in this text, for example, are carefully chosen to group information topics visually and to separate out new topics. These headings should be physically grouped in closer proximity to the information they introduce than to the unrelated paragraph above.

- Decide what kind of speed you want from your reader. A justified format is the quickest read; ragged right takes a little more intimate involvement on the part of the reader. A centered format is a very slow read, presenting itself line by line rather than as a grouped paragraph. Mixing these formats can be done to clue the reader visually about the content. The running text in a chapter may be justified, for example, while the photo captions are all ragged right.
- Every element that goes onto a page is important. Every element contributes to the whole. Take nothing for granted.

EXECUTION

Comping Type

In order to visualize a layout before the final typesetting, the designer may make an actual size rough. Headlines used to be indicated by hand, letter by letter, while text type was suggested by a procedure called *comping.* The width of each line should match the x-height of the proposed type. Type can be indicated by using a chisel-point pencil or gray marker or by drawing two lines that indicate the top and bottom of each line of type. Figure 6-27 shows comped type on an ad layout. Most contemporary designers simply set the copy (or dummy copy) on a computer, because format and style changes can be easily made. The danger with immediately turning to typeset copy is that it can look finished before enough thought has been given to design. Use the computer to generate a rich range of possible solutions, rather than to lock on to and refine one solution.

6-27
J. P. Sartori.
(UW-Whitewater design collection). Ad layouts using comped text to indicate typography.

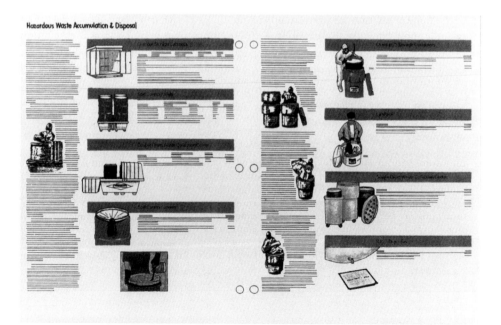

Delete	Close up
Insert here	Elevate a word
Move to left	Move to right
Lower a letter	Insert an Em space
Insert 2 Em spaces	Broken type, please reset
New paragraph	No new paragraph
Open up a space	Close up a space
Restore to original *stet*	Wrong font
Transpose	Set in caps and lower case
Set in all caps	Set in small caps
Set in boldface	Set in roman
Set in italics	Change to lower case
Insert period	

6-28
Proofreader's Marks

Specifying Copy

If the designer is not doing the typesetting, but is sending the copy to someone else, the next step is to specify the copy. When you *spec* copy, you provide all the information necessary to set the final type for layout starting with the original copy: type style, size, leading, format, line length, sometimes letterspacing, and special instructions.

Making Corrections

Almost always some corrections are needed in typeset copy, due to last-minute revisions or errors. Proofreading is an easier job now, with the spell check available on layout programs. Use it always.

You will need to know proofreader's marks to make corrections from a design point of view, such as damaged copy, poor breaks in words, or incorrect font. The standard proofreader's marks are shown in Figure 6-28. It is a good idea to use one color for corrections. The color you choose will come to be a visual symbol signaling your corrections.

Exercises

1. Study various magazines, newspapers, and other publications for samples of the different formats. Which are successful, and which are flawed?
2. Choose two of your less effective samples for analysis. Determine their line length, leading, point size, and type style. Figure 6-29 is a lovely sample of type design and layout.
3. Practice comping a page of type from this book. Then stand back, squint, and ask yourself if your comping matches the value of the actual typeset copy. How can it be improved? Are the x-height and leading accurate?

Projects

Typographical Illustration of a Poem
Select a poem or an interesting and emotive piece of prose that is no longer than twenty lines. Set it twice, using the typesetting equipment available to you. The first time, follow the standard guides for type design to

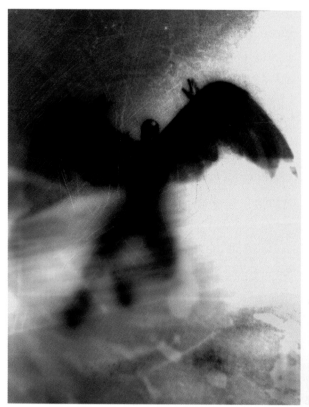
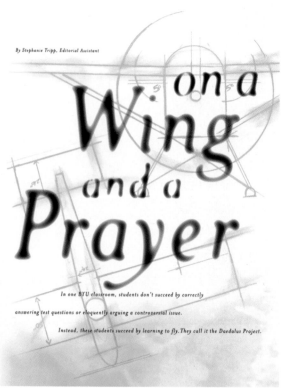

By Stephanie Tripp, Editorial Assistant

on a **Wing** and a *Prayer*

In one BYU classroom, students don't succeed by correctly answering test questions or eloquently arguing a controversial issue. Instead, these students succeed by learning to fly. They call it the Daedalus Project.

6-29
Spread from BYU Magazine.
Design studio: BYU Publications & Graphics, Provo, Utah. Art Director: Bruce Patrick. Designer/illustrator: Emily Johnson. John Rees photographer/johnrees@ qwest.net. *Courtesy of the artist.*

enhance legibility and pay close attention to leading, line length, spacing, and format. Select one type family, limit the fonts, and restrict the point size variation.

Set it again, breaking as many rules as you wish, while creating an effect appropriate to the piece and your feelings about it. Experiment with complexity and diversity. Freehand, Illustrator, Quark, or other vector graphics programs are suitable for these projects. If planning for online output, raster graphics programs can provide rich results (see Chapter 11).

Book Cover Design

Book covers are like small posters. They attract readers with their strong visuals. Create covers for two books that are part of a reissued series by a 20th-century author. The covers for this series should be visually united in a way to indicate they are part of a series. Consider similar color, layout, graphic technique, and so on. Be sure they are also varied enough to hold interest. Use a primarily typographic treatment, but consider including abstract or nonobjective shapes. Paula Scher's Great Beginnings series shown in this chapter is a good inspiration for this project.

Design the entire cover, including front, spine, back, and flaps. Include appropriate information. Print the finished pieces and fold them around an actual book for final presentation.

The research part of this assignment is important. Be familiar with the author's

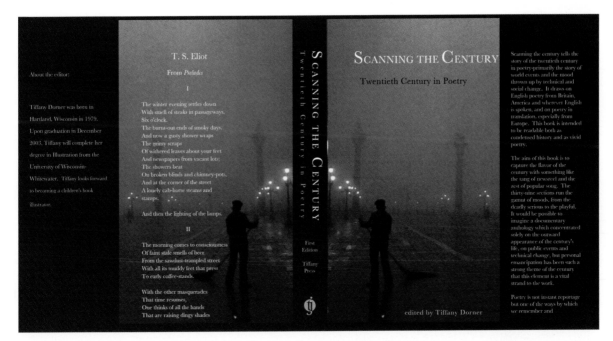

writings, so that your design reflects the content and tone of the writing. Spend time at a local bookstore, looking at the competition's cover designs. Look at a series, and consider how they are united. Look for designs that are primarily typographic.

Objectives

Learn to apply gestalt unit-forming principles to layout design.

Learn to integrate text and display type, while carefully orchestrating eye direction.

Learn to integrate typography and image to express a mood.

6-30
Tiffany Dorner created this cover design for her student portfolio using Photoshop and Illustrator. Her personal logo is include on the spine.

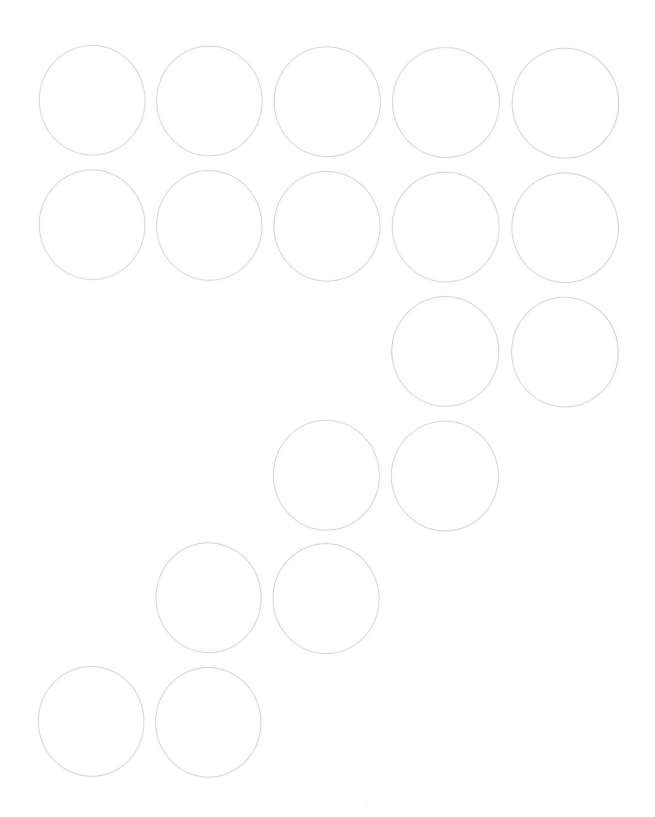

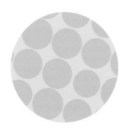

Chapter 7 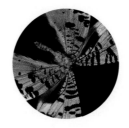 layout

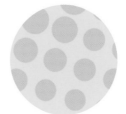

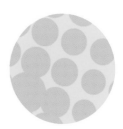

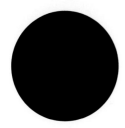

THE BALANCING ACT

Layout is a balancing act in two senses. First, it relates the diverse elements on a printed page in a way that communicates and has aesthetic appeal. Ideally, the form enhances the communication, no matter what style is being used (Figure 7-1).

Second, as in all design, every element on the page affects how the other elements are perceived. Layout is not simply the addition of photographs, text type, display type, or artwork. It is a carefully balanced integration of elements.

The layout artist must select an appropriate typeface from the vast array available. The format, size, and value contrast of the typographical elements must be closely related to accompanying photographs and illustrations. Layout may be the most difficult balancing act a designer is ever called on to perform.

Everything you have studied so far about creating a balanced visual gestalt holds true for layout design. A good relationship between figure and ground is essential. The careful shaping of the white ground of the page gives cohesion and unity to the figures or elements placed on it. No leftover space should be unshaped, undesigned. Open white space functions as an active, participating part of the whole design. Page design can be symmetrically or asymmetrically balanced. In either case, careful figure/ground grouping will enhance the readability of the page.

A careful balancing of contrast can give the page dynamic, unpredictable energy that will draw the reader's eye. Chapter 4 discussed contrasts in size, shape, value, and texture. A combination of similarity and contrast creates a balanced and successful layout.

SIZE AND PROPORTION

This difficult balancing act calls for sensitivity to proportion—the organization of several things into a relationship of size,

7-1

Terry Koppel.
(Koppel & Scher, New York.) Layout for *Fear of Flying* in "Great Beginnings" brochure. *Courtesy of the designer.*

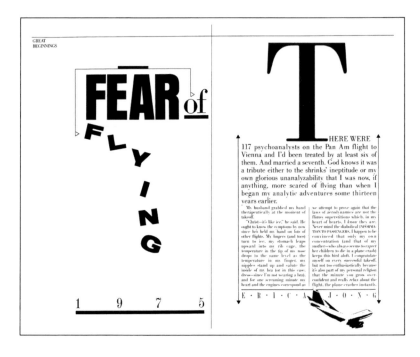

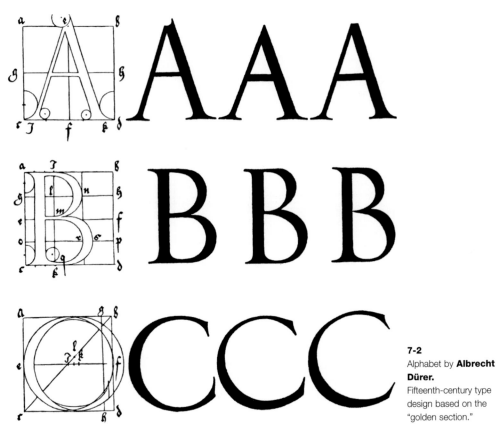

7-2
Alphabet by **Albrecht Dürer.**
Fifteenth-century type design based on the "golden section."

quantity, or degree. Artists have understood the importance of size relationships for centuries. The Parthenon expressed the Greeks' sense of proportion. It was based on a mathematical principle that came to be known as the "golden section." Albrecht Dürer used the golden section in the 15th century to analyze and construct his alphabet (Figure 7-2). The architect Le Corbusier applied the proportions of the golden mean or section to architectural design. It is based on a rectangle that can be subdivided into a square and a second rectangle with the same proportions as the original. Each resulting small rectangle can be subdivided to produce the same results. Figure 7-3 shows a diagram of those proportions. Ultimately, however, no mathematical system can take the place of

an intuitive feeling for proportion or a sense of tension and energy in contrast. When the contrast between elements is too great, however, harmony and balance are lost.

The division of a page into areas in harmony with one another is at the heart of all

7-3
The golden section.

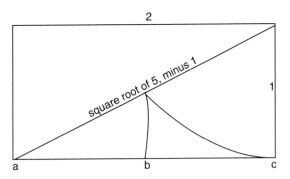

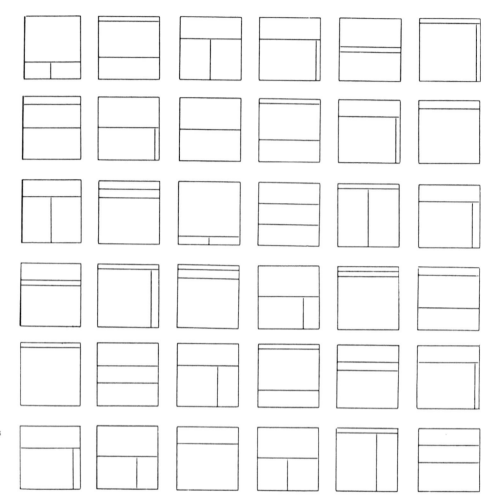

7-4
Emil Ruder.
Page areas in harmonious
proportion. *Diagrams
courtesy of Arthur Niggli
Ltd., Niederteufen,
Switzerland.*

layout design. Figure 7-4 shows how Emil Ruder, an influential Swiss designer of the International Style, worked with bringing a page and its elements into harmony. He felt the relationships between type sizes, between printed and unprinted areas, between type and image, and between various values of gray must all be harmoniously proportionate.

When we refer to size, we usually use words like *big* or *small*. These terms are meaningless, however, unless we have two objects to compare. A 36-point word in a page with a lot of text type will be large. On a spread with a 72-point headline, it will be relatively small. An element large or bold in proportion to other elements on the page makes an obvious visual impact and a potentially strong focal point. Do not be afraid to use an element really LARGE, as in Figure 7-1, where the letter *T* makes a bold graphic statement. Several magazines use a larger format than is standard. This is another example of size contrast. Next to other magazines on the news racks, they have the impact of a comparatively large and impressive display.

Another way of determining size is to have a standard expected size in mind. If we refer to a large household cat, "large" means

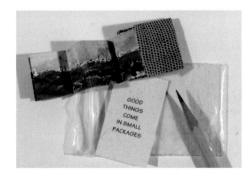

over 12 inches (30 cm) high. If we refer to a large horse, we have a different size in mind. Deliberately violating this expectation can create a dynamic, unusual effect. Mixing up standard relative sizes creates strong tension and compelling interest.

Another approach to confusing our sense of size and scale is by showing objects larger than life. On the printed page, viewers have come to expect things to be shown smaller than they really are. We have no problem accepting a photograph in which the Empire State Building appears 30 (8 cm) high; but magnify a tiny object, and we get a visual jolt that makes us pay attention. Imagine the photograph of a common housefly twenty times actual size. Figure 7-5 is a wonderful play on portfolio size by contemporary designer Karen Roehr.

VISUAL RHYTHM

Another important consideration in layout design is visual rhythm. Life itself is based on rhythm. There is a rhythm to the passing days and seasons. The tempo of our days may be fast or slow. The growth and gradual decline of all natural life-forms has a rhythm. Cities have particular pulsing rhythms. Different periods in our history have seemed to move to various beats. Our current age has an eclectic/quickened tempo compared with a hundred years ago.

Visual rhythm is based on repetition of shapes, values, colors, and textures. Recurrences of shapes and the spacing between them set up a pattern or rhythm. It can be quick and lively, lyrical, or solemn and dignified. Rhythm is crucial in the work of many visual artists including the illustration in Figure 7-6.

There are many ways to use rhythm in typography. Within a single word, a rhythmic pattern of ascenders and descenders and curves and lines is created. The rhythm might be symmetrical or asymmetrical in character. Letter and word spacing can set up a typographical movement of varying

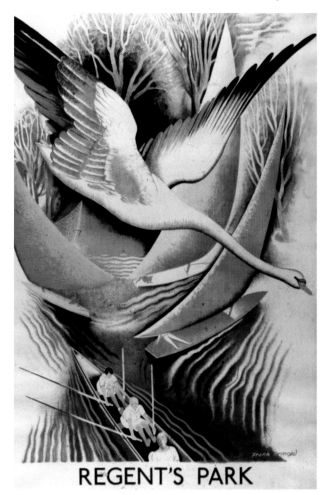

REGENT'S PARK

7-7
Letterspacing affects tempo.

tempo **o** **tempo**

t e m p o

tempos, as can changes in value and size (Figure 7-7).

The total layout of the page is another opportunity to form a rhythmic pattern. The lines of type can form a rhythm of silent pauses and rests, of leaps, of slow ascents and descents. Endless rhythms can be created this way (Figure 7-8).

The spacing and size of photographs can intermingle with typography. An alternating visual rhythm may reserve every left-hand page for a full-page photograph while the right-hand page is textured with smaller units of text and other elements.

7-8
Erik Peterson.
This student layout uses visual rhythm to deal with a difficult topic.

Another form of rhythm is progressive rhythm. The repeated element changes in a regular fashion. Text type might be used in changing values from regular to bold to extra bold and back again. A photograph might be repeated, each time with more of the image displayed. This rhythmic movement can take place on one page or on successive pages. Change in regular manner is at the heart of a progressive rhythm.

GRID LAYOUT

A sense of pacing and rhythm can be set up throughout an entire publication with the aid of a grid. A *grid* is an invisible structure underlying the page that is used as a guide for the placement of layout elements.

When and why is it appropriate to use a grid? Large publications usually require one to keep order. Grids may be used in single-page designs such as advertisements and posters. Figure 7-9 is an excellent example by the important 20th-century American modernist designer Herb Lubalin. They are also used to bring continuity to the separate pieces of a design series (Figure 7-10). A grid is most useful when it brings an organized unity not only to a single page, but also to facing pages, an entire publication, or a series of publications.

Layout design that utilizes a grid is as flexible and creative as its designer is. The grid has been accused of bringing a boring conformity to page design. Grids, however, can help generate distinctive, dynamic images. They allow for experimentation with all the forms of contrast. A grid functions like a musical instrument. A piano, for instance, has a limited number of keys of fixed tone and position. It is possible, however, to play many different musical compositions through placement, rhythm, repetition, and emphasis. Figure 7-11 by Herb Lubalin incorporates many different elements in seeming harmony through the use of a grid.

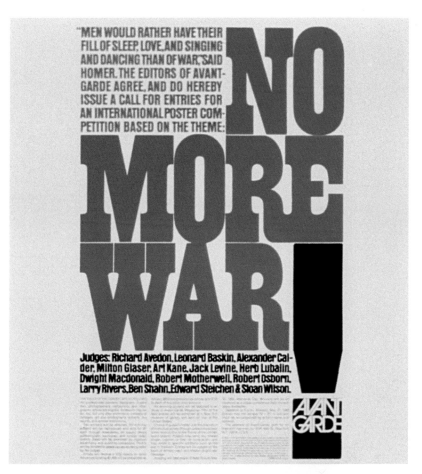

7-9
Herb Lubalin.
Advertisement for the magazine *Avant Garde*'s antiwar poster competition, 1967. An underlying grid and play on size contrast give a tight structure to this design.

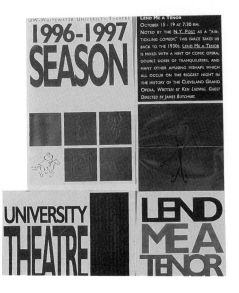

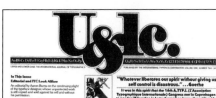

(left)
7-10
Design Studio 45, a student design agency at UW–Whitewater, created this series of publications promoting an upcoming theatre season. A grid layout integrates the various pieces.

(right)
7-11
Herb Lubalin.
Cover for *U&lc.* 1974. An underlying grid gives a clear structure to the many diverse elements in this layout design.

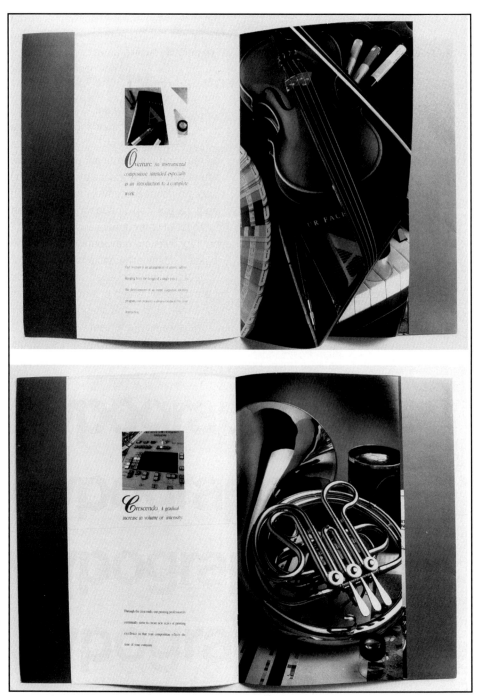

7-12, 7-13
Layouts for self-promotional brochure by 12Twelve Design, a division of Terry Printing. **Mary Hakala,** art director; **Dennis Dooley,** photographer. *Courtesy of the artist.*

Keeping the Beat

A musical composition has a timing or beat that pulses beneath all the long and short notes. In a visual composition, a grid often keeps this beat. Just as a four-beats-to-the-measure musical score would not be cut off at 3.5 beats, a grid layout that has four sections across will not end at 3.5. Whether the fourth unit is filled with an element or left as a white ground, it gets its full count and full visual weight. Within these four musical counts might be a mixture of quarter notes, half notes, or whole notes. The four-unit grid might hold one large four-unit element, two half-unit elements, or four quarter-unit elements. The beauty in any composition, whether visual or auditory, comes once the structure is set up and the variations in pacing, timing, and emphasis begin.

Playing the Theme

An underlying musical theme, like the one in Beethoven's Sixth Symphony (the "Pastoral"), will appear over and over in different guises, tying the symphony together into a whole. An underlying visual theme will accomplish the same for a visual composition. A layout for a publication unfolds through time, just as a musical concert does. Each page must be turned before the next is revealed. It cannot be seen and grasped at one viewing like a painting, an advertisement, or a poster. Unifying it requires a theme. Often this theme will include both a purely visual *design* theme

and an editorial *content* theme (Figures 7-12 and 7-13).

The editorial theme could be the repetition of quotations on a particular topic. It could be a contrast of "then and now," a set of interviews—anything that seems to tell an interesting story related to a common topic. Advertising campaigns are usually based on an editorial theme. Specialty publications such as annual reports, which revolve around one company, may also use an editorial approach.

A visual theme almost always accompanies the editorial theme. It might be the repeated use of a single thematic photograph on several pages throughout the publication. It could be a particular repeated arrangement of typography—or the grid itself. Figures 7-14 and 7-15 show a sensitive use of an underlying structure to bring unity to the pages.

Grids in History

The grid is by no means a new invention. It has been used for centuries by various

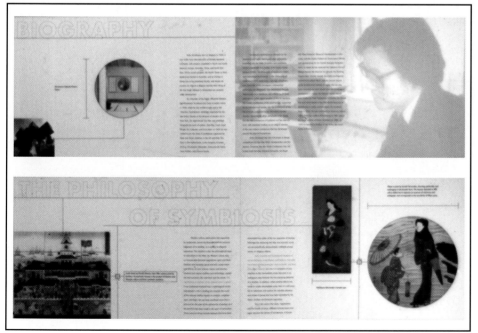

7-14, 7-15
Designer and educator **Daniel Kim** prepared these comp layouts for his portfolio, showing a creative application of grid layout. *Courtesy of the artist.*

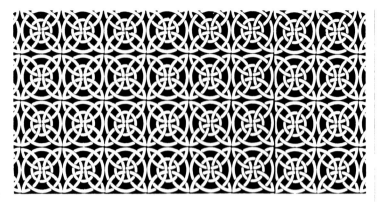

7-16
An ornamental grid design.

cultures to design ornamental screens and textiles (Figure 7-16). It has been the basis for quilt design, architecture, and navigation. Pakistanis, Native Americans, Africans contemporary designers, and a host of others have used it. The squared grid, in which each of the four sides of the unit is equal to the others, is the simplest variation, but it is capable of yielding sophisticated results whether used in quilts or layout design (Figure 7-17).

Renaissance artists developed a method of examining a subject through a grid network of strings and drawing onto a paper

similarly divided into sections. In the 20th century, the grid became of interest to artists as a shape in itself. Frequently drawings, illustrations, and paintings allow the grid structure to show through, just as Bauhaus architects insisted that the structure of their buildings show through.

Many layouts today that have a strong grid structure trace their origins to the de Stijl movement. Van Doesburg and Mondrian were both using dark lines to divide their canvases into asymmetrical patterns by 1918 (Figure 2-23, 4-2).

7-17
**Julius Friedman/
Walter McCord,** designers; **Craig Guyon,** photographer. Quilts: Handmade Color. *Courtesy of the artist.*

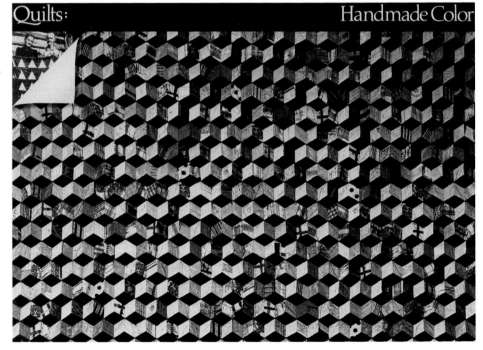

A more recent figure associated with the grid layout is Swiss designer Josef Müller-Brockmann. He had tremendous influence on the structure and definition of graphic design. "The tauter the composition of elements in the space available, the more effectively can the thematic idea be formulated," he stated. Copy, photographs, drawings, and trade names are all subservient to the underlying grid structure in this modernist approach that continues to have contemporary relevance (Figure 4-3).

Grid design is incorporated into our current technology. Dedicated page layout programs like Quark, do an excellent job of accommodating a grid-based layout. They allow the designer to construct an individually designed grid and specify type to fill the columns.

Choosing a Grid

Grids are as different as the minds that create them. They vary from the familiar three-column format, to a Swiss grid based on overlapping squares, to an original creation.

The first consideration when choosing a grid is the elements it will contain. Consider the copy. How long is it; how long are the individual segments; how many inserts and subheads? If the copy is composed of many independent paragraphs, the underlying grid should break the page area up into small units. If the copy is a textbook of long unbroken chapters with few visuals, however, a complex grid is wasted; most of its divisions will be seldom used.

Now consider the art. A publication that uses many photographs will call for a different grid than one that is copy heavy. Whenever many elements need to be incorporated into a layout, a more complex grid, broken down into many small units, is the most useful. It will give more possibilities for placing and sizing photographs.

You can create your own grid that corresponds to the number of elements and size of your page. The tinier the grid units, the more choices you will need to make about placement. The more placement options there are, the greater the chance the underlying unity will be lost. In other words, sometimes a simple grid is the best choice.

Both the vertical and the horizontal divisions in a grid are important. The vertical dividers determine the line length of the copy. Both the vertical and horizontal lines determine the size of photographs or artwork. Remember from Chapter 6 to relate line length and type size to make it easy for the eye to read and keep its place. Forcing large type into small grid units makes for slow, difficult reading.

Constructing the Grid

The vertical divisions of the grid are usually expressed in picas or in inches, as is the line length of copy measured for typesetting. The horizontal divisions are most frequently measured in points, as is leading. A 10-point type, for example, with 2 points of leading between lines would be set on 12-point leading. This type could be specified at a 21-pica line length or 3.5-inch line length. The column width would correspond. The structure is usually sounder if the elements themselves align with the grid edges and merely suggest the presence of the grid. With precise alignment, our eyes will draw an invisible line of continuation between elements that is a much stronger bond than the physical, inked line.

Grid structure and the path layout are both used to bring balance and harmony to page design. Both depend on the eye and mind detecting such unit-forming factors as repetition and continuation, tempered with a deliberate contrast or variation for effect.

PATH LAYOUT

The path layout assumes no underlying, unifying structure. Rather, the designer begins with a blank white sheet of paper and attempts to visualize the elements on it in

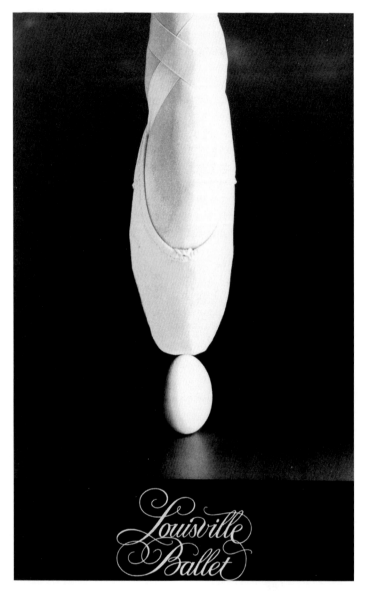

7-18
Julius Friedman, designer; **John Lair,** photographer. Poster for the Louisville Ballet. *Courtesy of the artist.*

for the eye. The goal is to guide the eye skillfully through the various elements. In order to do so, there usually is a clear entry point or focal point and a clear path to the next element and the next. A simple path layout is used effectively in Figure 7-18, a poster design for the Louisville Ballet by designer Julius Friedman.

Focal Point

The focal point, or the point of entry into a design, is the first area that attracts attention and encourages the viewer to look further. If at first glance, our eye is drawn equally to several different areas, visual chaos results and interest is lost. A focal point can be set up in many different ways, but they all have to do with creating difference or variety. Whatever disrupts an overall visual field will draw the eye. The focal point should not be so overwhelming that the eye misses the rest of the composition.

These differences could become the focal point:

- A heavy black value set down in a field of gray and white.
- A small isolated element in a design with several larger elements in close proximity to one another.
- An irregular, organically shaped element set next to geometric ones.
- A textured element set next to solid areas. Text type can often function in this manner.
- A pictorial image or word that is emotionally loaded.

PHOTOGRAPHY IN A LAYOUT

An important element in layout design is the photograph. A designer must learn what makes a good photograph and how to use it to best advantage. Copywriters, photographers, and designers depend on one another's skills. Poor page design can make a beautiful photograph lose all its impact and appeal. Sometimes, conversely, a poor

various arrangements. This complex approach can yield tremendously varied results. The underlying unity comes from a direct reliance on unit-forming factors. This reliance is sometimes unconscious, but beginning designers should learn and practice it on a conscious level. It can lead to excellent results.

The word *path* describes this less structured, more spontaneous approach because the designer is attempting to set up a path

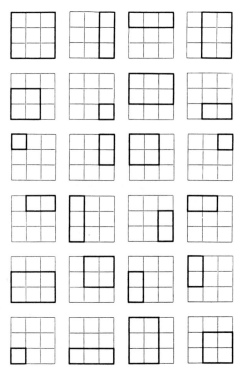

7-19
Emil Ruder.
Photo placements on a
grid. *Design courtesy
Arthur Niggli Ltd.*

on the remaining portion. Cropping is also used to fit a photograph into an available space by altering its proportions. When cropping to fit a space, use discretion. Cropping too tightly will destroy the mood of the image.

Sometimes a photograph, like an overwritten paragraph, can be improved by deleting excess information. The format is fixed in a camera, but the action being photographed might be taking place within a compact square area or a long thin vertical. Trimming away the meaningless part of the image on the sides will improve the impact, as in the newspaper image shown in Figure 7-20. It

photograph may be strengthened by a good design.

Dynamic photos strong in design and human interest can be made to look lifeless with certain design mistakes. One problem can be the paper choice. If it is too absorbent for the reproduction method, it will ink poorly, so the value contrast in the reproduced photos will be muddy. Another common mistake is lack of size contrast. When photos of similar sizes compete for attention; the eye will be drawn to none. Other elements on the page may also point away or detract from the photographic image.

Figure 7-19 shows some different ways of placing a photograph on a grid layout. Practice some variations yourself, attempting to establish a visual pacing.

Cropping

Many photographs can be improved by the designer's careful cropping. Cropping is eliminating part of the vertical or horizontal dimension of a photograph to focus attention

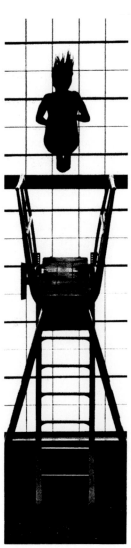

7-20
Gordon Baer
(Cincinnati, OH) Pepsi-Cola
Diving Competition.
Courtesy of the artist.

can also enhance a feeling of motion, as shown in this same photograph.

Sometimes cropping a photograph makes it dramatic. If you wish to emphasize the height of a tall building, for example, cropping in on the sides to make a long, thin rectangle will increase the sense of height. Cropping the top and bottom of a long horizontal shot will increase the sense of an endless horizon.

Cropping causes us to focus on the dramatic part of the poster image in Figure 7-21, a poster for the Cincinnati Ballet Company. The feet present a theme on repetition and variation and set up a wonderful visual rhythm.

Resizing

All the traditional resizing methods are becoming less important, as designers usually resize, crop, and experiment with the results on the computer. The important thing to understand is the concept of ratio. You must maintain the integrity of the original photograph, without expanding or distorting images to fit a space. Always maintain the original height-to-width ratio when rescaling a photograph. The software can help with that, if you check a retain proportion box or hold down the shift key when resizing.

Selecting

A designer may be given the photographs to work with or have the opportunity to order specific photos shot. You might also elect to shoot them personally. It is a wise idea for anyone considering a career in graphic design to take a course in photography.

Choose photographs for your layout on three grounds: *the quality of the print or digital file, the merit of the design, and the strength of the communication.*

Photo retouching programs make it easier to correct problems with print quality. It is helpful to understand what are good reproduction qualities in a photograph, in order to recognize and/or achieve them. Some of these qualities depend on the form of output. Generally, however, watch for good contrast between darks and lights, a full tonal range, sharp focus (where appropriate), and lack of scratches, dust spots, and other imperfections.

Multi-panel Design

Folders and brochures present a slightly different layout problem than magazines or books. A brochure is actually more a three-dimensional construction than a two-dimensional layout. Nevertheless, a grid may be used. Contrast of size and visual rhythm remain important.

7-21
Dan Bittman, designer;
Corson Hirschfeld, photographer; and the Hennegan Company, lithography. Poster for the Cincinnati Ballet Company.

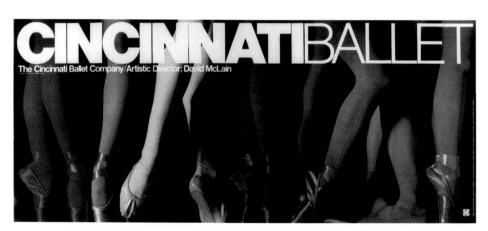

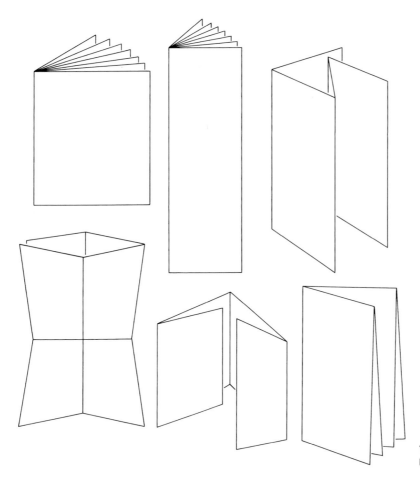

7-22
Brochure construction.

The additional element of the fold compli-
cates matters. Brochures may fold and
unfold into unusual shapes (Figure 7-22).
They may unfold several times and at each
successive unfolding present a new facet of
the design. Use this opportunity to tell a
story. Each panel can give additional information, with the front panel acting as a teaser.
Never give your punch line on the front panel.
Lead up to it. A successful front panel will lure
the reader inside. The succeeding panels will
build interest and develop a theme (Figure
7-23). If the brochure is a self-mailer, address
and stamp are placed directly on the back.

7-23
Anita Syverson created
this multipanel design for
Cummings Advertising
making creative use of
stock photography.

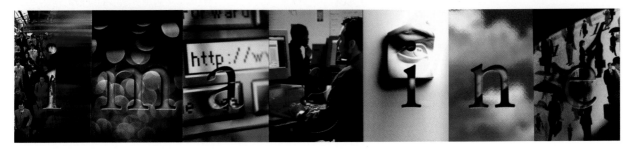

Other special decisions go into a multi-panel design: the size of the piece, the number of folds and their direction, and the flexibility of the paper. Usually when preparing a comprehensive, the designer will try to execute it on the same paper it will be printed on. Then the client can hold and unfold the design.

The brochure or flyer will often be part of a unified publication series. Then you must sustain the visual and intellectual theme of the series (Figures 7-24a, b.)

Layout Styles

During the discussion of design history presented in Chapter 2, you learned that the European-influenced modern style was imported to the United States during the 1940s. Characterized by sans serif typography and the belief in a universally shared aesthetic, the modern style saw order as the spirit of a modern, rational, technological civilization. The development of the grid system seen in the work of Swiss designer Josef Müller-Brockmann, Emil Ruder, and

others fit into this perception of design as a wedding of science and aesthetics in a rational world.

Design in the 1960s became more eclectic and inclusive. The 1970s saw a questioning of the rational Swiss design approach that led to the development of New Wave or postmodern graphic design. The designs of the International Typography Style and modernism were seen as too reductive. A new interest in complex, layered forms and meaning developed. April Greiman's work shows the exuberance of this inclusive, eclectic style that celebrates complexity and diversity. Greiman's work retains a strong sense of underlying structure (see Figure 2-36). As postmodernism grew, art and design history became a great visual resource for appropriation where all styles are potentially meaningful. Art nouveau, art deco, pop art, Swiss modernism, and personal intuition may all be combined to generate the postmodern design.

Katherine McCoy is an important figure in postmodern design who, as an educator and designer, articulates and defines the nature of the multiple layers of communication possible in the contemporary visual design. She writes about design criticism and consults in graphic design, marketing, and interior design for cultural, educational, and corporate clients. Her Web site at www.highgrounddesign.com contains an excellent discussion of contemporary issues.

7-24a, b
Connie McNish.
This unified series designed while McNish was a student includes a letterhead, envelope, business card, and a promotional brochure with an unusual and creative fold.

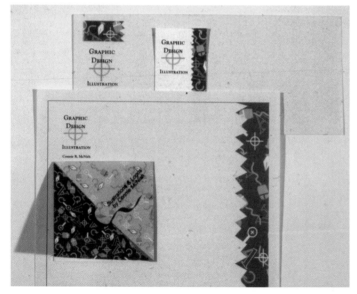

a

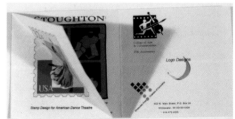

b

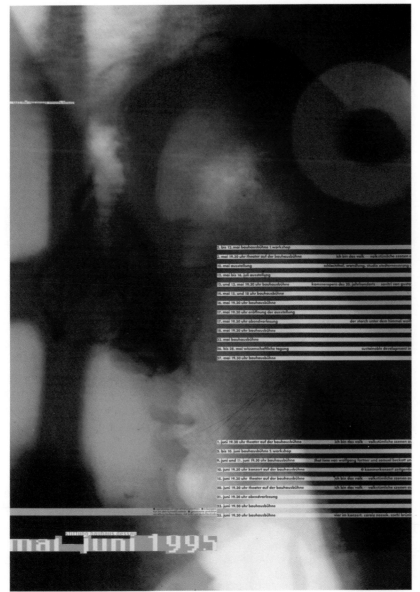

7-25
Cyan.
Sophie Alex, Wilhelm
Ebentreich, Detlef Fiedler,
Daniela Haufe, Siegried
Jablonsky. *Stiftung
Bauhaus Dessau, Jul-Aug
1995.* 1995. Offset
lithograph, printed in color,
33 × 23⅜" (83.8 × 59.4
cm). The Museum of
Modern Art, New York. Gift
of the designers.
Photograph © 2001 The
Museum of Modern Art,
New York.

Technological innovations contribute greatly to the changing face of design. The widespread use of computers in design that began in the 1980s was dominated by the IBM PC and Apple Macintosh. The computer brought a great deal of flexibility and made easy shifts of type size, shape, and style accessible to designers. Figure 7-25 shows this flexibility and rich visual texturing of typography by a contemporary German design group from the former East Berlin. They gained access to computer technology after the fall of the Berlin Wall in 1989. Much of their work is created for German cultural institutions.

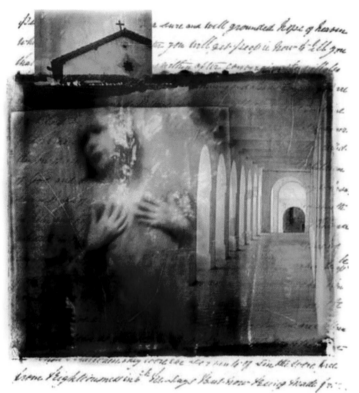

7-26

Diane Fenster.
1999. Illustration for Simon & Schuster using a visually rich integration of text and image. *Courtesy of the artist.*

Figure 7-26 by contemporary illustrator Diane Fenster shows an integration of type and image made possible by current technology. The ability to create such a powerful aesthetic, however, is ultimately in the eye and mind of the designer/illustrator.

Graphics are now generated and prepared for prepress with software that encourages complexity and reflects our society's complex structure and informational mix. Electronic mail, facsimile transmissions, and low-volume desktop publishing decentralize information processing.

The Internet is a great experiment in democracy because information can be disseminated and accessed beyond anything previously possible.

CONCLUSION

Layout is a balancing act that creates unity among the diverse elements on a page. An underlying grid can unite the many pages of a large publication. When combining copy, illustration, and photography, unity can also be established by finding similar shapes, angles, values, and type styles. Like a musical composition, a layout needs pacing, rhythm, and theme. This problem-solving approach stems from an understanding of visual language developed by 20th-century modernism.

Variety or contrast is important too. Many kinds of contrast—visual texture, value, shape, type style, and size—can create a focal point or visual path in a layout. A combination of contrasting historical styles is currently used to provide a rich, visually complex design. Multiple layers of communication created with this approach are a feature of postmodern style. Whatever the historical style, it is more than merely an affectation. Movements in art and design reflect the structure and values of society and help disseminate those values. Modernism and postmodernism are both informed and enriched by an understanding of how visual information is processed and meaning is derived. This understanding is fundamental to all forms of graphic design.

Finally, whatever the style, your layout should strive to do justice to the intentions of the copywriter, photographer, illustrator, client, and yourself.

Exercises

1. Use the sample grids in Fig 7-27 to do several rhythmic layouts. If you choose to use collage or pasteup, use old magazines, and cut out photographs, cropping where necessary and adding some version of comped type. If you use a computer, use a vector program such as Quark to establish grids and rectangles to insert typography and to indicate photographs.

2. Select several magazines or annual reports and figure out their grid structure. Can you find one with an interest-

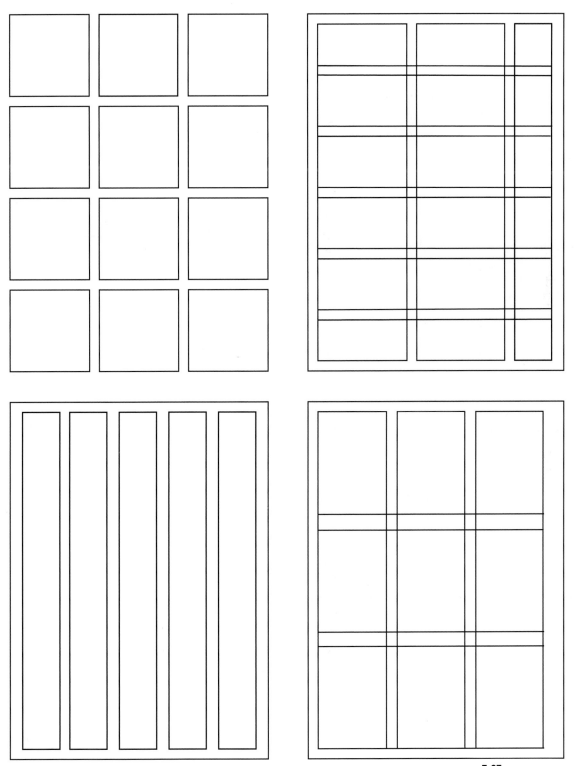

7-27
Sample grids.

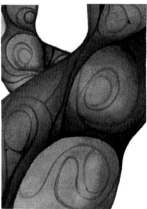
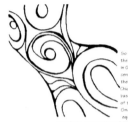

7-28
Natalie Krug.
"Heart" is a path layout integrated with a watercolor illustration that addresses the multiple meanings of the word heart.

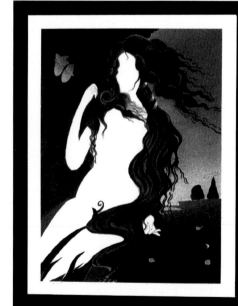

7-29
Ming Ya Su.
"Nymph." A grid layout in which both illustration and layout show a sensitivity to figure/ground relationships.

ing complexity and nuance? Look for stylistic influences. Bring these in for class discussion of strengths and weakness.

3. Save samples of brochure designs that appeal to you and study them for future inspiration. Look for interesting multipanel samples that unfold the message in sequential steps.

Project

A Two-Page Layout

Redesign into a two-page spread one of the unsuccessful layouts you found while doing the exercises. You need not include everything from the original. Each page of your redesign should be 8½ × 11" (21 × 28 cm). It should include a headline, three to five photographs and/or illustrations, and a minimum of 4" (10 cm) of body copy. All elements must be resized and cropped, as necessary. Establish a grid that suits your copy. Establish another grid and do a complete layout using each grid structure. After doing several roughs, choose the most successful. Prepare a final polished version using any method you prefer.

"Nymph" is a beautifully integrated grid layout with an air brush illustration. It makes a strong use of figure/ground relationships.

A Small Book

In consultation with your instructor, choose a short story, myth, or fable. Select a visual and conceptual theme appropriate to your story. Incorporate original imagery. Create a two-page layout (Figures 7-28 and 7-29). For a second option, design a multipage book, which can be bound in a variety of methods.

Objectives

Learn to chose an appropriate grid and fit layout elements to it.
Practice resizing photographs and typography.
Use all the information studied so far on balance, rhythm, unity, and contrast to create a dynamic and compelling layout.

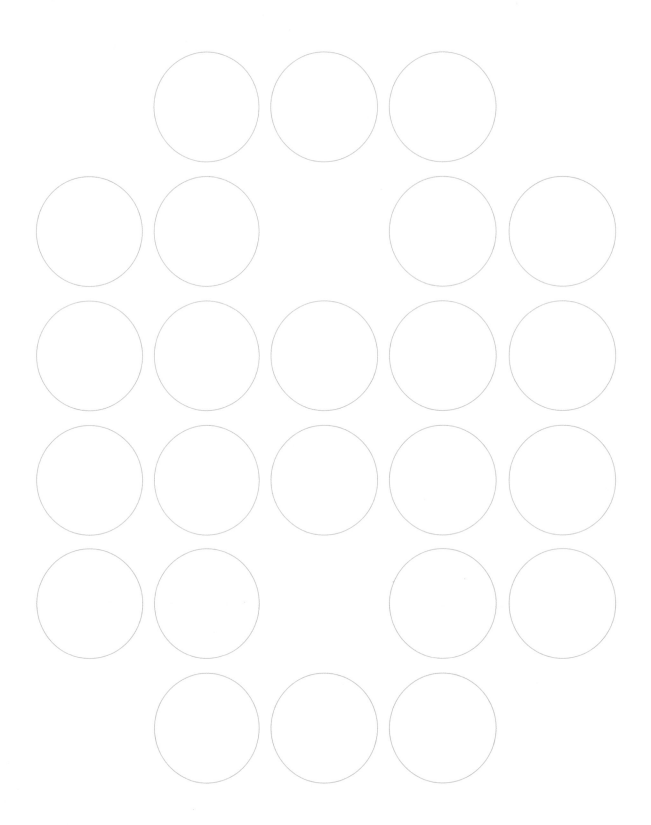

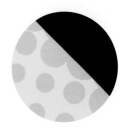

Chapter 8 illustration and photography in design

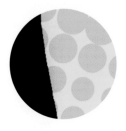

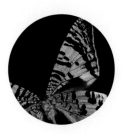

Oftentimes the graphic designer is called on to create or to acquire illustration and photography. The boundaries among these three disciplines are less rigid than in the past, especially as electronic media make photographic manipulation, drawing tools, and typography available to a broad range of professionals. It is advisable for every graphic designer to be familiar with the basics of image generation and utilization.

THE DESIGNER/ILLUSTRATOR

Illustration is a specialized area of art that uses images, usually representational or expressionist, to make a visual statement. Illustration is created for commercial reproduction, either in print form or as animation/motion graphics for various venues including Web delivery. Many drawings and paintings done as illustrations look and function as fine art and are exhibited and col-

lected as such. Many painters have worked as illustrators at some point in their careers and vice versa. Edward Hopper earned his living as an illustrator for the first half of his career; Pablo Picasso and William Blake illustrated books.

Some designers never actually do an illustration themselves; instead, they purchase freelance illustrations. Many illustrators are freelance artists who maintain their own studios and work for a variety of clients (Figure 8-1). Some studios have illustrators who do nothing but illustration, working with other designers who are in charge of typography, photography, layout, and art direction. But often the field has a need for illustrators who design and designers who illustrate.

Some people feel that editorial illustration is the highest and most artistic form of design. Nevertheless, however much an illustration created for print reproduction may resemble a painting, the restrictions an illustrator works under are similar to those in other areas of graphic design. The illustrator works with the guidance of an art director, must be concerned about how the work will be reproduced, has to meet a deadline, and is responsible for satisfying a client and meeting a defined purpose.

WHY ILLUSTRATION?

Illustration may be chosen instead of photography for several reasons. It can show something about the subject that cannot be photographed, such as detailed information about how photosynthesis works. Also, by enhancing details, illustration can demonstrate certain particulars more clearly than a photograph can. For example, it can enlarge tiny engine parts that are difficult to see or photograph and label them. Illustration can also eliminate misleading and unnecessary details that confuse an image, thereby forcing the eye to focus on important characteristics. Sometimes an illustrator is allowed

8-1
Dugald Stermer.
This magazine cover shown by the renowned illustrator integrates hand-drawn typography with a drawn/painted image. *Courtesy of the artist.*

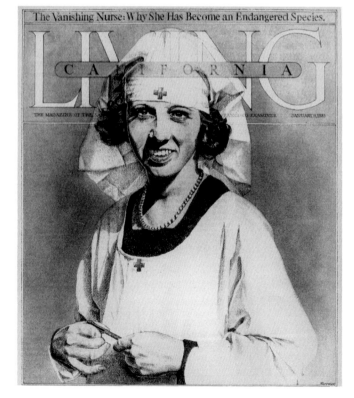

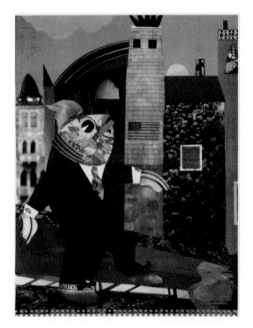

can be three dimensional or a combination of 2-D and 3-D imagery. The illustrator may use a revived art deco style, a New Wave or postmodern look, a highly personalized style, or a highly informational, descriptive rendering technique. Professionals usually concentrate on a consistent, personal style. Figures 8-3 and 8-4 show powerful sources of inspiration that can be found in both fine art and design history.

If the field of illustration is varied in medium and style, it also is varied in intent. The purpose for an illustration may be to present a product, tell a story, clarify a concept, or demonstrate a service. The following section lists these varied purposes. For detailed information about contracts, trade practices, and pricing, consult the Graphic

(top left)
8-2
Linda Godfrey.
"Fish Out of Water." The playful illustration created by this freelance illustrator as a student is collage, constructed with photographic textures.

(bottom right)
8-3
Romare Bearden.
Patchwork Quilt. 1970. Cut-and-pasted cloth and paper with synthetic paint on comosition board, 35¾ × 47⅞" (90.9 × 121.6 cm). The Museum of Modern Art, New York. Blanchette Rockefeller Fund. Photograph © 2001 The Museum of Modern Art, New York.

where a photographer and camera may be prohibited, as in a courtroom. Finally, it is a very effective way to present highly emotional material.

Although photography is capable of creating surreal and strongly emotive images, illustration is still more flexible. It is capable of turning out images of pure fantasy both by computer and by hand techniques (Figure 8-2). The hand-generated quality of illustration is considered by many to have a warmer, more intimate quality than other forms of illustration and photography. But the field of electronic illustration is growing as it branches into animation as well as images for the Web.

TYPES OF ILLUSTRATION

There are many examples of both contemporary and historical illustration throughout this book. Illustration has a variety of looks, depending on the medium, the style of the illustrator, and the purpose of the illustration. The artwork can be drawn, painted, mixed-media collage, or computer generated. It

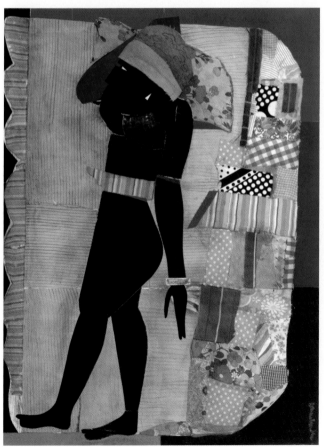

Commonplace objects must be shown with style and often enhanced with dramatic highlights and textures. Sometimes a creative concept leads to beautiful artwork that goes beyond simple product presentations. In the field of advertising illustration, illustrators work with art directors, account executives, and copywriters. Their work may need to please many people of varying opinions. The best prices for illustration are paid in the advertising field.

In editorial illustration, the artist may concentrate on the communication of emotion through an expressive treatment of line, shape, and placement. Editorial illustration can offer the freedom to experiment with media and to obscure details in favor of mood. Most importantly, illustration can convey a concept or story using a purely visual language. Some of the varied uses for both advertising and editorial illustration and other areas follow.

Fashion Illustration

Fashion illustration is a specialized area of advertising. A strictly literal drawing lacks the appeal of a drawing that presents the garment in a romantic, stylized manner. As a result, fashion illustration does not always simply convey information about the garment. It often attempts to persuade the viewer with the mood of the illustration. An important and interesting drape or texture of the garment or accessory, as well as the model's height, pose, and curves, are often emphasized for effect. Fashion photography shows a similar concern. A fashion illustrator draws from either a live model or a photograph of a model wearing clothes furnished by the client. The growth in the beauty and cosmetic areas, including related package illustration, has kept this field alive (Figure 8-6).

Recording Covers and Book Illustration

Creative packaging for recordings is an area that makes extensive use of illustrators. Many album covers have become collector's

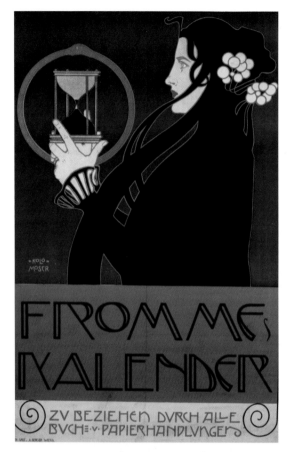

8-4

Koloman Moser.

Frommes Kalender. 1903. Lithograph, printed in color, 37⅜ × 24⁹⁄₁₆" (94.9 × 62.4 cm). The Museum of Modern Art, New York. Given anonymously. Photograph © 2001 The Museum of Modern Art, New York.

Artists Guild's *Handbook on Pricing and Ethical Guidelines.* It is a valuable reference updated yearly with information for illustrators as well as designers.

ADVERTISING AND EDITORIAL ILLUSTRATION

Advertising and editorial illustration are two important divisions in the field with quite different focuses. Advertising illustration is intended to sell a product or a service— almost anything that can be offered to a consumer. Figure 8-5 is a poster design that encourages the public to use the London mass transit underground system called the "Tube" to visit interesting places such as the Tate Gallery. The "paint" forms a map of the transit system that all Londoners are familiar with.

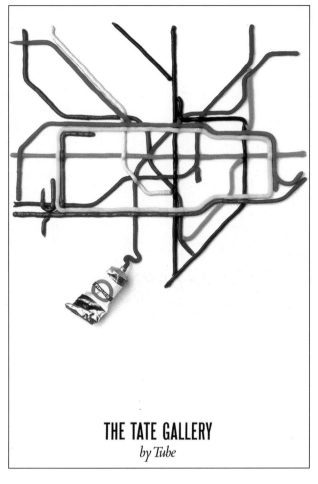

THE TATE GALLERY
by Tube

8-5
David Booth.
1987. 30 × 20". A highly effective photo illustration commissioned by the London Underground (subway) for traveling to the Tate Gallery.

items, and several books have been published on this area. CD covers are now a creative avenue for illustration. Although a smaller format, these provide an opportunity for multiple pages, integrating type and image. Payment varies widely, depending on the recording company, the recording artist, the complexity of the job, and the renown of the illustrator.

The book-jacket illustration is a vital part of the promotion and sale of a book. Publishing is a growing field. Some publishers give very specific instructions with detailed notes from the art director. The illustrator may be asked to read a lengthy manuscript. Pricing varies depending on these considerations, as well as whether the work is done for a trade book or textbook, in

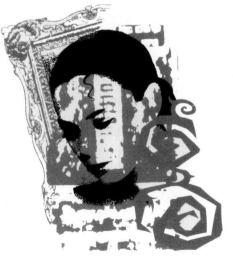

8-6
Margo Chase.
Logo/icon for hair care products signifies modern beauty. *Courtesy of the artist.*

(left)
8-7
Dugald Stermer.
Illustrator/designer. A skillful integration of painted word and image unifies this book jacket cover. *Courtesy of the artist.*

(right)
8-8
Genevieve Meek.
Unpublished drawing to a children's Halloween story by Joy Hart titled "Halloween Haunts." The drawing's title is "Halloween Bear." Pen and ink medium. *Courtesy of the artist.*

8-9
Arthur Rackham.
A children's book illustration from the period at the turn of the 20th century known as "The Golden Age of Illustration."

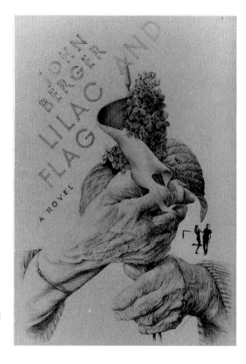

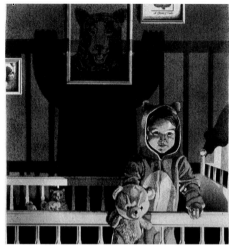

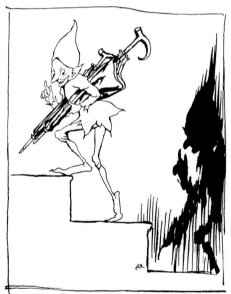

paperback or hardcover. Figure 8-7 is a cover by the well-known and influential illustrator and educator Dugald Stermer, who incorporates hand-drawn and airbrushed letterforms. When the illustrator also does the headline and type treatment, it is often well integrated with the artwork.

Artists who work on interior illustration add an important ingredient to the value of the book. Children's books often require illustration throughout, depending on the age group. The fee for illustration varies between a flat fee for books in which the illustrator's contribution is less than the author's to a royalty contract when the illustrator is responsible for a major part of the book's impact and content. Children's book illustration is a rewarding field because such books are illustrated throughout, unlike most adult novels. Artwork for young children must tell much of the story, with little reliance on the text. It is responsible for generating excitement and advancing the plot (Figure 8-8). Some of the best current illustration appears in beautifully designed and illustrated children's books. One of the many excellent children's book illustrators from the turn of the century is Arthur Rackham (Figure 8-9).

Magazines and Newspapers

Magazines depend on illustration to set a tone and pique a reader's interest. A single full-page image will often be expected to carry all the visual information for the accompanying story. The designer responsible for layout must integrate the illustration into the overall layout without detracting from the artwork. Ideally, treatment of the headline and text will reinforce the art through repetition, and careful placement.

Sometimes small spot illustrations are dropped into a page of text to enliven the visual presence. They are often black and white and executed in pen and ink.

Newspapers also use black and white spot art in editorial sections. Many different kinds of illustration can be found as you search through the sections of a newspaper. Fashion, sports, editorial, product, and technical illustration of charts and graphs are all there. The newspaper will often use color only on the front pages of each section or for special feature articles. Newsprint does not reproduce details and nuances in tonal quality well, and the newspaper industry does not pay as well as some other fields of illustration like corporate work for annual reports.

Often payment is not the driving reason people become artists and illustrators. The illustration in Figure 8-10a by artist David McLimans accompanies an article in *The Progressive* magazine. This publication and its contributors are concerned with political activism.

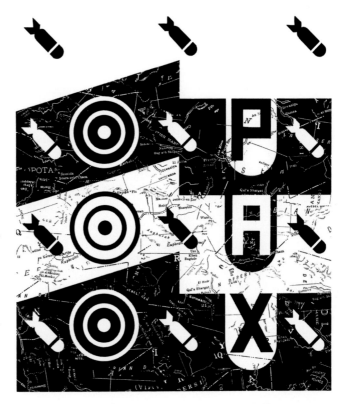

8-10a
David McLimans.
Line art illustration for the March 1991 issue of *The Progressive* magazine, accompanying an article on American political policy during the war in the Persian Gulf. *Courtesy of the artist.*

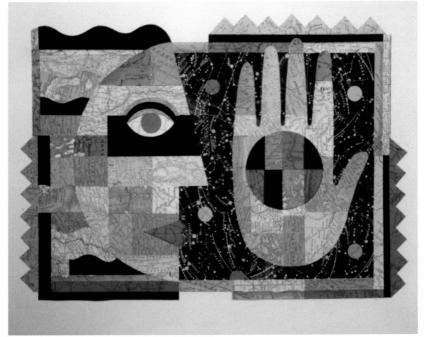

8-10b
David McLimans applies the same strong figure/ground and shape relationships in this annual report illustration.

Illustration for In-House Projects

Educational institutions, governmental agencies, corporations and businesses, and not-for-profit entities hire illustrators to generate material targeted at internal audiences. The assignment often calls for editorial illustration, that is, the communication of a concept. Annual reports, corporate calendars, brochures, posters, and an array of materials are produced to communicate the nature of the institution to its employees and constituents. Fees for illustration are relative to the size of the institution and the complexity of the job. Depending on the company, in-house staff designers may be asked to provide illustrations as a part of their regular job. Figure 8-11 is an excellent, highly creative piece done by an in-house department.

Greeting cards as well as medical and technical illustration are other markets where there is a call for illustration both freelance and in house. The *Artist's & Graphic Designer's Market,* published by F&W Publications lists over 2,500 companies that hire freelance designers and illustrators.

8-11
UCLA Extension Summer 1991 catalog. Art director: Inju Sturgeon, UCLA Extension Marketing Department. Designer: Eiko Ishioka. A playful and highly skilled integration of 2-D and 3-D enlivens this in-house illustration. *Courtesy of the artist.*

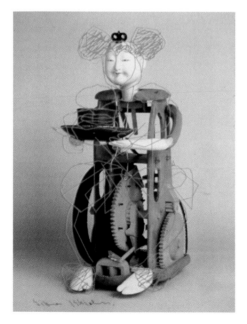

Greeting Cards and Retail Goods

Artwork in this category includes retail products such as apparel, toys, greeting cards, calendars, and posters. The major greeting card companies publish cards created by staff artists, but do commission some outside work as well. Seasonal cards, special occasion, and everyday cards are the major categories. A new direction for growth is cards targeted at specific lifestyle audiences, such as working women and seniors. Illustration for cards and retail goods may be paid on the basis of flat fees or royalties.

Medical and Technical Illustration

Medical illustrators are specially trained artists who often have a master's degree in the field, with a combined premed and art undergraduate degree. The accuracy of information as well as the clarity and effectiveness of presentation are vital in this field. The artist must be better than a camera in his or her ability to simplify, clarify, and select only what must be shown for complete communication. Illustrators should have a knowledge of the human body and a background and interest in science and medicine.

Technical illustrators create highly accurate renderings of scientific subjects, such as geological formations and chemical reactions, as well as machinery and instruments. They often work closely with scientists or technicians in the field, and they produce art for a wide variety of publications, advertisements, and audiovisuals.

Animation and Motion Graphics

Fields that are expanding are Web graphics and various forms of motion graphics. These fields use illustration, both through scanning print-based artwork and with artwork created electronically for online, CD-ROM, and film and video presentation. 3-D imaging is another expanding field that requires illustrators. The computer has an important impact in the field of illustration, especially for the designer/illustrator.

STYLE AND MEDIUM

Illustrators use a wide variety of techniques, such as mixed-media collage, cut paper, pen and ink, gouache or other painting mediums, sculptural constructions, and computer-generated work. Figure 8-12 shows a skillful integration of hand and electronic techniques.

Illustrator, Photoshop, and Painter get a lot of usage, and professional computer systems come with their own specialized software programs. Programs like Freehand and Illustrator are vector graphics (object-oriented) programs that allow the creation of clean, precise, editable images. Painter is a raster program that gives a more intuitive feeling to the process of creating an image. However the artwork is originally created, computer graphics allow an ease of editing that cannot be ignored. When the client says, "Can you make this change?" it is a lot easier to say "yes" when working with a digital image, even one that started with traditional media like Figure 8-12, created by a contemporary Milwaukee illustrator who operates his own business.

Computer-generated and photographically based work will not replace hand-created illustration, however, because many people feel hand-created illustrations are appropriate when a warmer, more human touch is desired. Computer technology can enhance and aid the creation of drawn and painted artwork. Artwork can be scanned and final touches or revisions completed electronically. It is also helpful in archiving and transferring files. What is currently threatening illustrators, however, is stock illustration that is readily and cheaply available electronically.

Whatever their artistic style, illustrators must be aware of all of the technical information concerning color separations and printing methods. Die cuts, embossing techniques, and specialty inks may also be a part of the final product.

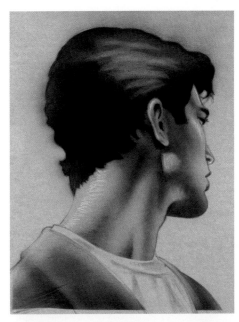

(top)
8-12a
Matt Zumbo, illustrator. created this black and white graphite and colored pencil drawing on toned board. *Courtesy of the artist.*

(bottom)
8-12b
Matt Zumbo composited and colorized his original drawings on the computer to generate the final illustration.

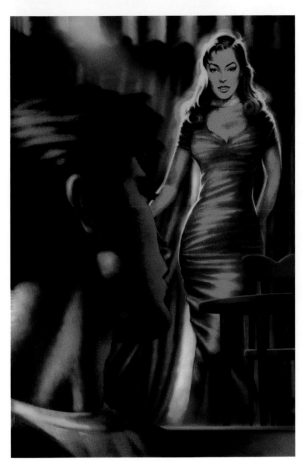

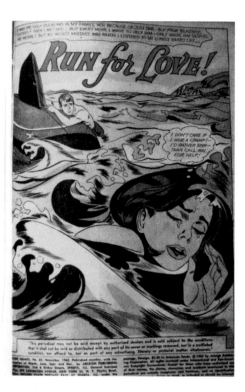

GETTING IDEAS

The illustrator goes through the same planning and visualizing procedures described in Chapter 1. The first step is getting to know the assignment. This research might call for reading a manuscript or understanding how a product functions.

Next comes the idea stage. Look at illustrations by other artists. Many annuals and periodicals show the most current illustrations. *Step by Step Graphics* and *How* present both illustrational ideas and techniques. The *CA Illustration Annual* and the many illustration sourcebooks like the *Workbook* and the *Graphic Artists Guild Directory of Illustration* are excellent sources to see the standards and styles in a particular field.

Classics from the history of illustration can also provide food for visual thought. Great artists from Dürer to Goya to Magritte have provided inspiration for illustrators. Look through books of photography, both fine art and simple descriptive photography, for subjects related to your project. Figures 8-13 and 8-14 show this process in reverse. Artist Roy Lichtenstein used art by D.C. Comics illustrators Tony Abruzzo and Bernard Sachs as material for his painting.

Thumbnail sketches should explore the subject from every angle, high and low, as well as tightly cropped and at a distance. Imagine different kinds of spatial treatment from a Western perspective to isometric to surrealistic. Sketch these ideas, trying them in different media. Exploration is especially valuable to student illustrators who have not yet developed a particular style. As you progress from sketches to roughs, you may need additional reference materials.

Another approach is to use semiotics. Analyze your subject from the point of view of creating an icon, a symbol, and an index. Again do several thumbnails of each. This method can lead to highly individual and creative problem solving (see Chapter 4). An icon is an image of the thing. A symbol shows cultural associations with the thing. An index indicates the presence of the thing. How would you illustrate America? Perhaps your choice of an icon or image is a field of wheat in the Midwest. Perhaps your choice of a symbol is an eagle. Perhaps your choice of an index is the shadow of an eagle on the field of wheat. This approach can lead to the creation of visual metaphors.

REFERENCE MATERIALS

Drawing from life means using an actual object, landscape, or human model. Drawing from life is most practical when using a still-life setup or a landscape. Models can get tired, and they can also get expensive. However, there is an immediacy and vitality to working from life that may give illustrations a different quality than can be achieved from working with photographs.

Drawing from a photograph is convenient for many reasons. The camera has already converted the subject into a two-dimensional language. Cropping is easily visualized by dropping a few pieces of paper around the photo edges. The subject never gets tired.

Reference materials can add authenticity to your work. An excellent source of photographs is the public library. Most major libraries keep picture collections. Once the source photos are obtained, adapt them to the particular situation (Figure 8-15 is a portfolio piece that uses multiple photographic references). It is a good idea for all designers and illustrators to begin a clip file of their own with images of many different subjects. Old magazines are a great source. You may be able to organize magazines by categories instead of cutting out the photographs. *Life, People,* and *Newsweek* magazines would fit into a "peo-

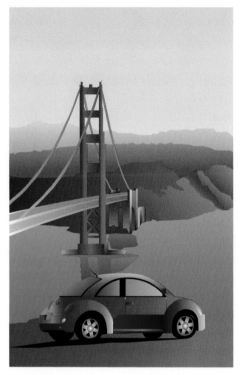

8-15
Steve Hojnacki.
This portfolio piece was created in Adobe Illustrator for a student portfolio using the gradient function and a combination of photographic references.

ple" category; the *Smithsonian, National Geographic,* and *Audubon* would fit into a "nature" category. The Internet is also a good source for an image search. The low-resolution files give vague visual data, but it can be helpful.

When working with photographs, respect the photographer as an artist. Do not duplicate a photograph exactly unless it has been shot specifically for you or by you. Copyright infringement laws concerning the use of photographs has gotten increasingly tight in recent years. The source photograph must be substantially altered before it will be legal to reproduce it as your own artwork. *Clip art* denotes copyright-free images that can be used as is or altered to suit your needs. Books and CDs of electronic and traditional clip art are available from many publishing sources such as Dynamic Graphics and Eyewire. Dover is the best print source for

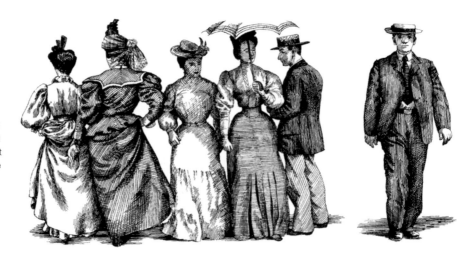

8-16
Copyright-free clip art is available from a variety of sources for reference and reproduction, both in print and CD. Stock art can be purchased by individual image with controlled usage or by CD or book with all usage rights transferred to the purchaser.

wonderful old line art engravings on every subject (Figure 8-16).

There can be disadvantages to working with clip art or relying too closely on photos. The preexisting image makes many decisions about composition, lighting, and size. The photograph can also provide only one kind of spatial representation. These limitations can be overcome by remembering to use the clip art or photo as a source, not as an answer. Reference sources need not be taken literally but interpreted creatively.

CONTEMPORARY VISION

The invention of offset lithography brought an explosion of illustration in the late 1800s. Coming into the 20th century as a vital force, and aided by new advances in printing technology, illustration retained its ability to draw inspiration from the fine arts. Painters in the early 20th century followed an investigation begun by Cézanne, and their art reflected the relativity of space, time, point of view, and emotional coloring. Discoveries in science, psychology, and technology supported their depiction of reality as changeable. It could shift, alter, and be processed in the human brain in a variety of ways. The artist could interact and help shape it.

Much of the art of the 20th century deals with picture plane space—the construction

of a flat pattern on the flat surface of the paper or canvas. There is less illusion to this work; it does not attempt to deny the flat surface it exists on. Constructivism and the de Stijl movement worked with picture plane space. Cubism presented reality from multiple points of view. An object might be portrayed simultaneously from the top, the front, and the sides. There is a similarity here to Egyptian art, but a different purpose. This picture plane space is a strong influence in contemporary illustration. Designers and illustrators have always been aware of the flat surface because they have also worked with typography, which encourages flat patterning. The representation of space is a varying cultural convention that contemporary illustrators draw on (Figures 8-17a-c). These poster illustrations by Michael Vanderbyl, an important illustrator and designer, make good use of a bird's eye view to render playful architectural forms.

The fauves and the German expressionists in the early 20th century also emphasized the flat patterning of the surface with bright, flat colors and with images that were personal and highly emotional. This expressive quality appears currently in editorial illustration in various forms. The emotionally charged image in Figure 8-18 by Alan E. Cober uses a visual pun to match the topic of tools of violence making up the face of

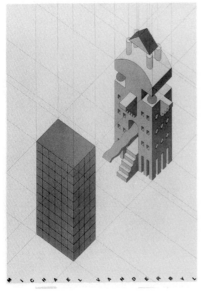

a

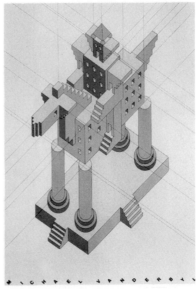

b

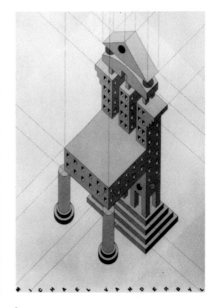

c

8-17a, b, c
Michael Vanderbyl.
Three self-promotional posters in conjunction with the publication of *Seven Graphic Designers* by Takenobu Igarashi. Printed in Japan by Mitsumura Printing Company.
Courtesy of the artist.

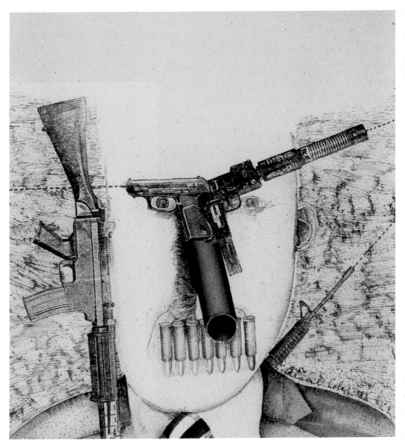

8-18
Alan E. Cober.
Illustration for the *Dallas Times Herald. Courtesy of the artist.*

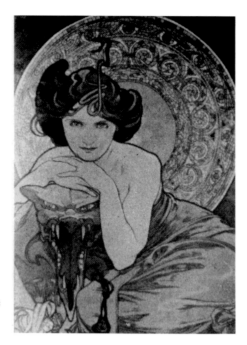

**8-19
Alphonse Mucha.**
Art nouveau poster design based on the photographic reference shown in Figure 8-20.

**8-20
Alphonse Mucha.**
Studio photograph of model.

violence. It becomes what it represents and is an example of editorial illustration at its best.

An interest in other forms of spatial representation began to appear in the mid–20th century. Trompe l'oeil artists revived an interest in life-size images inside a space that looks only inches deep. A French term meaning "fool the eye," *trompe l'oeil* works extremely well as an illusion of spatial reality. Our culture will probably never lose its admiration for this sort of artistic reality.

There are more artists, designers, and illustrators than ever before in history. We have the benefit of a mass communications network to keep us informed on what is happening now in art. We have a documented history of previous art and design movements, and our influences are more numerous than ever. Designers and illustrators are combining many materials and styles, concepts, and technologies to produce the rich variety of images and

techniques that make the 21st century a truly exciting time to be a designer and illustrator.

THE IMPACT OF PHOTOGRAPHY

Paul Delaroche, a French painter commenting on the invention of photography, exclaimed, "From today painting is dead!" While some artists shared that fear, others embraced the new medium as a tool and an opportunity. From its beginning, illustrators have used photographs as aids. The Art Nouveau illustrator Alphonse Mucha carefully posed models amid studio props and photographed them for reference in his poster designs (Figures 8-19 and 8-20). Such well-known 20th-century illustrators as Maxfield Parrish and Norman Rockwell have also relied heavily on posing and photographing models for visual reference in later paintings. Photographer Eadweard Muybridge (1830–1904) is well known in the design community for his photographic

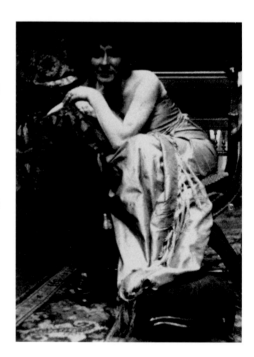

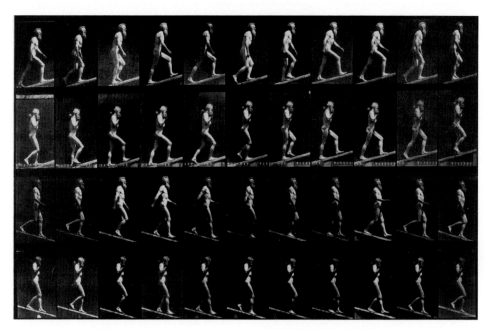

8-21
Eadweard Muybridge.
Excerpt from *Animal Locomotion,* one of the first photographic reference books. 1887.

series documenting the movement of people and animals. His books remain a valuable resource to illustrators today (Figure 8-21).

THE DESIGNER/PHOTOGRAPHER

Oftentimes the designer is called on to create, or locate, and integrate photography into a layout design. A working knowledge of how to evaluate photographs is very useful.

Photography is a strong, expressive tool with which to prove a point, explore a problem, or sell a product. Most people believe the camera does not lie. They believe an illustrator can change things around and make people or situations out to be better than they really are, but they fail to realize a camera also represents a point of view. It is this suspension of disbelief that makes the camera such an effective tool for persuasion and communication. It is also this belief in the "photograph as document" that is changing with the computer and the growth of photo illustration.

People want to know if they are looking at a manipulated image. In February 1982, the staff working on a cover for *National Geographic* magazine had difficulty getting a photograph of the Egyptian pyramids to fit the magazine's format. Because the information was stored digitally on a computer, it was a simple matter to move one pyramid over. When that photo manipulation became known (it was widely reported), our faith in photographic reality was badly shaken.

No photograph is truly candid. It is selected, framed, and shot by an individual who is interacting with the environment. Moreover, a situation will change just because a camera is introduced. Another editing and selection process occurs when the contact prints are viewed. Darkroom and computer manipulation may influence the last stages. All of these processes place photography firmly in the camp of an interpretative art. A photograph can tell the truth, but that truth is filtered through the eye and intent of the photographer. In the early 20th century, photomontage was a precursor to

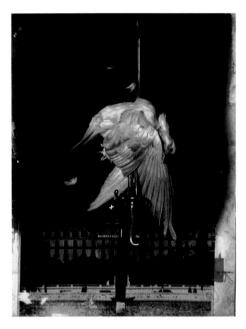

8-22
John Heartfield.
"The Meaning of Geneva."
Photomontage, 1932.
Copyright 1998 Artists
Rights Society (ARS), New
York/VG Bild-Kunst, Bonn.

the effects now possible with computer-mediated photography (Figure 8-22).

Designers use photographs and work with photographers throughout their careers. A photograph may be needed to document an event, illustrate a story, sell a product, or put across a point of view. In all cases, the photograph must be evaluated in terms of print quality, design quality, and ability to communicate. It is advisable to study and learn to appreciate good photos, and a class in darkroom work will help develop a feeling for print quality. Experimentation with digital photography can be an exciting and very accessible way to begin or to augment this learning process. A photograph communicates in a particular and powerful way. We have a special relationship with photography based on history, memory, and its similarity to the retinal image.

The criteria for good design in a photograph are similar to good design in layout or illustration. Figures 8-23a and 8-23b show a highly creative and effective use of photography for self-promotion. The photographer/designer mailed a series of ten postcards to clients around the country.

Digital Photography

The advent of digitized, computer-manipulated images makes this issue even more pertinent. Once the analog continuous-tone photograph is translated into digital data, it can be accessed, manipulated, and transformed with incredible speed and efficiency. Digital cameras are available that skip the analog stage entirely. Artist/educator Susan Ressler created the image in Figure 8-24 by digitizing original objects for a complex and rich series of manipulations.

Multiple variations of a single image can be generated when the image is digital, and color editing and retouching can be easily accomplished. Mistakes are never fatal, because the original is stored on disk. Materials intended for the offset press can be sent directly to film after retouching on a computer system. The impact of digital imaging on photography, especially in the growth of photo illustration, is tremendous.

A video camera can be cabled to a desktop computer and the resulting image captured as still data or as a manipulated live recording that will later be edited. It is increasingly necessary to honor and understand copyright issues. Appropriating photographers' or illustrators' images without payment or authorization infringes on their livelihood.

The most important aspect of photography remains in the eye and mind (and perhaps heart) of the artist. The concept, the design, the element of communication, and, finally, the output determine the quality of a photographic image.

SPECIALITIES

Photojournalism

Photographs fall into two general categories: candid and staged. Most photojournalism is candid. It is not shot in a studio or with hired models. Photojournalism attempts to capture a news event on location with immediacy and honesty. When a feature story is run

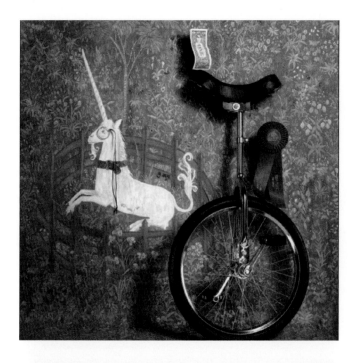

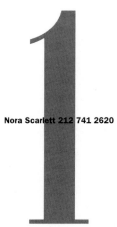

Nora Scarlett 212 741 2620

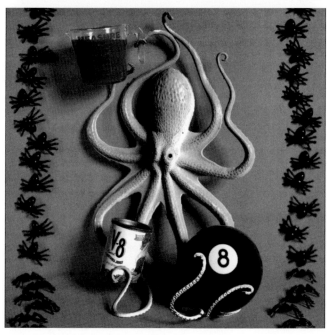

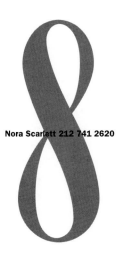

Nora Scarlett 212 741 2620

8-23a, b,
Nora Scarlett.
New York photographer, created these self-promotional direct mail pieces. She located or created all the necessary still-life props for this creative series. *Courtesy of the artist.*

in a newspaper, an art director or editor may ask for a picture essay that will illustrate a feature story with a sequence of images that give a sense of movement, establish a narrative, or set an emotional tone.

Staged photographs are often used in advertising and product photography. They are tightly directed and require elaborate studio lighting. Hired models can make shooting time expensive. Product photogra-

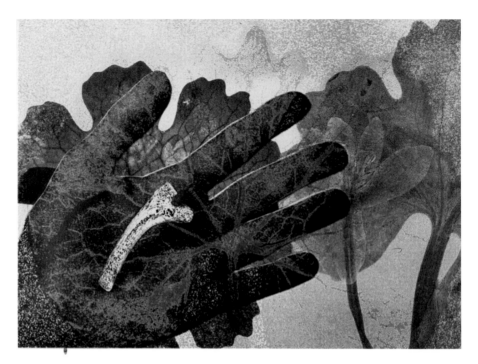

phers are usually less concerned with truth telling than the photojournalists and more concerned with presenting a product in the most favorable light.

Product Photography

Any area in which the intent is to promote or sell a product is called *product photography.* The product can be food, automobiles, furniture, clothing, fine art, or a wide range of other items. The metal sculpture in Figure 8-25 is captured in all of its surface texture and complexity through the art of the photographer. Still-life photographs enhance the beauty and desirability of many products. Often this sort of product is prepared for the camera with special gels and coatings that intensify lighting effects.

When the assignment comes from an art director at an advertising agency or directly from the client, the photographer is often told what to shoot within very narrow specifications. The challenge in this form of photography is to help sell or present the product in a way that is personally and aesthetically satisfying (Figure 8-26).

Most photographers doing this kind of work are freelance, and many work through an agent (a "rep") who solicits work from clients. The rep usually will get a 25 to 30 percent finder's fee from the assignment. Major catalog houses and department stores have their own in-house photographic staff and facilities. Regional advertisers, too, often make use of an in-house photographic staff. However, national advertisers usually hire dependable freelancers

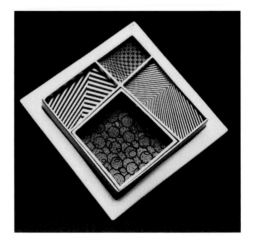

whose previous work suits the project at hand.

When shooting a fashion layout for a catalog, newspaper, or direct mail piece that calls for a model, the photographer will work with the art director and with assistants who help with the details of clothing, makeup, props, and so on. All people at a shoot should show respect for one another's professional abilities.

Corporate Photography

Large corporations need a great deal of photography for annual reports, presentations, and other publications. The company's art director or designer often hires a photographer for an individual assignment and offers suggestions regarding the project. The public relations executive also may become involved in the considerations. Sometimes an in-plant photographer on the staff does some of the photographic work. This photographer is often a generalist working out of the public relations (PR) department and shooting everything from candid news release photos to carefully composed and lighted architectural interiors.

Architectural photography calls for a special skill in handling building interiors and exteriors. Lighting an interior so the bright chandeliers as well as the details in dark corners of the room are all properly exposed and not distorted calls for considerable expertise. Photographing exteriors of tall buildings often requires special equipment that will correct for paralax. Architectural photography is a specialty in itself, and these photographic specialists work for a variety of interior design firms, landscape designers, and corporate accounts.

Editorial/ Illustrational Photography

Photography can illustrate an accompanying story—anything from fiction to a feature article on restaurant dining to CD covers.

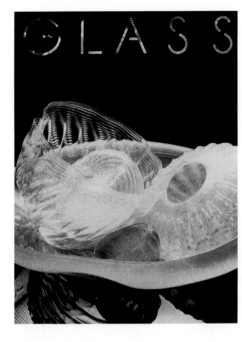

8-26
Poster by **Chuck Byrne** and **Julius Friedman** for the Detroit Institute of Art. *Courtesy of the designer.*

Photographic illustrations are sometimes closely art directed by the designer. The necessary props and set may be provided, or the photographer may be asked to find or construct them.

This form of illustration leaves room for creative interpretation, but communication remains the primary objective. Digital photography has made a great contribution to photo/illustration (Figure 8-27).

FINDING PHOTOGRAPHS AND PHOTOGRAPHERS

Stock photography agencies sell photographs to freelancers, advertising agencies, and in-house design departments. They have thousands of images on file that are constantly updated. Any type of photograph is available by transparency or CD-ROM, and agencies specialize in everything from architecture to current events to the history of civilization.

The *Bettmann Archives, Black Star Publishing Company,* and the *Free Lance Photographers Guild* are three of hundreds

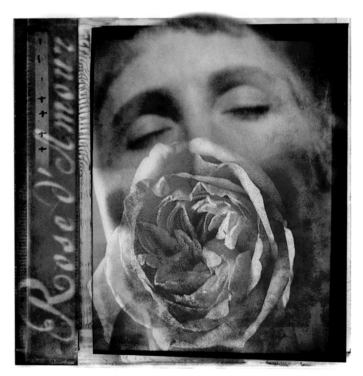

of varied services providing images and/or photographic services for use in editorial work, advertising, and television. The *American Showcase* is a full-color reference book used by advertising agencies, public relations firms, and others who want to hire freelance photographers and illustrators. Each portfolio page of images is accompanied by the name and address of the photographer who shot them. (You can order the book from American Showcase, Inc., 724 Fifth Avenue, New York, NY.)

Photographers specialize in a variety of areas, each of which calls for unique expertise. As a designer, you'll want to know how to communicate and work with a photographer. When appropriate, know where to locate and how to select available stock image. The designer in Figure 8-28 uses a combination of family and clip art images as part of her student portfolio. The designer in Figures 8-29 uses stock photography to

(top)
8-27
Diane Fenster, illustrator, created this sensual photo illustration in Photoshop. *Courtesy of the artist.*

(right)
8-28
Jackie Waylen
constructed this portfolio piece as a student in Photoshop using a combination of clip art and old family photos.

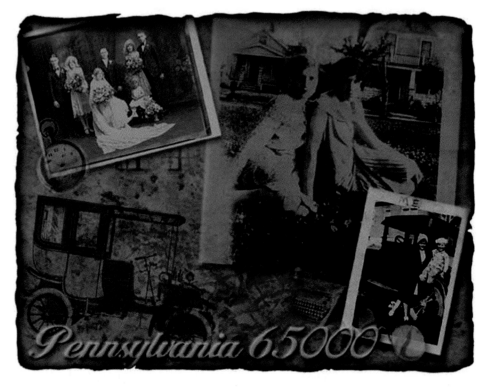

illustrate his proposed children's book. When the book is accepted for publication, the photographic images may be substituted for other similar, stock photographs, depending on copyright availability.

Project

Illustrate the cover of a tape or compact disc you enjoy, incorporating photography and/or illustration. Find several images that are appropriate (Figure 1-10). You may research and obtain authorized copies, shoot them yourself, locate copyright-free art, or generate the imagery through your own drawings. Do not appropriate a professional photographer or illustrator's work from magazines or other printed sources. Choose the images you will work from based on print quality, design quality, and visual information.

Combine the imagery with the title of the recording and the name of the artist.

Prepare your piece to actual size. You may need to use various traditional illustrator's mechanical enlarging and reducing aids, darkroom skills, or digitized images. Check with your instructor to see what medium you should pursue. Always keep your treatment appropriate to the subject matter and content, and remember to use the gestalt unit-forming techniques to integrate word and image. Complete the CD package, including all typography.

Objectives

Practice working with thumbnails to develop a variety of creative solutions. Practice creating and integrating imagery in a layout design with type and image working together.
Work to create an illustration that communicates visually, without dependence on words.

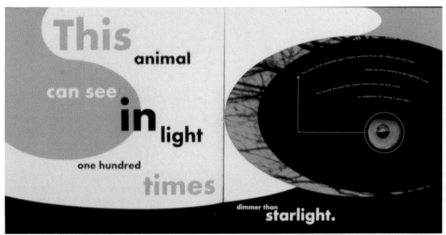

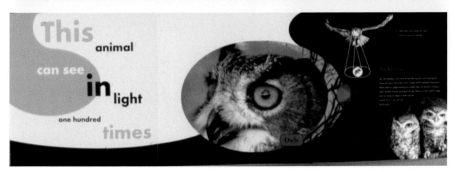

8-29
Dan Kim, educator and designer, created this proposal for a children's book using stock photography to complement his original design and editorial concept. These are two consecutive pages. *Courtesy of the artist.*

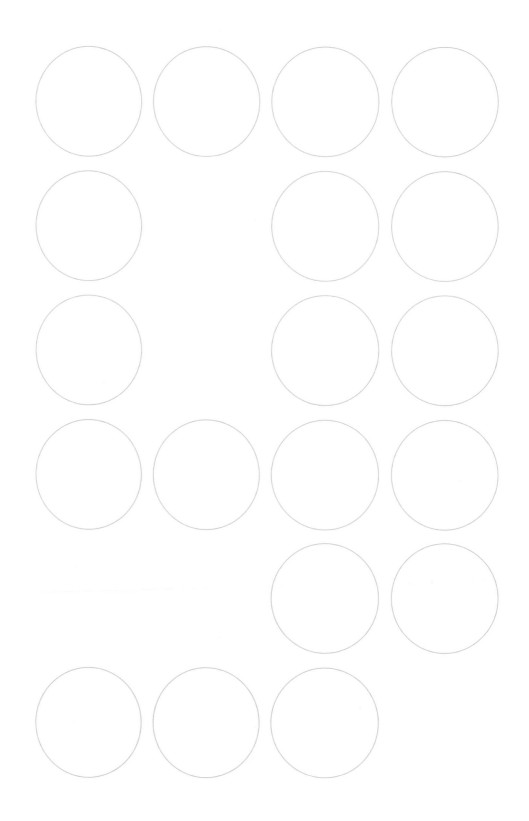

Chapter 9 :::: advertising design

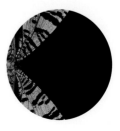

THE PURPOSE OF ADVERTISING

Advertising differs from pure graphic design in intent. It primarily seeks to persuade, and the presentation of information is secondary to that intent.

The successful advertisement (1) attracts attention, (2) communicates a message, and (3) persuades an audience. Advertising can have many different looks. It may appear in television, newspapers, direct mail, magazines, billboards, outdoor displays, Web sites, and point-of-purchase displays. Whatever the medium, it is characterized by an attempt to persuade an audience, with the intent to boost sales, profits, and share of the market.

There are elements of information in an advertisement and elements of persuasion in pure graphic design. Those who believe "advertising is information" assume the consumer initially buys the product based on information supplied by advertisements. Future purchases are based on firsthand assessment of the quality of the product. This theory states that the persuasive element in advertising is secondary to the information supplied.

To what extent is this view of advertising true? Probably the ads most useful in informing consumers are those on a regional level announcing events such as plays, concerts, and meetings. The consumer might miss an opportunity to participate without an advertisement. Another example is advertisements for equipment, which often come with information about specific attributes that are important in the decision to purchase.

Those who believe the function of advertising is persuasion maintain that advertisements exist to change perception. Advertising induces the consumer to believe product has certain desirable qualities or associations. Soda pop and blue jeans become associated with youth, zest, and popularity. Ads that use them "sell" an attitude and a lifestyle. Associated products have youth and zest "rubbed off" onto them.

The purest example of advertising for persuasive purposes can be found in national advertising, especially of long-standing and leading products. The public no longer needs a lot of basic information on these products. What sells such a product to the public is the associations they have with it. Many of these associations are generated by advertising and have nothing to do with the actual product (Figure 9-1).

Many advertisements have both persuasive and informative qualities in their advertising. The closer an advertisement comes to pure information, the closer it comes to pure graphic design. The closer a graphic design such as a poster comes to not only announcing an event, but also persuading ticket purchases, the closer it comes to pure advertising. Figures 9-2 and 9-3 are part of an integrated campaign created for the Minnesota Zoo by Rapp Collins Communications, a well-known contemporary design firm in Minneapolis, Minnesota. Several examples of this wonderfully humorous and effective ad campaign are used throughout the chapter.

9-1
Ad layout courtesy of Apple Computer. **Gavin Milner/Bob Cockrell,** art directors; **Harold Einstein,** writer; **Ed Adler,** producer; **Tom Nelson,** photographer. Prepared by BBDO, Los Angeles, CA.

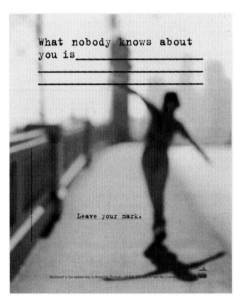

TYPES OF ADVERTISING

Retail and national advertising are two major categories of advertising. Each can be divided into several major areas according to dollar volume: television, newspaper, and direct mail and the Internet.

Retail advertising is so named because it is often sponsored by a retail establishment. It tends to be informational, especially when announcing special discounts or availability. It often attempts to get people to go to sponsoring stores to buy items they have seen advertised nationally. Studies show that retail advertising encourages price competition.

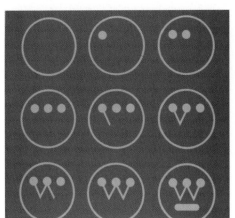

NUMBER TWO IN A SERIES OF SIX

Why The Red-eyed Assassin Is As Dangerous As It Sounds.

If you guessed that an insect named "the assassin" just might be dangerous, you're right. The red-eyed assassin possesses a powerful venom, which it can spray up to 18 inches to stun its victims. For survival, the red-eyed assassin injects this liquefying venom into its victims— and then sucks their insides out.

Ironically enough, even though the red-eyed assassin does have keen eyesight, it does not have red eyes. "Red-eyed" refers to the two red dots on its back that resemble eyes, which keep potential predators at bay.

The red-eyed assassin of West Africa. Just one of more than 5,000 spiders, beetles, butterflies, and other exotic bugs. Each with a story to tell.

For more information about the BUGS! exhibit, call the Zoo-To-Do Hotline at 612-432-9000.

BUGS!

At the Minnesota Zoo. Now through Labor Day.

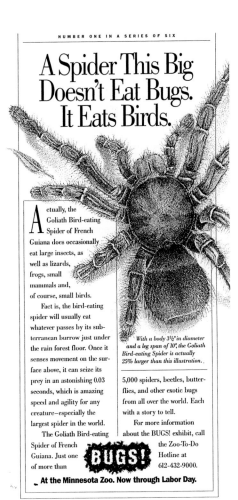

NUMBER ONE IN A SERIES OF SIX

A Spider This Big Doesn't Eat Bugs. It Eats Birds.

Actually, the Goliath Bird-eating Spider of French Guiana does occasionally eat large insects, as well as lizards, frogs, small mammals and, of course, small birds.

Fact is, the bird-eating spider will usually eat whatever passes by its subterranean burrow just under the rain forest floor. Once it senses movement on the surface above, it can seize its prey in an astonishing 0.03 seconds, which is amazing speed and agility for any creature—especially the largest spider in the world.

The Goliath Bird-eating Spider of French Guiana. Just one of more than

With a body 3½" in diameter and a leg span of 10", the Goliath Bird-eating Spider is actually 25% larger than this illustration.

5,000 spiders, beetles, butterflies, and other exotic bugs from all over the world. Each with a story to tell.

For more information about the BUGS! exhibit, call the Zoo-To-Do Hotline at 612-432-9000.

BUGS!

At the Minnesota Zoo. Now through Labor Day.

National advertising is advertising run by manufacturers with a nationwide distribution network for their product. It tends to be persuasive. It began when manufacturers wanted to differentiate their brands from similar or identical brands, and when there was a national delivery system for advertisements. Figure 9-4 shows the national TV presentation of the trademark designed by Paul Rand as part of the Westinghouse corporate identity system.

9-2, 9-3
Two advertisements created as part of the BUGS! ad campaign prepared for the Minnesota Zoo by Rapp Collins Communications. Creative director **Bruce Edwards,** art director **Bruce Edwards,** copywriter **Chris Mihock.**

9-4
TV storyboard of an animated logo designed for Westinghouse Electric Corporation by **Paul Rand.** 1961.

Television

A large amount of total advertising dollars are spent on television. The content of national television advertising is strongly persuasive. Commercials may be a network advertisement, shown on national shows; a spot advertisement, prepared nationally and shipped to local areas; or a local advertisement, prepared and shown locally.

Market research is an important part of all advertising, especially in heavily persuasive advertising. The two primary marketing considerations in television advertising are program attentiveness and viewer volume.

Program attentiveness is how strongly viewers concentrate on a show. The maximum attention assures maximum recall. Unlike the Web, or newspaper, direct mail, or other print media, the television ad occurs in time and cannot be reread.

The second marketing consideration in this area is the number of persons viewing television programming. Certain hours are considered peak viewing periods. These prime-time slots cost prime dollars. Because so much money is at stake, a great deal of research goes into ad effectiveness.

The television advertisement is usually prepared initially in the form of a storyboard. When prepared two dimensionally, it consists of two frames, one carrying a visual depiction of the scene, the other carrying words being spoken by an announcer or cast. The storyboard depicts only key scenes (Figure 9-5).

The visual is often prepared so it will carry the message even if the volume is muted. The product name is often superimposed over the screen at the end of the ad. The audio is also written to carry the message alone, in case the viewer is temporarily out of the room or unable to see the screen.

Newspapers

Newspaper advertising carries both regional and national ads. National advertising often arrives as an "ad slick" ready for insertion. The creative work has been done at the company's ad agency. Regional display advertising often requires designing by the newspaper's staff of artists and copywriters. Most newspapers now have a Web presence and hire designers to create and maintain those sites.

Advantages and Disadvantages

Some challenges face the designer in newspaper advertising. First, the designer often must include diverse art elements and typefaces into a single ad. The logo and elements relating to a national campaign must often be incorporated into an ad for a local sale. Often the cost of an advertisement will be shared among manufacturers if their logos appear in the ad. This diversity can make the task of creating a well-designed, attractive advertisement a real challenge. Secondly, the designer must also create around the limitations of cheap, absorbent newsprint and hurried printing to meet daily, sometimes hourly, deadlines.

Single-item ads or large institutional clients like banks may use a full page with room for white space. These ads allow more leeway for design. *No matter how many elements are in the advertisement, whether it is a national or retail ad, whether it is reproduced on newsprint or expensive glossy paper, good design will always aid communication.* Given some creativity, it will also attract attention and help persuade the audience.

The advantages of newspaper advertising are many. The paper is widely read. Circulation rates are available to help advertisers plan the number of people their ads are reaching. Moreover, the circulation is localized. It is therefore easy for a retail outlet to reach those people most likely to be interested in and able to travel to a sale. Finally, the copy may be changed daily, and

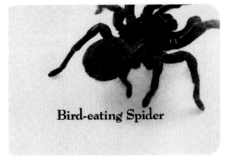

Bird-eating Spider

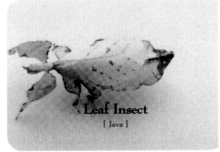

Leaf Insect
[Java]

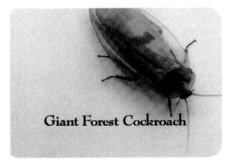

Giant Forest Cockroach

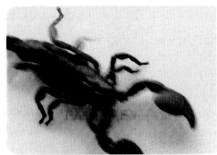

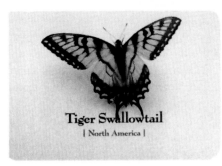

Tiger Swallowtail
[North America]

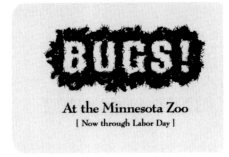

At the Minnesota Zoo
[Now through Labor Day]

9-5
Storyboard of a TV advertisement created by Rapp Collins Communications for the Minnesota Zoo. Creative director **Bruce Edwards,** art director **Bruce Edwards,** copywriter **Chris Mihock.**

the updated ad will still reach its audience within a day.

The Audience

Newspaper readership is varied in character. People from all age groups and from every social and economic group read the paper. When a product is of interest to a limited group, newspaper advertising is not advisable, because so small a percentage of readers would be potential buyers.

Newspaper advertising can be targeted to a limited extent, however, by considering the type of reader attracted to a certain type of paper. The *Wall Street Journal,* for example, has a different readership than the *New York Post.*

Advertising rates are based on the size of the ad, the circulation of the paper, and the position of the ad within the paper. The sports page, the society page, the home section, and the financial section are areas where advertisements allied to special subjects are likely to be seen by the desired group of readers. Advertisers pay extra dollars to ensure the appropriate audience sees their ad. Other positions within the paper that are worth extra money are on the

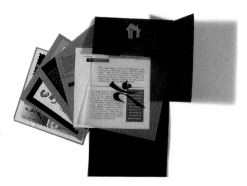

9-6
Studio 45. A direct mail piece created by the University of Wisconsin–Whitewater student design agency announcing an open house in their computer lab.

outside pages, at the top of a column, and next to reading material.

Direct Mail and Internet

Direct mail advertising comes in many forms. It is an exciting and growing area of advertising that has boomed partly as a result of credit cards and partly as a result of today's busy lifestyle. Direct mail accounts for most

9-7
Cover for annual report designed for Westinghouse Electric Corporation by **Paul Rand** in 1971. *Courtesy of Mrs. Marion Rand.*

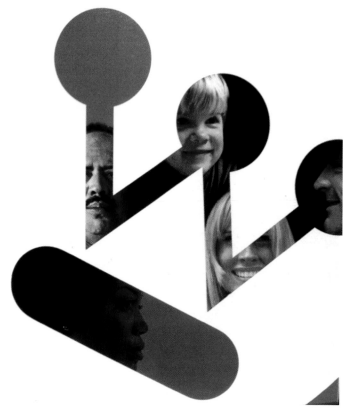

third-class mail and a considerable amount of first-class mail. Increasingly, the Internet is an important way for advertisers to target specific audiences with tailored messages.

Direct mail is advertising in which the advertiser also acts as publisher. The advertiser produces a publication (rather than renting space or time in someone else's), selects the mailing list, and sends the publication directly to the prospects through the mail (Figure 9-6). A highly targeted form of direct mail includes printed communication to investors in the form of annual reports. Often these are very high-quality, high-dollar publications that carefully present the integrated corporate identification. Figure 9-7 shows the Westinghouse Electric annual report cover from 1971, utilizing the logo design by the 20th century design leader, Paul Rand.

Online delivery of sales material is a fast growing market as corporations increasingly find it appropriate to communicate with their audience via the Internet. This media also calls for an integration of the corporate identity program into the pages of Web sites.

Advantages and Disadvantages

The advantages of direct mail are substantial. First, the advertiser can use a mailing list that has been compiled to reach a specialized audience. Businesses sometimes develop their own mailing list. The primary sources of names, however, are mailing-list brokers. They are in the business of building and maintaining lists of individuals likely to have an interest in a given topic. Lists are usually rented for onetime use because they go out of date quickly and must be constantly updated. Secondly, direct mail does not have to compete for attention with other ads on a newspaper page or surrounding a television commercial. Thirdly, it is flexible in its format. This feature makes direct mail challenging to the designer. The size, paper, ink color, and folding characteristics are all additional variables to be designed. A piece that folds is a three-dimensional problem. It must succeed visually from a variety of positions. The design develops from front to back, building interest and encouraging the reader to continue.

One of the disadvantages of direct mail is that people are often hostile to it. If the audience throws away the envelope or catalog without even opening it, communication has failed. Studies have shown that a mailing requiring participation, such as a lottery, will increase effectiveness. Copy and graphics that present specific offers and a clear, simple message succeed well.

Forms of direct mail include letters, flyers, folders or brochures of varying dimensions and formats, catalogs, and booklets. A single mailing may consist of several pieces, such as an outside envelope, a letter, a brochure, and a business reply card. It might be part of a campaign of related pieces that are mailed out over a period of weeks.

Internet forms of advertising include Web sites for catalogs, e-mail messages alerting customers to sales opportunities, and banner ads that may include movement and sound.

Other Forms of Advertising

Magazines also offer a forum for advertising. A wide variety of magazines are published. There are general-interest magazines, such as *Newsweek* and *Life,* and specialty or "class" magazines, such as computer, religious, sports, and health publications. There are trade and professional magazines, such as *Print, CA,* and *ARTnews,* as well as professional publications for doctors, engineers, and so on. With magazines it is possible to target a specific interest group. Also, if advertisers have a regional or national product to promote, they may choose magazine advertising because many magazines have national circulation (Figure 9-8). Some of

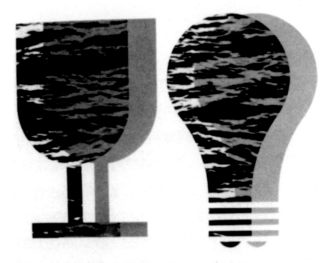

Fresh water and electricity...from one super-factory

Imagine a modern factory that can produce 300,000 kilowatts of electric power—and at the same time take water from the sea and make it drinkable at the rate of 50 million gallons a day. That's enough power and water for a population of half a million.

No such super-factory exists anywhere in the world. Not yet. But Westinghouse is building a small-scale version of the system for an electric utility in the Canary Islands. Waste heat from the electric power turbines will convert sea water to fresh by a flash distillation process, providing abundant electricity and water for industry, agriculture and home uses. And at a lower cost than now exists in many parts of the world.

Westinghouse can build large or small sea water super-factories for electric utilities in any coastal area. And as research continues, scientists may find a practical way to harvest chemicals from sea water in the same process. You can be sure ... if it's Westinghouse.

We never forget how much you rely on Westinghouse.

9-8
Magazine advertisement for Westinghouse Electric Corporation designed in 1962 by **Paul Rand.**
Courtesy of Mrs. Marion Rand.

those national magazines have regional versions, targeting different parts of the country.

Another form of advertising is billboard display (Figures 9-9a, 9-9b, and 9-9c). When designing for billboards, remember that the message will be seen from a moving vehicle at a distance of at least 100 feet (30 m). The visual and the copy must be kept simple. It is surprising how many billboards violate this principle. Type for billboards should be at least 3 inches (8 cm) high at 100 feet (30 m) and 12 inches (30 cm) high at 400 feet (120 m). A message of more than about seven words is difficult to read. A single image is easiest to grasp. An easily recognizable silhouette makes a strong visual that can carry much of the

9-9a, b, c
Billboard created by Rapp Collins Communications as part of the BUGS! campaign for the Minnesota Zoo. Creative director **Bruce Edwards,** art director **Bruce Edwards**, copywriter **Chris Mihock.**

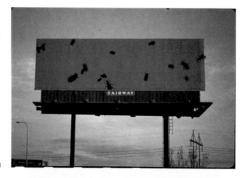

a

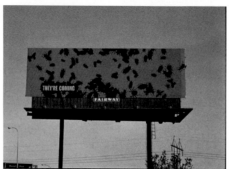

b

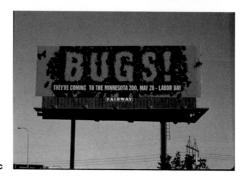

c

other promotional materials established for the product (Figure 9-10). The term *point of purchase* describes the display that is present along with the product in the store. Studies have shown that purchase of many items is based on impulse. More than one-third of purchases in department stores and almost two-thirds of the purchases in supermarkets result from display of the product. The display in the store, especially supermarkets, consequently plays an important part in advertising products. Package design can be considered a form of point-of-purchase design and is an interesting area to investigate.

Personal Promotion

A special form of advertising that brings out the most creative and delightful work samples is personal promotion. This is the campaign an individual creates to advertise freelance services or to promote a small design firm. The goal is to design a creative sample that shows the best of concept development, illustration, and design skills. It must reach and appeal to an appropriate audience (Figure 9-11).

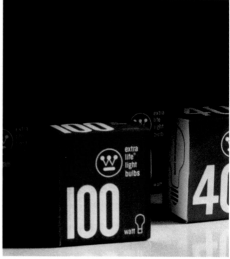

9-10
Bulb packaging designed by **Paul Rand** for Westinghouse Electric Corporation in 1968. *Courtesy of Mrs. Marion Rand.*

message. A strong intellectual and visual unity is important. The problems presented by transit advertising and outdoor advertising in general are similar to those for billboards. The audience is always in motion. The form of the appeal must be bold and simple, with details eliminated.

Point-of-purchase advertising and package design is another area of importance. Both are primarily three dimensional and should present a look consistent with the

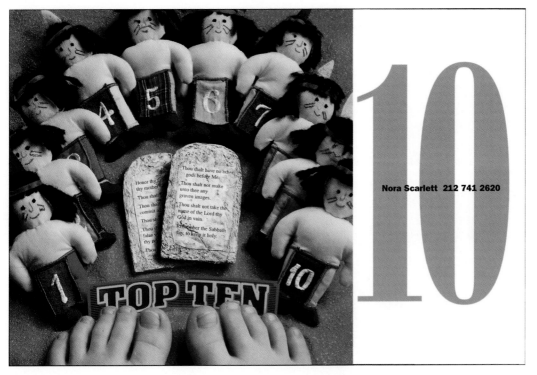

Nora Scarlett 212 741 2620

9-11
Personal promotional campaign designed by contemporary photographer **Nora Scarlett** for direct mail delivery. *Courtesy of the artist.*

CORPORATE IDENTITY

Companies have used trademarks to identify themselves since the early Renaissance, as discussed in Chapter 5. This practice grew and flourished with the Industrial Revolution and culminated in the 1950s with very complete visual identification systems. Names associated with this golden age of corporate identity include Paul Rand, Saul Bass, and Lester Beall, among others.

Large companies and institutions now often have a master corporate identity plan that coordinates all of their designs. This plan begins with the trademark and applies it to the layout of business cards, letterhead, advertisements, product identification, and packaging. Even the company uniforms and vehicles are a part of this identity program. The accompanying illustrations from J. I. Case Company show their strong corporate logo applied to signage, package design, and vehicles (Figure 9-12). Corporate identity is a specialized branch of advertising and design that works by creating a unified image through a systematic application of constant elements. Every aspect of typography, imagery, and application must be considered part of an integrated presentation.

This integrated image presents the corporation to the public in a positive and memorable light. It not only communicates an image, but attempts to persuade the public that the company, hence the product, is superior. A graphics standard manual is presented to company personnel detailing the appropriate use and placement of the trademark and related materials. The identity program must be flexible enough to be adapted to future needs. It is one of the most comprehensive applications of design and advertising.

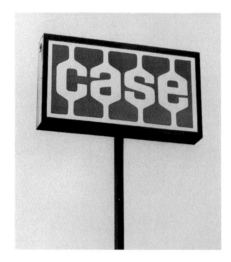

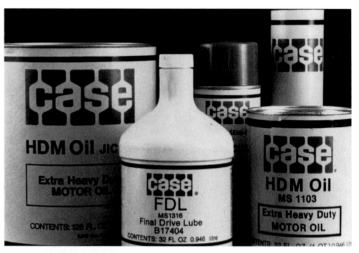

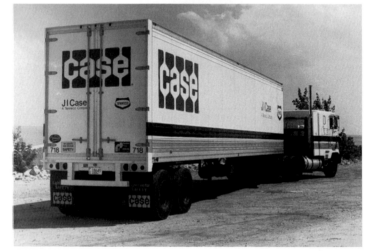

9-12a, b, c
J.I. Case Company
corporate logo applied to
signage, packaging, and
vehicles. *Courtesy of J.I.*
Case, Racine, Wisconsin.

WORKING WITH OTHERS

Advertising takes teamwork. You must communicate closely with copywriters, photographers, illustrators, clients, and market researchers. Either the visual or the verbal element may be the departure point for developing the message. An integration of form and content, of design and communication is at the heart of good advertising.

Work with others to establish key information. Who is the audience? What is the nature of the product? Where will the ad appear? What is the purpose of the ad? What is the budget? Once you have answered these questions, you can begin to translate this information into visual form.

A successful ad attracts attention, communicates through its unified arrangement of elements, and persuades through the interaction of strong and appropriate copy and layout.

Exercises

1. Find some persuasive ads in a magazine. How do they catch their intended audience? What associations with the product do the ads induce? How?

2. Find an ad for a product that targets different audiences by appearing in two

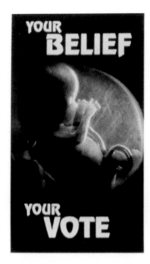 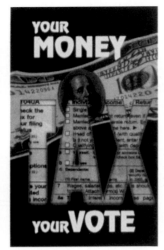 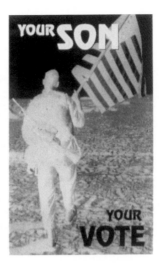

9-13
Terri Breese.
Integrated ad campaign created to encourage voter participation.

magazines in a different format. Try looking at "African American" and "senior" and "youth" publications.

3. Turn off the sound and watch some television commercials. Does the visual convey a complete message? Now try listening without viewing the advertisement.

4. Scan your local newspaper. Which advertisements attract your attention? How do position and design affect their success?

Project

Magazine Advertisements

Design two magazine advertisements in an 8½ × 11" (20 × 28 cm) format for a non-profit, public service organization. Your task is to warn readers of the hazards of alcohol or smoking abuse. The primary audience for the first ad is 18- to 24-year-olds. The second ad should communicate with the underage drinker or smoker. Identify the magazines in which your ad will appear. Research and discuss in class some of the problems that might be targeted, such as drunk driving.

Prepare the ads for black and white reproduction, including an image, a headline, and a few lines of body copy. In your thumbnails, try various approaches, including a path layout, grid layout, and a simple dominant image. Figure 9-13 is a student solution to a similar problem.

Personal Promotion

Prepare a personal promotional campaign. Create a logo for yourself as an independent designer/illustrator, apply it to a business card and letterhead, and prepare a brochure for your promotional mailing. The research stage of this assignment primarily involves looking at other personal campaigns. Set your standards very high. Try to top the professionals.

Objectives

Experiment with researching and targeting (or appealing to) a particular audience. Practice both communicating a message and persuading an audience.

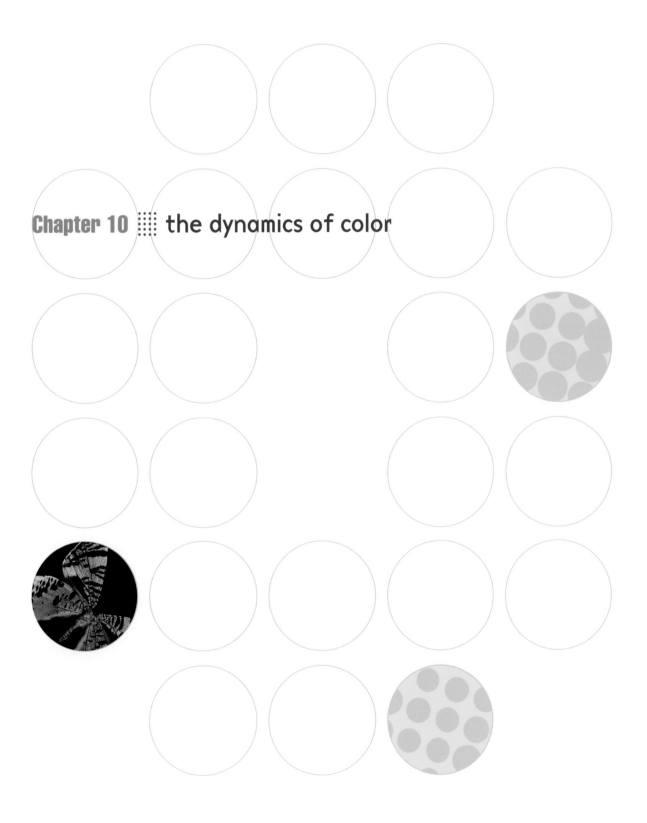

Chapter 10 ::::: the dynamics of color

Color for the designer and color for the fine artist is similar at the creative stage. A basic knowledge of color theory is useful to both. Later, in preparing art on the computer for the Web, or for the printing process, the designer needs to be familiar with how color is influenced by its intended publication venue. A great deal of new terminology must be understood. Let us first brush up on color as a creative and expressive communication. Then we will consider color from the computer and the printing perspectives. Web color is discussed in Chapter 12.

DESIGNING WITH COLOR

Every student who has completed an elementary course in art has heard that color is a property of light. Many people do not fully understand those words, however, until years after their art degree is completed. A young painter several years past her B.F.A. tells a story of looking around her living room for a composition to paint. "I considered the objects in the room and the space they occupied; the corners of the ceiling and the negative spaces in the staircase. I looked at the carpet and saw the standard 'landlord green.' And then I looked at the carpet again and realized that my mind was processing 'landlord green,' but my eyes were actually looking at black geometric shapes swimming beside a shining pastel/fluorescent color of fresh spring leaves. The sun was shining in the window of my dark living room and transforming my carpet. Color is a property of light, I thought. Oh!"

Color has been accurately described as both "the way an object absorbs or reflects light" and "the kind of light that strikes an object." The painter's carpet would appear to have a different color had it a deep shag texture or a slick, shiny surface. It would appear to have a different color under an incandescent or fluorescent light, under bright natural sunlight or light overcast cloud cover. Even the angle from which it is viewed has an effect.

Isaac Newton first passed a beam of white light through a prism and saw it divide into several colors. The colors of the light wave spectrum are red, orange, yellow,

10-1
Light waves of many colors join to make white light.

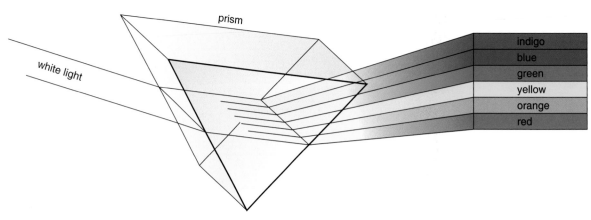

green, blue, and indigo (Figure 10-1). In physics, mixing the colors of the light wave together produces pure white light. It is these light waves, bouncing off or being absorbed by the objects around us, that give them color.

The three primary colors in white light are red, blue, and green. They are called *additive* primaries because together they can produce white light. The eye contains three different types of color receptors, each sensitive to one of the primary colors of the light spectrum. This seems to suggest an active connection between our physiological makeup and the world in which we live (Figure 10-10).

The designer needs to understand that color depends on light. *Color is not an unchanging, absolute property of the object. It is dynamic and affected by its environment.*

The Color Wheel

For the artist and designer, mixing pigments will never produce white. Black is the sum of all pigment colors. Several color wheels have been developed to help us understand the effects of combining pigments.

The traditional color wheel, developed by Herbert Ives, begins with *subtractive* primary colors of red, yellow, and blue. Mixing these hues produces secondary colors. Mixing the secondary colors with the primary produces a tertiary color.

The Munsell color wheel is based on five key hues: red, yellow, blue, green, and purple. Secondaries are formed by mixing these primaries. Although these two classification systems differ, the basic look of the resulting colors is similar. The color wheel is only a workable system, not an absolute (Figure 10-2). The CMYK process colors used in offset printing are also a pigment-based subtractive gamut.

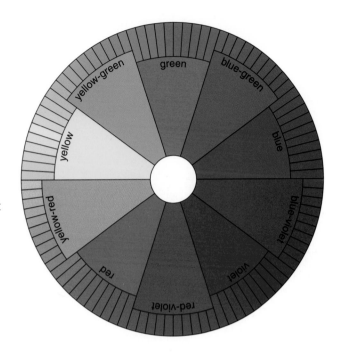

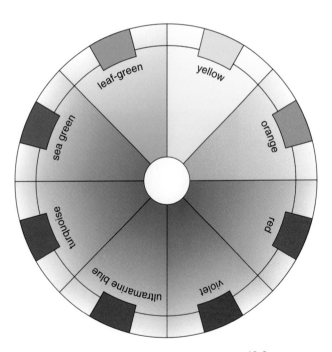

10-2
Two possible color wheels.

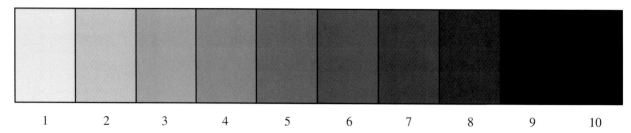

| 1 | 2 | 3 | 4 | 5 | 6 | 7 | 8 | 9 | 10 |

10-3
Changes in value.

Properties of Color

Every color has three properties: hue, value, and intensity. *Hue* is the name by which we identify a color. The color wheel is set up according to hue.

Value is the degree of lightness or darkness in a hue. It is easiest to understand value when looking at a black and white image. The darkest value will be close to black, the lightest close to white, with a range of grays in between. Value also plays an important role in all color images. Every hue has its own value range. Yellow, for example, is normally lighter than purple. Its normal value in the middle of a yellow value scale will be lighter than purple. In a value scale, the color values lighter than normal value are called *tints;* those darker than normal value are called *shades.* When working with pigments, the addition of white lightens a value, whereas the addition of black darkens it (Figure 10-3).

The third property of color is *intensity,* or saturation. It is a measure of a color's purity and brightness. In pigments there are two ways of reducing the intensity of a color: Mix it with a gray of the same value, or mix it with its complement (the color opposite on the color wheel). Low-intensity colors have been toned down and are often referred to as *tones.* Colors not grayed are at their most vivid at full intensity (Figure 10-4).

Color Schemes

Color combinations are grouped into categories called *color schemes.* Colors

10-4
Tom Girvin, art director, designer; **Anton Kimball,** illustrator; **Mary Radosevich,** production. Bright Blocks is a package design by Tom Girvin Design, Inc. This colorful package uses highly saturated color to target its young audience. The colorful design increased sales dramatically. *Courtesy of the artist.*

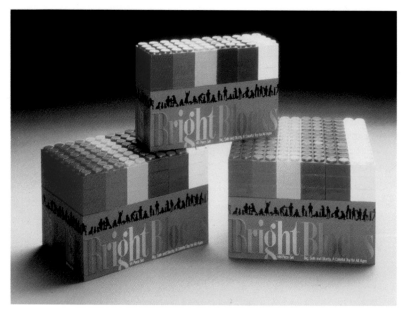

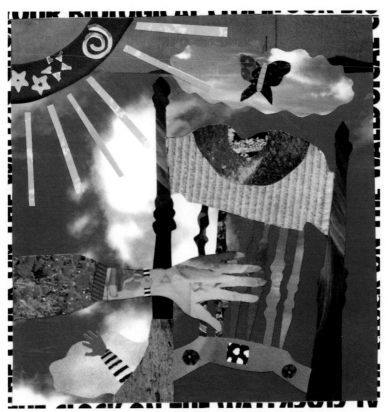

10-5
Linda Godfrey.
This freelance illustrator while she was still a student created a whimsical collage using photographic textures. The strong use of blue is accented with complements, and repetition is used throughout this creative design.

opposite one another on the color wheel are called *complements.* Art that combines these colors is said to be using a complementary color scheme. Figure 10-5 uses a range between blue and gold/brown/orange. Complements heighten and accent one another. They often are used to produce a bold, exciting effect. A split complementary scheme includes one hue and the two hues on either side of its direct complement. Colors next to one another on the color wheel are called *analogous.* An analogous color scheme is generally considered soothing and restful. A *monochromatic* color scheme is composed of one hue in several values.

In color there are no real absolutes. That is why this information is often called *color theory.* It is unusual, but quite possible, to produce a tense, dramatic effect using analogous colors or a soothing, harmonious

effect using complementary colors. Remember, these principles are not rules, but useful guidelines. An artist or designer may choose to deliberately violate them for effect.

THE RELATIVITY OF COLOR

Our perception of color is colored by many considerations. For example, the way each color looks to us is strongly affected by what surrounds it. This phenomenon is known as *simultaneous contrast.*

We automatically compare colors that sit side by side. When complements (such as red and green) are placed side by side, they seem to become more intense. They complement one another. A gray placed beside a color appears to have a tinge of that color's complement in it because our eye automatically searches for it. Therefore a

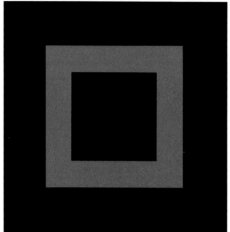

10-6
Simultaneous contrast gives two boxes of the same gray appear to have different values.

neutral gray beside a red will appear to be a greenish gray; the same neutral gray beside a green will appear to have a reddish cast.

Value also is affected by simultaneous contrast. A gray placed against a black ground will appear to have a lighter value than the same gray placed against a white ground (Figure 10-6). Our eye makes a comparison between the black and gray and judges the gray as much lighter. In the other sample, our eye looks at the white and judges the gray as much darker.

One designer first experienced this effect when she was a child, visiting her aunt for dinner. Butter in her own home was a yellow stick brought home from the store. On the aunt's farm it came straight from the cows, after a little churning. This fresh butter did not have yellow food coloring added to it. When her aunt placed it on the table on a yellow plate, the niece would not eat it. It looked white and could not be the real thing. Who would eat white butter? The aunt, however, knew about simultaneous contrast, although not by that name. She whisked the butter plate away and returned with the same butter, this time on a white plate. The young girl was delighted with the

10-7
Bridget Riley.
1969. Gouache study. H 62 cm W 98 cm. Each red stripe is altered by the band it encloses. Victoria and Albert Museum, London.

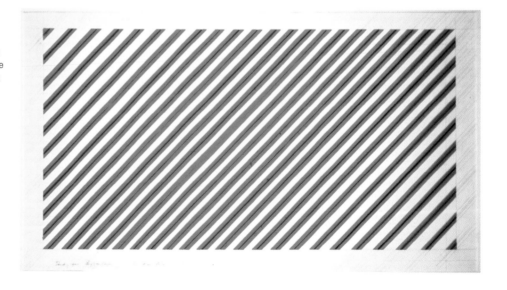

"new" butter. This time, compared with the white plate it sat on, the fresh butter looked yellow.

Simultaneous contrast means that color is relative to the colors surrounding it. This fact was first discovered in the 19th century when a French chemist named Michel-Eugène Chevreul, also a merchant who dyed fabric, was disturbed by apparent inconsistencies in his bolts of cloth. He discovered that his dye remained consistent, but the viewing conditions did not. Bolts of the same color appeared to be different colors depending on the color of the fiber samples around them. He went on to research and document color properties. In the 20th century, Josef Albers made a further intensive study of color. Albers experimented with simultaneous contrast and contributed greatly to our understanding of that effect. Figure 10-7 by Bridget Riley uses the optical effects of color in this painting.

THE PSYCHOLOGY OF COLOR

Relativity also holds true in the psychology of color. Colors have the power to evoke specific emotional responses in the viewer—some personal and some more universal. In general, for example, warm colors stimulate, whereas cool colors relax most people. Interior designers pay close attention to this relationship when they consider the color schemes for a dentist's waiting room or the newsroom of a daily paper. Can you imagine sitting in a dentist's chair staring at a bright red or yellow wall?

Red, yellow, and their variations are referred to as warm colors, perhaps because we associate them with fire and the sun. Blue and green are considered cool colors. They also happen to be the colors of sky, water, and forests. The difference in the wave lengths of these colors may also account for our reactions to them.

Associations

Personal memories play a part in color perception as well. If your mother usually wore a particular shade of blue, and you loved your mother (and she loved you), that shade of blue has good associations for you. It seems a warm, friendly color, although to other eyes it might look cool.

Along with personal associations, we have cultural associations with color. They often appear in our language: "black anger," "yellow-bellied coward," "feeling blue," and "seeing red" are a few examples. To her wedding a bride wears white, the color of purity; to a funeral we wear black, the color of mourning. These are not absolute; they change from culture to culture. For example, people in India wear white to a funeral. For a wedding, they favor yellow. But these cultural preferences are changing with global awareness.

We can describe our culture's general color associations. It is by no means a description to be memorized and taken as gospel. Color psychology is complex, affected by many considerations, but if you can combine this information with a light hand and sensitive eye, it may prove useful.

Red

Red is a dramatic, highly visible hue. It is associated with sexuality and aggression, with passion and violence. It is also an official hue found in most national colors. Red is often the favored color of a sports car or a sports team. A dignified, conservative executive, however, is unlikely to choose red for a car or a corporate logo unless its intensity is toned down or its value darkened toward black.

Blue

In its darker values, blue is associated with authority. Our executive might likely favor a navy blue car, suit, and logo. A middle-value blue is generally associated with cleanliness and honesty and has a cooling, soothing effect. It is used as a background color in package design because of its quiet, positive associations. Even at full intensity, blue retains a calm quality.

Yellow

Yellow is used in food packaging a great deal because it is associated with warmth, good health, and optimism. There remain in English the reminders that yellow also has been associated with cowardliness and weakness. That does not appear to be the case currently, however. Even our cultural associations are subject to change.

Green

Green is associated with the environment, cleanliness, and naturalness. Soothing and cooling, it is consequently a favored color among manufacturers of such products as menthol cigarettes and noncola beverages.

Selecting Color

Consider the psychology of the audience in a choice of color. A game or toy intended to appeal to children should have different colors than one intended to reach adults considering retirement plans. Our color preferences change as we grow older. In general, youth prefers a more intense color that signals urgency and excitement. The subtle color preferences of age are associated with restraint and dignity.

The institution you are designing for should also affect the selection of color. Banks tend to prefer the darker values and the blues and grays associated with authority and stability. A physical fitness club would probably want more vibrant and intense colors. A restaurant may choose complementary colors that are toned down to an attractive and intimate level (Figure 10-8).

As a designer, individual color preference is not the only or even the primary consideration. Choice of color should reflect five psychological factors:

1. Cultural associations with color.
2. The profile of the audience and its color preferences.

10-8
Julie Talcott.
Freelance illustrator. This computer-generated illustration uses complementary colors and strong repetition of line and shape to create this integrated design.
Courtesy of the artist.

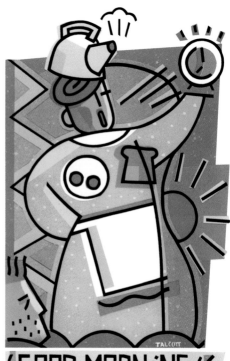

3. The character and personality of the company represented.
4. The designer's personal relationship with color.
5. An awareness of current color trends.

UNDERSTANDING ELECTRONIC COLOR

Color on a computer monitor is created in a manner much like a pointillist painting by Georges Seurat. Computer images are composed of individual dots called *pixels*. The pixel is a rectangle of light on the computer screen that can be set to different colors. The more pixels, the better the resolution and clarity of the image. The resolution is determined by the hardware (Figure 10-9).

Many designers work with a 24-bit system. In such a system, each pixel is represented by 24 bits of color information: 8 for red, 8 for green, and 8 for blue. There are 256 possible values of each of these three

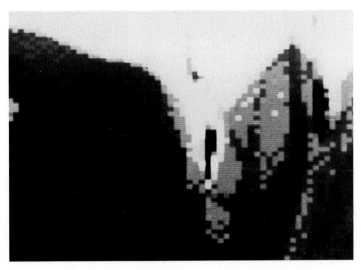

10-9
This enlargement of a
digitized flower also shows
the pixel structure.

colors. These differing values of red, green,
and blue can be combined to produce more
than 16.7 million colors.

Color Models

Designers study color theory in order to use
it effectively. Color theory remains the same
whether it be applied to a traditional or electronic design. But when using electronic
color, it can be helpful to study its practical
differences. We must understand the various
ways color is created in order to see the
final design printed and looking the way we
intended. The previous section of this chapter discussed creating color using pigment-
based subtractive primaries. There are three
color models you need to be familiar with
when using computer graphics. These are
the most prevalent color models.

RGB

The image on the computer monitor is displayed in the additive primaries RGB (red,
green, blue) and is a back-lit image made by
adding light. An image on the monitor may
display colors in RGB that cannot be duplicated in the reflective copy of CMYK printing.
Be prepared if the printout does not match
the computer screen. They are displayed in
different color *gamuts,* or models. Calibrating
the monitor will help (Figure 10-10).

CMYK

All of this electronic color is quite different from
mixing and blending paint or colored pencils.
When the monitor's colors are transferred to
paper or the file is ripped for offset reproduction, it is printed in the subtractive model of
CMYK. The CMYK model is the basis for four-
color process printing comprised of cyan,
magenta, yellow, and black inks. (The K
stands for black, which is added to give

10-10
Red, green, and blue are
the primary colors in the
additive system. Red,
green, and blue together
produce white. In this
system, cyan, magenta,
and yellow are secondary
colors.

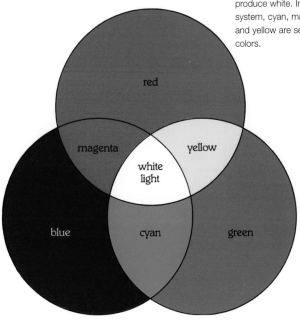

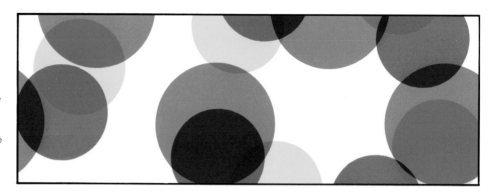

10-11
In the subtractive color system, cyan, magenta, and yellow are the primary colors, and their overlapping produces the red, green, and blue of the secondary colors. Cyan, magenta, and yellow together produce black.

density to the final print.) For additional information on CMYK, see "Process Colors" later in this chapter (Figure 10-11).

HSL

Hue, saturation, and *lightness* (HSL) are terms familiar to us from the world of color theory and a discussion of the properties of color. Photoshop allows the user to manipulate colors using this model and other models, by moving popup menu sliders. The intensity of a color diminishes when its saturation slider is moved (Figure 10-12). The lightness control varies a color from white to black (this corresponds to value in pigment-based color models). If you are not concerned about preparing a file for four-color (process) printing, this can be a satisfying color model to use because it is

the most intuitive and closest to the way mixed pigment color is used in painting and drawing.

Another Color Wheel

The RGB/CMY color model positions the two sets of primaries equidistant from one another. Each secondary color is between two primary colors, each color on the wheel is between two colors that are used to create it, and each color is directly opposite its complement. This is a helpful model to study in order to understand what is happening on the computer monitor.

Red and blue make magenta. In order to decrease magenta from an image, the red and blue must be decreased. Whatever is done to a color, it has the opposite effect on that color's complement. In other words, decreasing red will increase cyan (Figure 10-13).

Various computer programs that allow designers to do color correction have popup menus allowing this kind of manipulation. Photoshop is an effective color correction software in common usage by designers, although there are other dedicated color management programs. Its sliders allow the user to manipulate color quickly and see the resulting effects. It also allows the user to work from numbered percentages in order to specify colors that will match a CMYK print. And, finally, it allows the user to switch

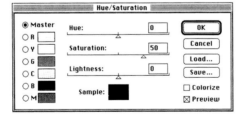

10-12
Photoshop slides allow careful control of hue, saturation, and lightness (value).

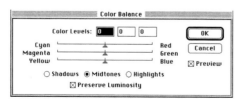

10-13
Photoshop sliders control and demonstrate the relationship between RGB and CMY color systems.

between color models, specifying that an image be created in RGB, CMYK, spot color, black and white, or duotone modes.

Color Gamuts

The visible color range of a color model is called a *gamut.* As Figure 10-14 shows, the eye can see more colors than can be created in either the RGB or CMYK color models. The gamut of RGB, however, is larger than that of CMYK. That means that if a design is created with the RGB mode, some of those colors probably cannot be printed using CMYK process colors. Photoshop will give you an alert symbol (a triangle with an exclamation mark inside) in the Picker palette if your color is not printable. This allows you to substitute a printable color before sending the file for reproduction.

COLOR IN PRINTING

In addition to applying the psychology of color theory to design work, you must stay within restrictions imposed by the technology of mass reproduction. Designs must be created within the limitation of the budget, equipment, expertise, and time available for a particular project. *The designer's use of color must be not only creative and appropriate, but practical and printable.*

Tint Screens

In mixed pigments, color changes are created by adding a different pigment-based hue. White is altered to gray by the addition of black; red is altered to a light pink by the addition of white; and green is created by mixing blue and yellow.

Additive color on the RGB computer monitor is created though varying intensities of light, as just discussed. When the file is sent to press, in order to create a tint or a light value of a hue, the printer cuts back on the density of the ink through varying

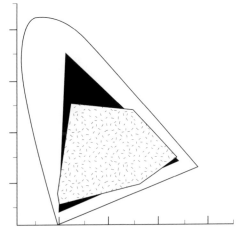

10-14
The exterior shape represents the colors the eye can see. The black triangle represents the colors that can be shown on the monitor; the texture represents colors that can be printed on coated paper.

screens. Screens are available in gradients from 10 to 90 percent. There is a similarity between the tint screens of printing inks and the application of transparent watercolor. In both cases, white is made by allowing the white of the paper to show through, and lighter values are made by applying less pigment or ink.

In appearance, the value scale of printer's screens is similar to a value scale mixed by an artist combining pigments. However, if you look at the printer's scale under a magnifying glass, the screened dots will show up (Figure 10-15). All commercial printing is a form of optical illusion achieved not by sleight of hand, but by dot screens. The same black ink is applied to paper for a 90 percent gray or a 10 percent gray, but the

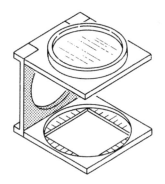

10-15
A linen tester magnifies screened dots.

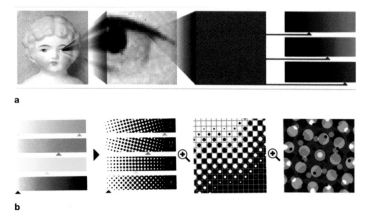

a

b

dot screen fools the eye into believing it is different. Where there are more dots, the ink looks blacker. A solid ink is not screened but printed at 100 percent.

There is an analogy here with the computer screen. The image on screen is composed of dots, or pixels, of varying colors. The image the printer creates is also composed of dots, this time of solid colors of ink. The monitor uses varying intensities of light to create (additive) color, and the printer uses varying densities of ink (subtractive pigment (Figures 10-16a and 10-16b).

Figure 10-17 shows 10 to 100 percent tint screens of the three process colors: yellow, magenta, and cyan. Try looking at them with a magnifier. Changing the hue or making an ink appear darker is done by combining screened percentages of different colors. To change a cyan to purple, for example, a tint screen of magenta could be laid over it. The new color effects generated by using screens of process colors are referred to as *fake colors* (Figure 10-18). Figure 10-19a is a Pantone Guide that shows process color combinations; Figure 10-19b shows an array of solid spot colors. When creating such colors electronically, or specifying by traditional pasteup mode, reference guides like these charts and specify ink percentages or numbers rather than "going by eye."

10-17
Changing tint values with screens. Material furnished by Hammermill Papers Group for plates 4 and 5.

It is important to visualize these screened color combinations correctly before sending them to the printer. The comp may have been generated on the computer and shown on screen or it may be output as a proof print. The goal is to arrive at a printed piece that matches your expectations.

	MAGENTA	YELLOW	CYAN
10%			
20%			
30%			
40%			
50%			
60%			
70%			
80%			
90%			
100%			

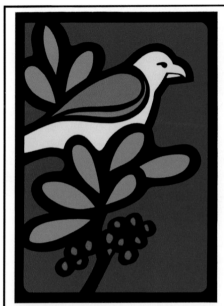

Four-color pre-separated art

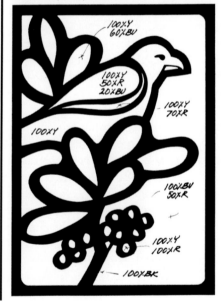

number that the printer can match, using a reference guide. This is much more scientific than specifying a logo be printed in a bright cool red. Each ink color has its own number. Choose the ink color from the guide and enter it on your computer, or tell the printer its number. The printer then prepares the ink you have specified. To get the desired blue for your two-color design, you might specify a spot color of Pantone 313 with a 20 per-cent screen of black. A variety of reference books show screened percentages of these ink colors. They also show what happens when you combine two different ink colors in screened percentages. Using spot colors is usually less expensive than full process colors.

Spot Color or Process Color?

If you are using one to three spot colors, several numbered guides are available to assist you. The most complete, the Pantone Matching System, consists of a full line of color specification books, coordinated by numbers. These formula guides, first devel-oped in 1963, enable you to specify a color

(left)
10-18
Tint screen percentages of the four process colors are combined to create this illustration.

10-19a
Pantone Process Color System Guide.

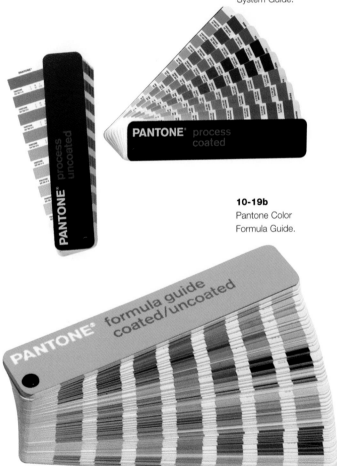

10-19b
Pantone Color Formula Guide.

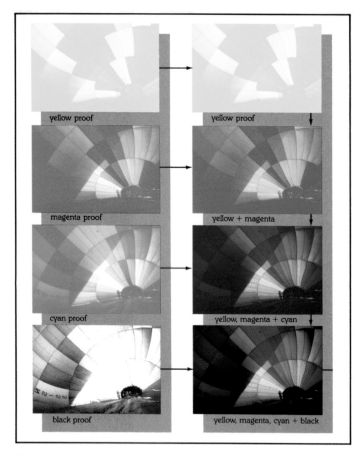

10-20

Yellow, magenta, cyan, and black proofs and their combinations.

Process Color Separations

The offset reproduction of a full range of color, rather than just two or three colors, is done with CMYK process color. The three primary colors in process printing are yellow, magenta, and cyan, as we have discovered. The addition of black as a fourth color gives depth and solidity to the image. These four printer's inks produce the visual effect of full color (Figure 10-20).

Once the designer has given the printer a full-color illustration or photograph to reproduce, either traditionally or electronically transferred, the printer separates out the process colors. Artwork is separated into three color exposures from which the printing plates are made. A black separation is also made. When the press is inked with

each of these four colors, and the color is laid down from the plate onto the paper, an illusion of full color results. The varying densities of halftone dots overlap and lie beside one another, mixing optically. It is a truly effective illusion.

As with spot color tint screens, the mixing happens not within the pigment, but within the eye of the viewer. Unlike the even dot coverage of tint screens, a process color separation is made of dots of varying densities that correspond to the color density in the original image. This variation is why such a complex range of color can be produced from only four process colors. Examine the full-color images in this book with a linen tester magnifier (see Figure 10-15).

Cutting Costs

Each additional ink used in a design means the printer must do additional work preparing plates, negatives, and the press. The more ink colors you use, the more printing the design will cost. Combining screened percentages of inks will enable you to get the most out of each color you pay for and can decrease the cost of the job.

Another way to get more color into a job without increasing the cost is by printing on colored paper. Excellent reference books (often from paper companies) are available on using colored inks on colored papers. The color of the paper will show through, subtly altering the look of the ink. For this reason, white ink is seldom used in the printing industry. Opaque white is difficult to achieve. A study of how tint screens, ink, and paper interact will help achieve the desired effect at a minimum cost.

Halftones, Duotones, and Tritones

Photographic prints used for halftones should have an extended tonal range with good contrast. If your negative has good detail, it can be converted to a good halftone. Although a poor negative or print

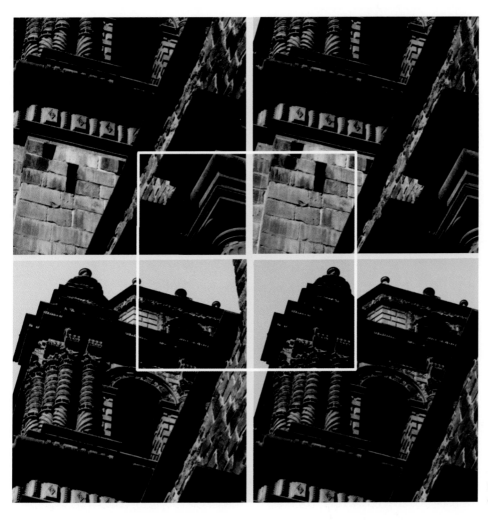

10-21
Duotone and tritone
combinations.

with loss of detail can be improved, it cannot be converted into a high-quality halftone.

Duotones and tritones are commonly used techniques for printing black and white photography using spot colors. Although these halftones are limited in color, there are many options to consider (Figure 10-21). Electronic scanning can selectively enhance the tonal range, and different line screens can be employed from coarse to very fine. A halftone can be printed over a solid color or over a screened color to create a fake duotone effect.

A duotone is created by generating two halftone negatives from the same image. By printing these negatives in varying colors, you can achieve different effects (Figure 10-22a). Duotone effects depend as much on how you use the two colors as what colors you specify. For example, a black and violet duotone can be run with the black dominant or the violet dominant. The density range of each plate can be extended or compressed, producing shadow detail in one color while the other accents the highlights.

The tritone uses three colors for still more creative options. Black combined with two colors yields a new effect, as does printing with a warm black instead of a true black. A tritone can also be created during printing

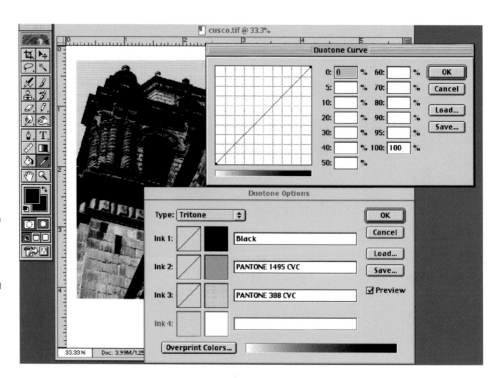

10-22a

Photoshop popup menu showing a duotone curve on one of the colors that will be used to create a duotone. It controls the distribution of color throughout the darks and lights of the image.

10-22b

Photoshop popup menu showing a tritone combination of inks.

using varnishes as a third color (Figure 10-22b).

Whereas designers used to be dependent on reference guides and their instincts to specify these techniques, now it is possible to simulate them quite accurately on the computer. The effect of varnishes and various paper surfaces on ink color, however, are still difficult to visualize before printing.

Technology is changing fast in the design and printing industry, but many principles stay the same. A good design sense and a working knowledge of color theory, coupled with a basic foundation in computer graphics, will see you through.

PROCESS COLOR SEPARATION SUMMARY

When a computer is used to generate four process color separations, a scanner first digitizes your photo into a fine grid of rectangles called pixels (see Figure 10-8). A higher quality scanner gives a finer grid with a higher resolution and more pixels. Each pixel is assigned a value for each of the three additive primaries (red, green, blue, or RGB).

The scanned image can be previewed on a color monitor. This display also uses RGB colors, but the final image is printed with subtractive primary colors (cyan, magenta, yellow, or CMY), with the addition of black (K).

Translating the three RGB values into four CMYK values results in variations caused by switching from an additive (RGB) system to a subtractive (CMYK) system. This entire translation process can be done on a personal computer as well as on higher end systems.

The final step is to turn the CMYK values (which are continuous tone separations) into four halftone films. The halftones are translated into film for making printing plates. In the halftone film, color shades are simulated by varying sizes of halftone dots. In a digital press environment the film step can be skipped. Files are sent directly from computer to plates.

Exercises

1. Find printed samples of monochromatic, analogous, and complementary color schemes. Search for samples of color used in graphic design, advertising, or packaging that convey a particular mood and reach a particular audience.

2. Find an example of a two-color design that uses tint screens to achieve a multicolor effect. Analyze how this design was prepared for printing. Make notes and discuss them with your instructor.

3. Find a duotone or tritone and compare it under a magnifying lens to a traditional process color photograph. Then compare these halftone effects to the tint screen you analyzed.

4. Using a program such as Photoshop, practice converting from RGB to CMYK to HSL and manipulating the colors using slider controls (see Figures 10-22a and 10-22b).

Project

Word and Image Poster

Prepare two full-color posters that combine the image of a famous person, place, or thing with a related word. The word related to each image can be a name or an association the image brings to mind. Pay close attention to integrating the typography with the image through various gestalt unit-forming techniques and color choices (see Figure 10-23).

Choose a complementary, split complementary, or analogous color scheme, and create two color versions of the poster. Use tint, tone, and shade to give your color schemes different personalities. Be creative with color choices. *Local color* designs try to keep realistic color (a sky is blue), but there are other choices. The use of arbitrary color frees you to assign whatever color seems desirable. The sky may become yellow to

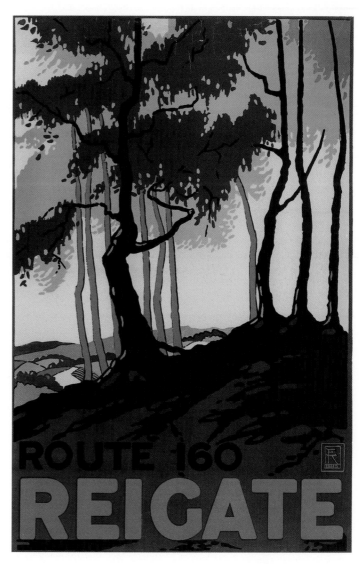

**10-23
E. McKnight Kauffer.**
Reigate, 1916. 24.4 × 20"
(62 × 50.8 cm). The
London Transport
Museum. This influential
painter and designer used
complementary colors to
create this striking poster
for London's subway
system.

enhance the purple backlit tree trunks, or hair may become dark blue in an analogous color scheme of cool hues.

Objectives

Practice using color to express a mood appropriate to an image.

Practice integrating word and image from the standpoint of both pure design and content.

Control color and learn more about it by using different models and creating variants of tint, tone, and shade.

Chapter 11 ::::: production: the tools and process

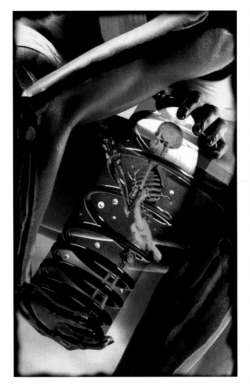

11-1
Patrick McDonough.
SpringMan. This portfolio piece created in 2000 is part of a series exploring the metaphor between humans and their creations.

11-2
Patrick McDonough.
Skeleton Towers. Further explores the Photoshop potential for image manipulation.

A DESIGNER'S TOOL

Computers are at the core of contemporary design and production, and it is worth spending a little time at the beginning of this chapter to understand how this invaluable tool works. Its applications in the design field are constantly expanding. Many new avenues of nonprint design and communication are opening up as computers continue to develop. This technology has the power to reshape our perception of ourselves and the world in which we live. Wonderful as this electronic tool is, for an artist and designer the greatest tool of all is a flexible, curious open mind. Education is a lifelong process—especially now, as changes come ever more quickly and challenge our understanding of the world and how we function in it.

There are many computer applications in design. These include CAD/CAM (computer-aided design and manufacturing) systems that can generate three-dimensional models of a new automobile with the designer never touching anything but the computer. Other print applications allow designs to go from the designer's computer to the offset press, all as digital files. Beyond print applications, the World Wide Web knits us together with an exchange of visual information and other data sharing like never before. The readily available multimedia and animation programs like Premiere, Director, Flash, and After Effects allow the designer to generate animation, interactive environments, and presentation graphics in a desktop environment (see Figure 2-42). Solid information about good design basics will continue to be vital in all the new fields created through the continuing development of computer graphics.

The flexibility and convenience of this powerful tool are revolutionary. A designer can create multiple variations of an image or page layout, experimenting with color, shape, or grid effects. Changes from the client can be accommodated quickly. Special effects in overlapping, tint screens, collaged and manipulated imagery are read-

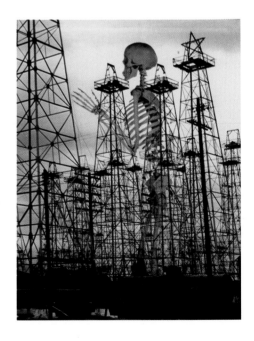

ily achieved (Figures 11-1 and 11-2). *Now, more than ever, there is need for a designer's eye to be well educated and highly discriminating.*

Keep experimenting and asking yourself, "What is the relationship between the elements of the design? Does the form of the design succeed in conveying the message?" Special effects can be seductive. Always ask, "Are they also good design?"

ANALOG AND DIGITAL DATA

Many users are unaware of the structure of the hardware they are manipulating. A basic knowledge of what makes it all work will help you prepare your files most effectively, and a background in the terminology will help you communicate clearly about projects.

What is it that makes computers so different? They deal in digital information. The analog world is full of continuous tone photographs, long-playing records (remember?), and clocks with smoothly moving hands. We ourselves live in an analog world, with time flowing smoothly past, as day fades to night, as we grow up and gradually age.

The digital world, however, is full of discrete units of information, like music on CDs and digital clocks. Each piece of music or unit of time is a separate, discrete entity that can be accessed and manipulated. When a black and white continuous tone photograph is examined under a magnifier, all that is there is a close-up of continually changing gray values. When a digitized photograph is examined close up on a monitor, individual picture elements or pixels give the illusion of a continuous gray or color tones (Figure 11-3). Each of those separate pixels can be manipulated, adjusting value, hue, and luminosity, giving the designer, photographer, or photo retoucher total control over the image.

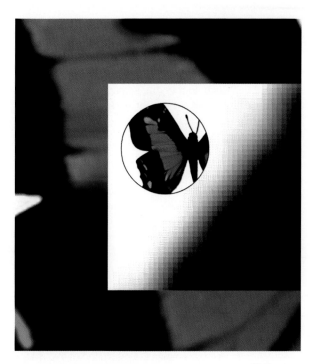

11-3
Enlarging a raster image on the monitor will reveal its pixel structure.

Analog to Digital Conversions

In a scanner or a digital camera, analog to digital converters (ADC) convert analog voltage signals to digital RGB values. In a flatbed scanner, for example, a page is placed face down on the scanner and a scan head moves along the page, illuminating it. The light reflected from the page strikes a series of mirrors that redirect it to a lens. This lens focuses the beam of light into a prism that splits the beam into red, green, and blue components. The red, green, and blue light beams strike rows of photosensitive CCD cells, where they are converted into an analog voltage level. Finally, the analog to digital converter changes these voltage levels to digital information, storing the RGB levels for all the individual pixels in the image that are seen on the screen.

The Screen Image

Raster graphics create the video display the same way a traditional home television does. A raster beam shot from electron

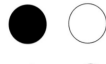

11-4
All computer graphics are created by "on" and "off" commands, represented here as 1 and 0, or black and white.

guns illuminates the display line by line. As it moves across the screen, the raster beam's brightness and color is determined by instructions from the computer hardware.

Each spot on the screen, called a *pixel* (indivisible visual unit), represents a location in memory. A digital image is broken down into pixels, each of which can be individually accessed and manipulated. Each pixel location in memory is composed of a bitmap that has an "on" or "off" command stored several bit plane (layers) deep. All computer graphics comes down to "on" and "off" commands (Figure 11-4).

The resolution of a screen controls its sharpness and clarity. You may have noticed the jagged edges on some computer displays. Because each spot on the visual display is a pixel corresponding to a spot in memory, the number of individual pixels in the file determines the resolution of the image (Figures 11-5a and 11-5b). The screen, the file, and the printer may all have different resolutions. For print graphics, a high resolution file and output is mandatory. The online viewing, however, is in low resolution.

Object-Oriented and Bitmapped Graphics
There are two kinds of image files in computer graphics. Vector graphics and raster graphics are also known as object-oriented and bitmapped graphics. Quark, Illustrator, and Freehand are vector graphics programs. Images are created by lines drawn between coordinate points and are not composed of pixels. These images can be selected and moved separately from other objects. Vector graphics programs create images with clean, sharp edges. Remember René Descartes? He was a 17th-century philosopher whose most famous words were "I think, therefore I am." Descartes also created the Cartesian coordinate system that vector graphics is based on. In this coordinate system, X and Y are a two-dimensional graphic, and X, Y, and Z are three dimensions (Figure 11-6). It is amazing to realize that computers use information developed that long ago. Objects created in vector graphics like the Illustrator image in Figure 11-7 are easily selected and manipulated through pushing, pulling, adding, and deleting points.

Bitmapped programs use raster graphics to create images. This means each pixel is individually manipulated through color and size to create a "map" of your image. This is done by accessing the individual bits in each pixel. Photoshop and Painter are both bitmapped graphics programs. These programs seem to have a more intuitive feeling,

11-5a, b
This bitmap shows the on-and-off commands represented on the monitor as pixels forming a simple "x."

1	0	0	0	1
0	1	0	1	0
0	0	1	0	0
0	1	0	1	0
1	0	0	0	1

a

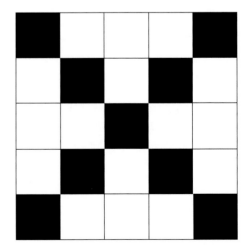

b

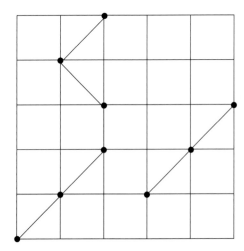

illustrations, and photographs are compiled for printing. QuarkXpress and Adobe's InLine Design work with outline vector graphics fonts to give sharp, clear, resizable typography.

Hardware and Software

The hardware are the physical components that make up a computer graphics system. This hardware is driven by software programs that tell it what to do. The central processing unit (CPU) is the main part of the system that houses the hard drive. This hard drive, along with the built-in floppy disk, CD-ROM, and/or Zip and DVD drives, give access to personal file storage. There are various forms of external storage. The visual display terminal (VDT) shows the images as they are created.

11-6

Vector graphics are created by lines drawn between coordinate points.

Memory

All of a computer's ability to store, recall, and display images is based on the simple notion of on or off (Figure 11-4). A single piece of information like this is called a *bit.* It can be used to represent a black or a white pixel. Hence the term *bitmapped graphics.* A group of bits can handle grays and even complex colors. Eight bits are called a *byte* and can store 256 different grays or colors per pixel. Three bytes (24 bits) gives the capability of rendering 16.7 million colors. Full-color effects are achieved when 24 bits represent each pixel within an image. A full-color image, especially in high resolution, will take up much more memory than a gray scale image because it uses more bits of information (Figure11-8).

11-7

The selection points in this vector graphic are easily manipulated to rescale or reshape the object.

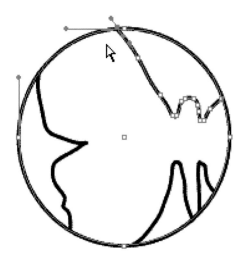

operating much like painting or drawing materials. Bitmapped images lose data when changed in size, unlike vector graphics that retain their clarity as they are scaled up or down.

   Page layout programs accept both forms of graphics. This is usually where type,

11-8

A bit of information is organized into groups called a *byte. A group of bytes* make up a "word."

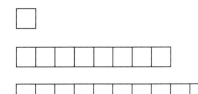

RAM and ROM

There are two kinds of memory in a computer. An integrated circuit chip on the computer's motherboard has a permanent memory called *ROM* (Read-Only Memory). It holds the computer's essential operating instructions. The *RAM* (Random Access Memory) is the memory used to actively create your files. When you launch an application or open a document, it is loaded into RAM and stored there while you work. Enough RAM is needed to hold the software you are using and the data you generate. RAM needs are constantly escalating. Buy as much as you can. RAM chips also range in speed (measured in ns, or nanoseconds). Be sure to buy the ones specified for your computer.

Most RAM chips are soldered onto Memory Module boards. They are fairly easy to plug in and can be added to your system to increase its memory capacity. Each system has a particular configuration of SIMM (Single In-line Memory Module) or DIMM boards. Make sure any RAM chips will fit your particular board.

Storage Devices

Where do you store these large files you have created? Hard drive space is always too short, but a few gigabytes is a good base. You can add an internal drive to most machines. Designers resort to a wide array of external portable storage devices that allow them to get their images to the service bureau or to archive files (see the section later in this chapter on the production process). Obviously, whatever route you choose, the vendors you deal with must be able to support it. Some current alternatives include Zip drives, and CD and DVD storage drives. Electronic file transfer is now a valuable, timesaving reality.

INPUT/OUTPUT DEVICES

Data In

Many peripheral devices are capable of capturing data for a computer. Scanners come in many varieties, from flatbed to transparency to drum scanners. Their operation is discussed later in this chapter, related to prepress. The higher the resolution a scanner can produce, the more it will cost to purchase and the better the scan data.

Digital cameras and video cameras are two other forms of input. A digital camera captures a continuous tone analog image and converts it to digital data, saving it to a hard drive as bits and bytes. Still video cameras can be mounted next to the computer system, used for still capture, and take the place of more expensive 3-D scanners. Digital video is now commonly available at the consumer level in the United States, complete with simple editing programs. Higher end video cameras are often used in the field by news organizations. A transceiver allows images to be transmitted anywhere in the world.

A tremendous variety of input devices are available, and careful background research will help determine which will meet your particular needs and budget.

Data Out

Will you want a print of your design for a portfolio? That image on the screen needs to be output in a usable manner, unless you plan to use it for a Web site or to download to a digital CD portfolio for viewing. It is wise to plan on an electronic as well as a print portfolio.

A variety of printing technologies are available for your studio or computer lab, and each creates a slightly different kind of image. A basic description follows.

A PostScript-equipped printer that can read EPS files is an important piece of equipment for a professional design studio that is creating type and image files using various software. PostScript is a device-independent format that means the file will print out at whatever dpi the printer is capable of delivering.

The Inkjet printer sprays ink drops onto the paper where they form characters or shapes. Epson sells archival ink sets for some of its product lines, producing a high-quality, long-lasting image. Inkjets are very cost-effective printers, and suitable for most color proofing and student portfolio prints.

Dye sublimation printers heat up colored ribbons until the pigments turn into gas, which is absorbed by the polyester coating on the paper. The output from these printers is continuous tone and thus can simulate a traditional photograph.

An imagesetter is a high-resolution device found at service bureaus and commercial print shops that exposes the image onto film that is then chemically developed, in preparation for offset reproduction. Now let's look at prepress.

PREPARING FOR PRESS

The Process

The first step in preparing art for the printer is the job of the graphic designer. You are responsible for decisions about the placement of elements, the location of color, the choice of imagery, and the typographic treatment. Once the design is approved, the job is sometimes turned over to a pre-press artist who prepares the design for printing. Many entry-level jobs for designers are in prepress production, although many designers who generate their own electronic designs also prepare their own prepress files.

Preparing art for the printing process has changed a lot in recent years. In the United States, this preparation is done primarily with electronic techniques. An understanding of the terminology will provide a strong foundation for the new designer. It is possible to better understand the computer language and printing process when we begin with a historical knowledge of traditional techniques. Much of the terminology from the older hand-done method and the electronic method is the same.

An Overview

Before computers, the traditional pasteup artist prepared a black and white version of the design that was *camera ready*. All of the components of the design were assembled in black and white, and colors were specified before sending the job to a process camera to have film shot and plates burned. If any artwork was to be reproduced in full (process) color, it was sent separately to be color separated by a camera. All black and white photographs were also sent separately to be screened into halftones.

A process camera produced negatives of the black and white artwork including all text and image materials. These negatives were prepared for plate making by a technician called a *stripper*. He or she would cut, trim, and tape the negatives into position on a carrier sheet. The plate would then be exposed, put on the printing press, and the final printed copies of the original layout produced on specified paper in specified colors.

In the current digital prepress version, all scans whether done by the designer or at a higher quality professional bureau, are placed on the computer file to be sent to the printer, where the final composite file is created by *ripping* that data onto a negative

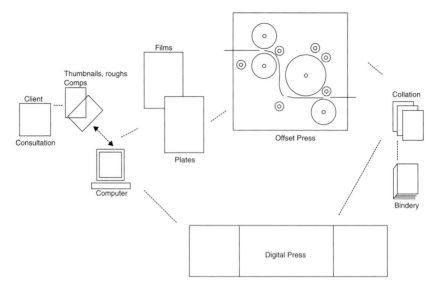

11-9

From concept to printed piece.

and then burning it to a plate. If the press is digital, the file goes directly to press (Figure 11-9). The inking process on the offset press remains essentially the same as it was before digital file creation. Spot or process color inks are put on the press rollers, and the color is printed onto paper.

The prepress and printing process require high standards and good communication skills from everyone involved. Often the printer can answer a designer's questions about the equipment a job will be run on, which will influence preparation of the artwork. This chapter discusses the preparation of artwork for the offset press, the most common method of reproduction.

Terminology

To the printer, the terms *art* and *copy* refer to all material to be reproduced. The copy is the typeset material, whereas art is everything else. All photographs, illustrations, and diagrams are called art. In general, they fall into two classifications: line art and continuous tone images.

Line Art

Line art is made up of a black and white image with no variation in grays except those created by optical mixing. In the old traditional prepress process, any line art could be pasted up directly onto a board. It was ready to be photographed for reproduction. Anything not line art was

11-10

From left to right, line art, gray scale, and three-color image, underlined with an enlarged halftone dot pattern.

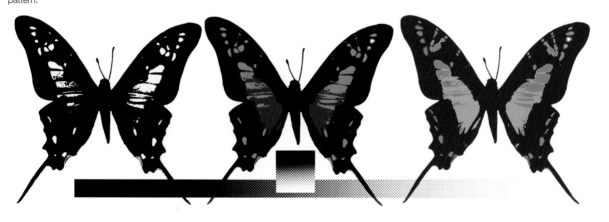

handled separately because it needed to be converted at the printer's or via electronic prepress into line art dots called screens or halftones. The printing press will only reproduce line art. Figure 11-10 shows line art, gray scale and spot color images with an enlarged dot screen pattern beneath.

Typeset copy, pen and ink drawings or diagrams, high-contrast black and white photography, India ink solids, and line art scans are all forms of line art. Screens printed on a desktop laser printer do not generate clarity of reproduction. If working with a traditional paste-up, do not send a laser-printed screen or halftone. Instead ask the printer to strip in a screen at the negative stage, unless you are working with large special-effect dots that you want to show.

Continuous Tone Art

Art that produces a graduated or blended variety of values is called *continuous tone* art. It includes photographs, illustrations, or diagrams done with pencil or paint, and any other method that produces a variety of values. When creating such art on computer, the image is scanned and incorporated into the digital file, and the resolution is an important factor (discussed later).

The electronic prepress artist sends a file with the process or spot colors prepared and with line art or continuous tone art in place, often on software layers. The final offset color printing is done by making a separate negative and plate for each necessary color. The different inks are laid on the paper by the press in succession. As mentioned earlier, direct digital imaging can skip the negative and plate stages and go directly to press.

Spot Color Variations

Reversals and tint screens are some line art variations that can add interest to your one- or two-color art (also called spot color). This is discussed in Chapter 10. They should be planned out at the design stage. A reversal can also be converted to a tint screen (Figures 11-11a, 11-11b, 11-11c, and 11-11d). The screen percentage and color

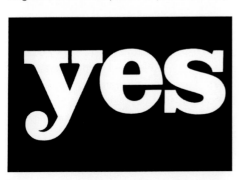

a

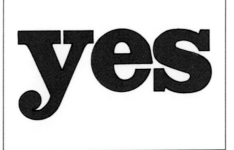

b

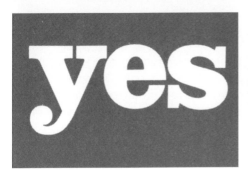

c

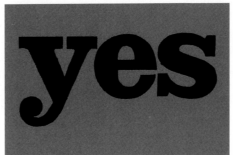

d

11-11a
Line art reversed.
11-11b
Specify percentages for screen tint.
11-11c
A dropout—line art reversed out of a tint screen.
11-11d
A surprint—line art superimposed over a tint screen.

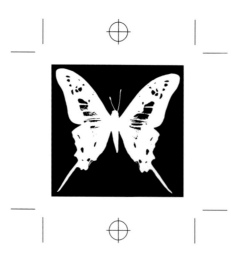

11-12
Accurate registration marks
are important.

can be created by the electronic artist on the file or specified by the precomputer procedure on an overlay. Crop marks indicated on the prepress file show where the end of the page should be, and they tell the printer where to trim the sheet. Registration marks indicate how the layers of color should overprint (Figure 11-12).

Registration

There are three types of color register: nonregistered, commercial register, and hairline register. *Nonregistered colors* do not abut. *Commercial register* (sometimes called *lap register*) means slight variations in placement of color of about one row of dots are not important. *Hairline register* is a term for extremely tight registration, where the tolerance is not greater than half a row of screen dots. Traditional acetate overlay separation is appropriate for nonregistered or commercial registration. It is not suitable for hairline registration. When preparing an electronic file, trapping becomes an important consideration to ensure successful tight registration of colors that lie side by side. Some software programs, such as Quark, do automatic trapping, inserting *choaks* and *bleeds*. However, these issues are getting easier. In most cases the printer or prepress service

bureau will trap your file for you. It is important to clarify expectations.

Quality Issues

Careful consideration of LPI, dot gain, and paper quality is necessary to ensure quality output.

Dot gain occurs when a halftone dot prints larger than intended. It causes a printed piece to look very dark and full of high contrast. When examined under a magnifier (a linen tester or loupe), the halftone dots appear to be large and bleeding into the white spaces. An absorbent paper can cause dot gain, as can problems with the press itself. A poor photographic halftone can also be responsible for dot gain. The fewer the reproduction steps between the original photo and the printed image, the less opportunity for a dot gain problem to occur.

Lines per inch (LPI) refers to the screen frequency of the actual printed piece. Again, your printer is a good source of information about the recommended LPI for your job. The higher the lines per inch, the finer the printed image because the rows of halftone dots are closer together and are very small. However, the higher the LPI, the more tendency there can be toward a clogging of halftone dots, or dot gain. Coated papers will handle higher screen frequencies than uncoated or newsprint:

120–150 LPI for coated paper stock
85–133 LPI for uncoated paper stock
60–80 LPI for newsprint

DIGITAL PREPRESS

Computer technology is continually changing how images are created and reproduced. We can merge design and production into a much more integrated process than before. Designs can be previewed on the computer screen (or in a proof stage), changes suggested by the client, adjustments made by the designer, and the final design sent to the production people via electronic files. Color correction, photo retouching, and color separations can be done on a desktop system before sending to a service bureau or printer for a high-resolution output to film or to press. Once the design is in digital form, there are vast possibilities for reutilization.

This all may sound simple, but it is actually quite complex. There are lots of ways to corrupt a digital file and confuse the printer. *Clear communication between designer, prepress technician, service bureau, and printer is a must.*

The RIP

The designer may generate all the elements of an electronic file or may hire a service bureau to create the high-resolution scans for images. Once the publication is assembled, the designer or someone he or she designates needs to verify that the file is ready for *raster image processing* (RIP) on an imagesetter. A typical computer monitor has a resolution of 72 dpi (dots per inch); a typical laser printer has a resolution of several hundred dpi. The imagesetter that will send a file to film, however, usually has a resolution of 2,400 dpi or higher. The pages might print fine on a laser printer, but fail to print on an imagesetter, because it calculates pixels by a different method. It is a safe bet that if the pages do not print on a laser printer, they probably will not print on an imagesetter either. How do you ensure those pages are ready to RIP? Many of these considerations are especially important when using imported elements and multiple programs.

Some Do's and Don't's

It is important to keep an electronic file clean and neat. If you do not need something in a

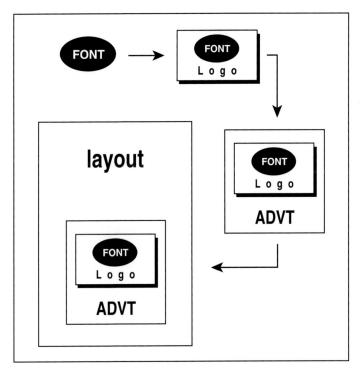

11-13
Avoid *nesting* electronic files as shown. Import each element directly into the page layout program.

file, delete it. Do not cover it with a white rectangle or leave it on a hidden layer.

Avoid putting files into files and then putting these files into yet more files. This process is referred to as *nesting,* and it can snarl the RIP by requiring many unnecessary steps of electronic memory (Figure 11-13).

When using multiple programs, it is best to assemble all the elements in your final output program.

Do any manipulation of those elements in the original file before importing. Rotate and resize the image in Photoshop, for example, before sending it to Quark. Do not plan to resize, mask, or rotate an imported graphic. They make the RIP work much harder. When you use a large graphic, build a new file with only that graphic to the right scale. Then import that into your layout for fine tuning.

Avoid scaling graphics up or down by large amounts. The data may stay the same, and you can end up with a very tiny, very high-resolution image, or a very large, relatively low-resolution image.

Scan an image at approximately the size it will be in the final publication. If it is necessary to drastically reduce the size of an image, plan to also use the software program to reduce the resolution (dpi).

Fonts

Fonts are composed of a *printer font* and a *screen font.* The printer (PostScript) font allows typography to output to print; the screen font is a cruder version that shows up on the monitor. The RIP needs to find and use exactly the font used to create the document. It cannot be some other vendor's version of Helvetica. It has to be the exact one used in your publication in order for the line breaks to work out correctly. Send all printer and screen fonts along with your document (Figure 11-14).

Do not rely on popup menu styles to create bold, italic, or condensed versions of your font. These variations are not specially designed typography. They are computer-generated distortions and will not RIP well. Use the real fonts in the font menu. Avoid Truetype fonts, which do not RIP well for print graphics.

Scanning

In the old method of traditional printing, the designer sends a continuous tone photograph or transparency along with the pasteup or mechanical, and specifies where the image should be inserted and resized. The printer then creates a halftone negative at the correct lines per inch (LPI) for the press and the paper choice. Traditional photographic halftones, however, are less and less common. The primary tools for creating a halftone today are the computer and imagesetter.

When the designer is creating the publication electronically, the photo is usually scanned on a desktop scanner or sent to a prepress service bureau for a high-end drum scan. The designer needs to be familiar with terms such as LPI and dpi, and understand their relationship in order to ensure good quality results.

A higher resolution has more dots per inch (dpi). That refers to how many dots fit within each inch to recreate an image. More dpi produces more data and potentially a finer reproduction of an image or typography. A 72 dpi *low res* scan can show jagged edges of pixelation when printed. However, avoid scanning at a higher resolution than is needed, which wastes time and file size.

LPI and dpi

When the continuous tone photograph is halftoned in the traditional process, it is converted into dots on a photographic negative. When a continuous tone photograph is scanned via the digital process, it is converted into dots on an electronic file. The more dots, the higher the resolution, or dpi.

There is a relationship between the resolution of your scan and the lines per inch of the final printed piece. For a good quality

11-14

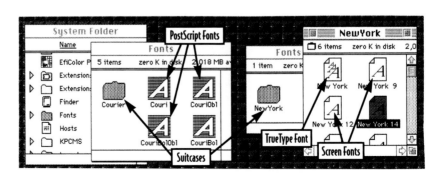

printed piece, pay attention to this relationship.

Do you know the optimum LPI (lines per inch) of your printed piece? If not, ask the printer and look at the list on page 202. LPI is sometimes called *screen frequency* or *screen ruling.* For halftones, a final dpi resolution of 1.5 times the LPI usually works well. The formula is LPI $\times$ 1.5 = dpi scanning resolution. (Remember that resizing the image can change the dpi, and plan accordingly.) LPI will vary depending on the paper used for printing, as mentioned earlier in this chapter. This is true whether preparing traditional or electronic files; but in traditional mechanical preparation, it is usually the printer's problem to figure out. It is still best to consult with the printer about LPI.

Scanning Suggestions

Using a retouching program to sharpen an image will produce a cleaner looking file. A blurry scan may not be improved with higher resolution, but it will look better when software sharpening filters are applied, such as Photoshop's Unsharp Mask filter.

When scanning, crop away the white borders. They create data that adds to the file size. If cropping is desirable, do that in the scanning stage to save memory and reduce file size.

A line art image will not need to be halftoned when it is scanned. When printing line art scans, use very high resolution and use sharpening. Image resolution does not need to be higher than the output resolution, but if the file is going to an imagesetter for a RIP, try for at least 800 dpi on a line art scan.

Every time material is duplicated photographically, some image degeneration, or loss of information, occurs. Provide film from the imagesetter to the printer in the proper format to avoid a duplication step. Ask the printer if film should be provided emulsion side up or down, in negative or positive, and provide that information to your imagesetter

bureau. Oftentimes the imagesetter is operated by the printing company, which simplifies communication.

File Links

To insert scans or other graphics files into a layout program, the computer must find those files. To find a file, the computer searches along a path established when the graphic was imported into the layout program. This path is known as a *link*.

There are several reasons why this link may not be found. If the graphic was renamed, or moved to another folder, that can break the link. All graphics files should be sent to the service bureau along with the job, which is usually assembled in a page layout program. These files should be located in the same folder that uses the graphics.

File Formats

The way the image is stored on the disk determines which programs can open, read, and edit that image. Two of the primary formats for storing graphic images on disk are TIFF and EPS, although there are many more formats. If an image is not stored in the proper format, it will not appear as an option to open or import into another program.

TIFF (Tagged Image File Format) is a widely used bitmapped file format. It is appropriate for scanned images. Almost every program that works with bitmaps can utilize the TIFF format.

EPS (Encapsulated PostScript) is an object-oriented file format that is excellent for storing graphics of any kind. You need a PostScript printer to print an EPS graphic. A PostScript file is a series of text commands that are a page-description language. It is a programming language created to put type and graphics on paper. EPS is a refined form of PostScript that will allow an object-oriented *or* bitmapped program to open the file for editing.

GIF (Graphics Interchange Format) supports 256 indexed colors; most image-editing programs can read and write GIF image files, but it is not compatible with page-layout or illustration programs. It is useful for multimedia and Web page design, since a special plug-in is not needed to view its animation.

PICT is a Mac object-oriented file format. It handles bitmap and vector images well. They should be converted to TIFF or EPS before placing in a page-layout program such as PageMaker or QuarkXpress.

Once you understand the basic concept of file links and file formats, it clears up a lot of questions about why an image may not appear on screen when imported into another program. At a more advanced level, you will be learning more about this topic.

Compression

Sometimes a file is simply too large for the storage device. In that case, data can be compressed to shrink the number of bytes needed for storage. Two methods are used to compress bitmapped data: *lossless compression* and *lossy compression.* Lossless gives less compression, but preserves the original image. Lossy methods give high compression, but lose information in the original file. For example, JPEG is a lossy compression method that throws away some of the high-frequency variations in color. RLE is a lossless method that depends on batch processing adjacent pixels with identical values.

CONCLUSION

There is a great deal to know about preparing artwork for reproduction. The better you as a beginning designer can understand the tools and procedures of prepress, the better you will comprehend the problems and solutions involved in producing a quality design. Figure 11-15 was created for a large glossy poster, at a high LPI and corresponding dpi. All art prepared for offset reproduction must be clean and accurate, whether prepared by traditional or electronic means.

Preparing Electronic Files for a Service Bureau

- Assemble your file in a page layout program like Quark or Pagemaker. It is easier to RIP (raster image process) files from a layout program rather than an image manipulation program.
- Bring all your images from Illustrator, Freehand, and Photoshop into the final document as EPS files.

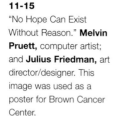

11-15
"No Hope Can Exist Without Reason." **Melvin Pruett,** computer artist; and **Julius Friedman,** art director/designer. This image was used as a poster for Brown Cancer Center.

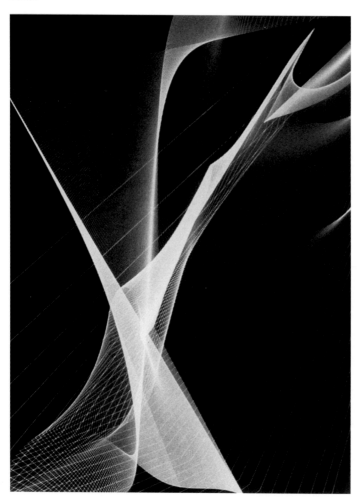

- Check the automatic trapping option in Quark and Pagemaker, and ask the service bureau to check your trapping.
- All files must be CMYK before they are assembled into Quark or Pagemaker (if you are doing full color output).
- Only CMYK colors will print accurately. If you are using Photoshop, check the color picker menu for an alert symbol. If the triangle has an ! in it, the selected color will not print accurately.
- Include all your original EPS scans and vector graphic files.
- Be sure all documents are linked. Check the links menu in Quark and Illustrator. If files are missing, locate and include them.
- Supply all fonts used in your document. Supply both screen and printer fonts. To do that, look in the system folder; find fonts. Locate your font with a suitcase icon by it. Inside this are the screen fonts. Find your printer font. It will have a page icon and be identified as a PostScript file.
- Organize and label these files on a disk. Do a "print window" from the desktop menu of your file folders on the disk. Highlight the file to print from. Send this print, along with a black and white proof print of your file, to the service bureau.

Review

Common Prepress Terms

art
copy
line art
continuous tone art
halftone
LPI
spot color
process color
registration marks
trim marks
dot gain
font
film/plates
mechanical (traditional)
camera ready (traditional)

Electronic Prepress Terms

dpi
electronic file
software layers
scanned image
analog
digital
vector graphic
raster graphic
printer font
screen font
file links
file formats
RAM
ROM

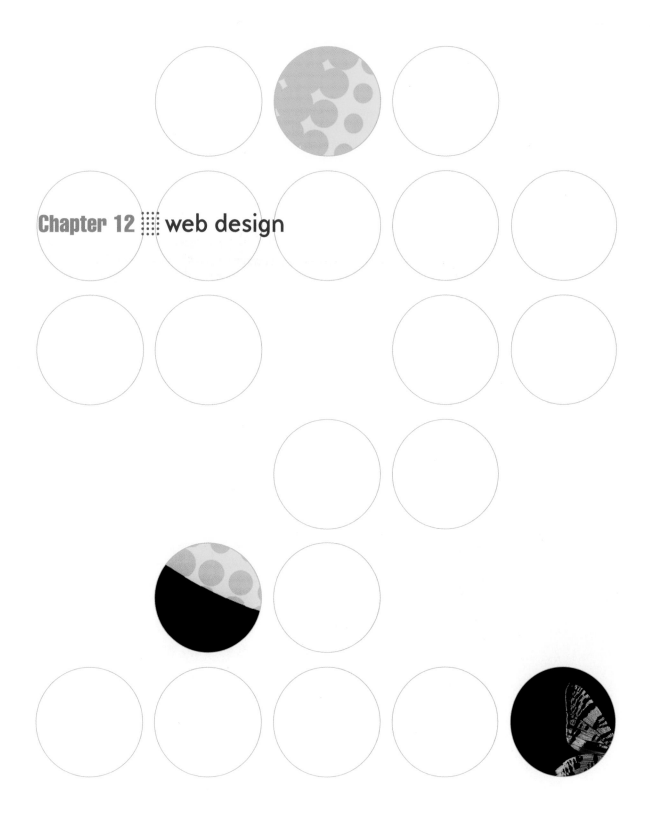

Chapter 12 ::: web design

The Web has quickly become one of the most powerful and exciting tools for designers today. The first sites were created by technical people using an early, relatively limited version of HTML (hypertext markup language). These sites were linear, text based, and not hampered by fine distinctions in typography because users set their font viewing preferences on their own computers.

In the 21st century, the new media of Web as well as motion graphics takes us beyond both text and image. As we know, human perception is a blend of sensory input from sight, sounds, touch, and smell, all shaped by memory. Increasingly, new media can involve the senses of the human body, including sound and movement. It can help us develop new ways of visualizing reality and sharing data. The Web is an interactive medium with few geographic boundaries.

GLOBAL VILLAGE

Media and new technologies are linked to changes in social structure. Increasingly, as the new media of the World Wide Web allow ease of international communication, our communication and design issues become a shared, worldwide experience. Our new technological media are vitally linked to the actualization of Canadian theorist and media philosopher Marshall McLuhan's concept of a global village. These new media are also linked to the establishment and redefinition of cultural and personal identity.

The telephone, the microscope, and the telescope are earlier examples of new technologies that extended the range of our senses. Now we can see inside storms and along chains of molecules, From book to photography to video/computer disc, our storage and retrieval system has grown. New technologies rely strongly on visual communication, requiring grounding in visual literacy. You must be knowledgeable both about the production and the consumption of images. We all need to be prepared to continually retrain and renew our knowledge base with new media throughout our professional careers.

Web-based media is very different from print because it is nonlinear and interactive. CDs can also be prepared with nonlinear, interactive information flow, using programs such as Macromedia's Director, but the Web is the most powerful of the interactive media. Web data can be delivered simultaneously around the world, freed from the physical restraints of traditional media. Time and space are easily traveled with these new media.

HOW DOES THE WEB WORK?

When you type an address into a browser like Netscape Navigator or Internet Explorer, the user's computer sends a request over the Internet for a specific URL address. The file is downloaded over the Internet to the user's computer. The Web browser displays the file. The URL (Uniform Resource Locator) is the address entered to access a particular

12-1
Online page in
Netscape Navigator.

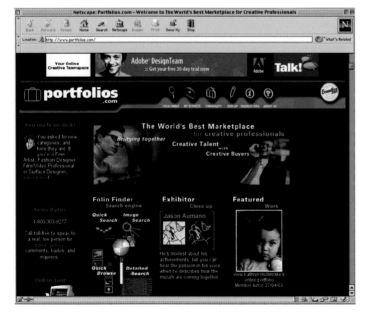

site. This URL consists of 3 parts:

Protocol = http://
Domain name = www.server.com
Pathname = folder/filename.ext

The protocol is the communications language the URL uses. The domain name is the server where the desired file is located. The pathname is a particular file in a site. For example, http://www.portfolios.com takes you to a site for viewing artists' and designers' portfolios (Figure12-1), and http://www.portfolios.com/search/search.html# quick-browse takes you to a particular page in that site for a quick browse of their offerings.

There are many similarities and differences between print and Web-based design. Let's begin by examining the similarities and then look at the differences.

COMMON METHODOLOGY

1. Begin any publication by defining the message and the audience.
2. Familiarize yourself with the competition.
3. Research and analyze the available resources.
4. Organize the content. In Web design that means developing a flow chart for content. Figure 12-2 shows a typical student flow chart for a portfolio site.
5. Design the visuals, developing a look and feeling tied by a common visual/conceptual theme.
6. Produce the web site or print piece.

DESIGN SIMILARITIES

A book or magazine presents information in a sequence of pages, as does a Web site. These pages should be tied together with a similar visual treatment such as a uniform grid, consistent choice of font, and alignment of typography.

A successful publication, whether online

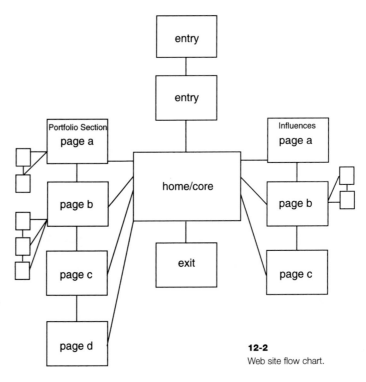

12-2
Web site flow chart.

or in print, often also uses a visual and conceptual theme that unites the publication. Consistency in placement and treatment of items such as page numbers and navigation bars or buttons is important. Figure 12-3 uses a pebble that generates animated water-like waves as a navigation button. The color for this site is carefully chosen to set an overall tone. Remember, color sets a mood and communicates a message, whatever your method of output. Each section of a Web site or a print publication can be color coded.

The 20th century produced wonderful examples of graphic design. A study of basic design principles applied to the field of graphic design/communication shows a number of visual principles that seem to cross cultures and decades. The Gestalt unit-forming principles of visual perception form a base for design of Web graphics as well as print media. Repetition and variation, rhythm, continuation, and figure/ground

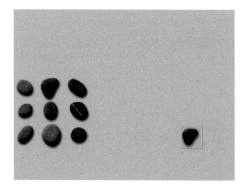
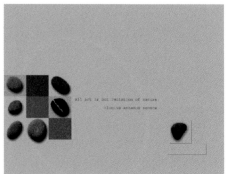
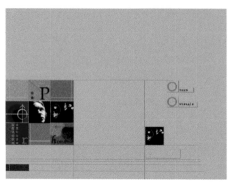

12-3
Pages from **Leah Shea's** Web portfolio show her use of a consistent, unifying style as well as highly interactive buttons and links.

treatment are fundamental to the design of any publication. Although various cultures have unique design solutions using these visual components, all cultures deal with these visual foundations.

PRODUCTION SIMILARITIES

A bottom-line production similarity is that when the Web site is mounted online or the print piece sent to press, all elements must be prepared correctly in order to function properly.

DESIGN DIFFERENCES

A book or magazine presents linear information. The pages sequence from front to back. The structure of the information flow is one directional and reasonably simple to create. Information on the web is nonlinear and interactive. Figure 12-4a shows a student Web portfolio with multiple choices on its home/core page. Figures 12-4b and 12-4c show a

direction pursued; Figure 12-4d shows an interactive show/hide behavior on a button.

The structure of the information flow is often complex and should be diagrammed before creating the site. It is possible to get stuck out on a limb in a Web site, with no links back into the information flow, causing a viewer to end the session. A successful flow leaves the viewer only a click or two from the home/core page.

Time, motion, and sound are important components of Web design. You will want to learn the design sensibilities and the production skills necessary to create animation and sound files that communicate the intended message. All design communicates a message, but it may not have the intended and desired effect, if the designer lacks skill.

PRODUCTION DIFFERENCES

Many, many differences exist in production considerations. The dpi of image scans, availability of fonts, appropriateness of file

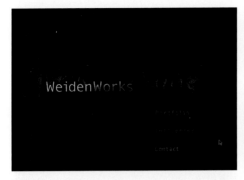

a

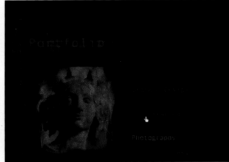

b

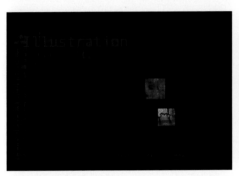

c

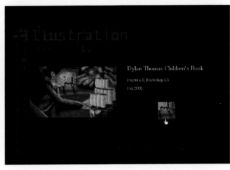

d

12-4a
This home page offers a choice of three directions.
12-4b
One direction leads to the portfolio section, which again offers three subcategories.
12-4c, d
Following the Illustration subcategory takes the viewer to a page with interactive show/hide behaviors on the buttons.

formats and sizes, and color gamuts of RGB versus CMYK must all be learned anew for their application to Web graphics. Consider the ephemeral quality of the online environment with its varied user environment versus the concrete reality of the printed page. This is a very important difference. Download time is also a crucial issue in Web design that does not exist in print graphics. Naming conventions must be understood and rigidly adhered to in Web graphics.

The Web is a picky medium, and it is vital to understand its rules in order to reach the audience with the intended message.

WHAT ARE THE RULES?

Naming Your Files

Filenames use different conventions and restrictions depending on the operating system (Windows, Mac OS, Unix). Because the server computer mounting your site may run a different operating system than yours, name your files so they can be used on the server computer. Use filenames that are no longer than eight characters, followed by a three- or four-character extension. Do not use spaces or other special symbols; use only lowercase letters and numbers. For example, a Web page would have an html extension. Name your first page index.html, and your image and GIF animation assets with recognizable eight or fewer character names followed by the extension .JPEG or .GIF (Figure 12-5).

Keep all files related to your site in one folder, with sections grouped together either by folders or naming conventions.

Resolution

Prepare final Web files at 72 dpi. Often, however, the best results come from scanning or otherwise preparing images at a larger resolution and reducing the file down later. Keep an unflattened, high-resolution version of your image files, so you can go back and make all changes on the original.

Print graphics at a resolution of 72 dpi

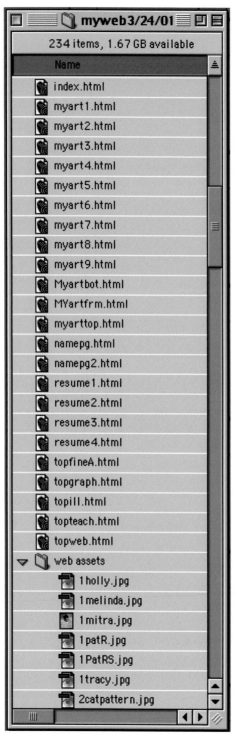

12-5
Web site directories follow strict naming conventions.

look terrible. However, Web graphics are displayed on monitors. The Mac monitor is around 72 pixels per inch (ppi), while the default on a PC is slightly higher. The bigger your monitor is, the more pixels it can display on screen. However, the ppi does not change, so Web graphics are prepared at 72 dpi. A larger monitor simply displays a bigger image, not a higher resolution image.

File Size

The file size is measured in bytes, and refers to the amount of disk space required to store the file. The larger the images, and the more complex and numerous the elements added to a page, the longer that page will take to view in the browser window.

Keep graphics as small and concise as possible to avoid long download times and frustrated users. Reuse graphics on your site. Once a graphic is used it has been downloaded. Downloaded graphics are cached in memory, eliminating the need to download a graphic again.

Flat, solid areas of color reduce a file's size considerably. If you are creating gradations, top-to-bottom creates a smaller file size than right-to-left gradations.

Monitor Size

For the most conservative size, guaranteed to reach all users, keep important elements, text, and graphics of your Web page within a 600 × 350 pixel area. Some users still have 13" monitors with a 640 × 480 display space, leaving online display beneath the Web address even smaller. To check the approximate way your file will look on various monitors, go to Chooser>Monitors>Resolutions and change the default, or use the size popup at the bottom of the Dreamweaver page. As shown in Figure 12-6, the bottom of the window contains information on the file's download speed based on your Internet connection, as well as screen size viewing

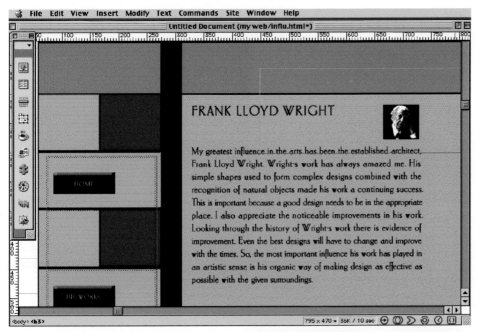

a

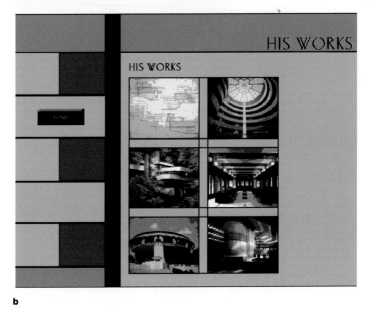

b

12-6a, b
Tracy Landowski's
Influences section of her personal Web site shown (a) inside a Dreamweaver window and (b) at full size. This site is unified throughout by its visual treatment.

options.

If your monitor is 640 × 480, and you change its default resolution to 800 × 600, you'll have more pixels, but they'll be smaller. A setting of 1024 × 768 gives even more pixels, showing more image. The converse is also true. A Web file you create to fill the screen on your 1024 × 768 will be too large to view on someone's 640 × 480 monitor.

File Formats

A file format tells the computer what kind of file it is dealing with. The Web accepts GIF and JPEG. These are both compressed file formats, producing graphics with smaller file sizes. The GIF file format is used for images featuring type and flat-color images. It is a lossless file format which means that it compresses graphics without eliminating detail and is designed for 8-bit (256 colors or less) graphics. You can reduce file size and improve loading time by saving solid color graphics as a GIF.

Use JPEG for graduations or photo-graphic images. Complex graphics with photo-based imagery reproduce better as JPEG. It is a **lossy** file format which removes data from the graphic image. Designed for displaying 24-bit true color, it does not support transparency, but can describe a larger more photolike image with less data, making for smaller files and faster downloads. PNG (Portable Network Graphics) are also a compressed, lossless file format. Not all browsers support PNGs, but one of their advantages is 256 levels of transparency.

Transparency

GIF files support transparency but JPEG does not. To create and save a transparent file in PhotoShop, choose File>Export>Gif89a. The popup allows you to select the area to be transparent with an eyedropper. You can easily save these GIF files and

12-7a, b

The PhotoShop "Save for Web" popup allows the user to specify JPEG or GIF, as well as transparency and color palette.

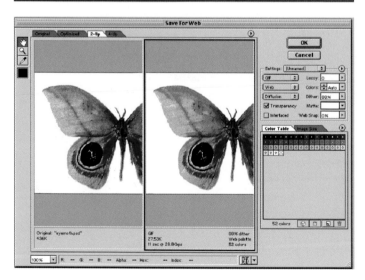

place them with a transparent background. Or you can use the File>Save for Web function and specify transparency by checking the appropriate box in the resulting popup menu. PhotoShop is an invaluable tool in preparing Web graphics. New versions continue to make these procedures easier.

Color

Converting files to the RGB color palette is the final image production step. Rerendering an image with a limited number of colors produces a pixelated effect called dithering. To avoid dithering of solid color GIF files, use Web-safe colors from a 216 Web-safe color table. (This produces an 8-bit file.) Current versions of PhotoShop let you "save for Web" and help you through a popup window of choices to specify the format and color table (Figure 12-7 shows a JPEG and GIF option). You can also create a GIF with a reduced color palette by choosing Image>Mode>Indexed Color. Then choose Web from the Palette menu and save as CompuServe GIF.

Changing an image from RGB to Indexed Color reduces an image's color usage from RGB's 16.8 million colors to a smaller palette. You can choose from a number of standard color palettes. The 216 Web-safe colors, the 256-color Mac and Windows systems palettes, or custom palettes such as Adaptive are available.

When preparing a GIF image, the two palettes to consider are the Web safe or the adaptive. Both are accessible from the PhotoShop Mode/Indexed color command from the Image menu. If the graphic contains photographic imagery and some flat-color elements filled with Web-safe colors, choose an adaptive palette. It is made up of colors most appropriate for the particular image. Dithering is most noticeable in solid flat-color areas. Choosing colors from the reduced Web-safe palette as often as possible when creating flat-color graphics helps reduce dithering. When composing background colors in PhotoShop that need to match the background of your Web site, it is advisable to use Web-safe color. Increasingly, PhotoShop makes these choices for you, as editions are updated.

WEB COMPONENTS

Pages and Sites

A Web site is composed of separate, linked pages. The site must be mounted on a server if it is to be viewed anywhere but from a disk.

Links

A link (also known as a hyperlink) is an active part of a document.

Clicking a link can take you to another part of the same Web page, other Web pages on your hard disk, or to a location on a remote computer. Every link contains the Web address for the page that the link refers to. This Web address is called the page's URL.

Tables and Frames

Tables allow you to precisely align layout elements into columns and rows. And they keep data from jumping around when the window is resized. Think of tables as similar to the underlying grid that provides structure to a print publication design.

Frames are very different from tables, although they look similar. A frame splits the page into sections. Typically one stationary frameset on the left side has links that call varying content into the frame on the right side. Each frame is actually a separate Web page. Frames are an excellent device for controlling the presentation and flow of information.

Animation and Sound

GIF files can be used to create animations. Adobe's ImageReady, which comes packaged with PhotoShop, is an excellent program for creating small animations. Flash is

the top program on the Web capable of generating sophisticated motion that downloads quickly, as well as interactive sites. Interactivity means that something happens in response to a viewer action. For example, clicking on an image or button can cause a sound file or animation to run. There are many forms of interactivity in Web sites. The simplest one is a button link to another page. Figure 12-8 is a Flash interactive file that shows a new image and a connected song as each of three buttons is clicked.

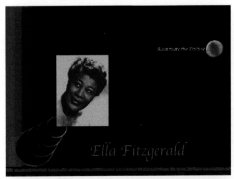
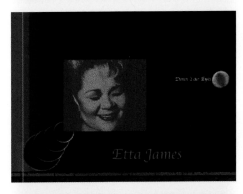
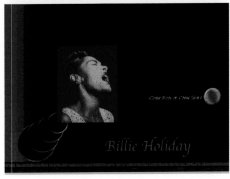

12-8
Dawn Disch created this interactive sound animation in Flash as a tribute to women and the "blues."

Web Software

All Web sites are actually created with HTML. Designers do not necessarily need to know this language, but a little background is advisable. Many software packages write the HTML for you invisibly. Third semester Graphics students using Dreamweaver produced most of the examples in this chapter. It is an excellent professional design and production tool for the Web from Macromedia, although several on the market also do a good job. Simpler programs include PageMill and FrontPage; Netscape Navigator comes packaged with Netscape Composer, an introductory Web program that many people already have on their computers.

Web Publishing

A great variety of online services for Web publishing are available. America Online or CompuServe are familiar to most. Many local Internet service providers also provide access to the Web, e-mail, and free space for a Web site.

www.geocities.com is a free location to publish your Web site. Like commercial television, it runs advertisements to turn a profit, so be prepared to have ads running along with your pages. But it gives excellent practice in trouble-shooting and mounting a site.

IN SUMMARY

Characteristics of good site design

1. Appealing entry page or sequence that attracts viewers
2. Clearly marked navigational devices
3. All elements (links and assets) work
4. Integrated design with possible use of metaphor or symbol
5. Good use of design basics
6. Acceptable download time
7. Communicates an appropriate message to an identified audience

The Web is a postmodern format, full of layered information. Its values may encompass modernism's rational, ordered organization of information, but the structure of the Web also encourages a postmodern mix of layered information.

Critique

The critique of a print or Web based creation should be based on issues specific to that medium. It is also important if possible to integrate into critiques the larger issues of medium and message and cultural impact.

- Consider the overall complexity of the site. How many JPEGS, GIFS, animations, links, and so on, are there?
- How complete is the research on the site's topic?
- How successful is the visual/conceptual theme?
- Is there a clear logic to the navigational structure?
- Are the files error free?
- Does the image fit the intended screen size well?

Discussion Questions

1. How is the computer a tool like any other throughout history? How does it present ways of seeing and shaping reality that are significantly different from the past?
2. What are the constants we bring to the use of new technology?
3. What is truly new about the new media that cannot be duplicated by any other media?

Assignments

1. Web Site Review

Choose a Web site to critically evaluate. Use the terms found throughout the chapter to identify elements. Use the Characteristics of good site design to help your evaluation. Refer to the Critique section for additional ideas. You'll also want to use these references to evaluate your own design work, and that of your classmates if you continue to assignment 2 and 3.

2. Beginning Web Page Design

Refer to the methodology discussed earlier in this chapter to plan and design a small Web site of about six pages. The topic is design history, and you are asked to research and prepare a short presentation on a designer from the history of design chapter. Gather and prepare several images for the Web. The Internet is a good research tool. The pages can be assembled in PhotoShop. Write a brief amount of copy. Be sure to include buttons intended to act as links between pages. Print these pages for presentation. Discuss their navigational structure and overall design

If you have enough time to spend on this assignment, either now or in a later class, you can "slice" the PhotoShop pages in Image Ready and insert them in a Web program. Figure 12-9 shows a PhotoShop image ready to be inserted into a Web program. In this file, "Follow the Movement" is a separate image that will be used as a link button.

3. Beginning Web Site Design

Assemble your buttons, images, and text in Netscape's Composer, ready to mount online. Include active links and tables. View this site on the monitor for final critique. Consider using Geocities or other sites to actually post your design on the Internet. Both Composer and Geocities are free and come with tutorials.

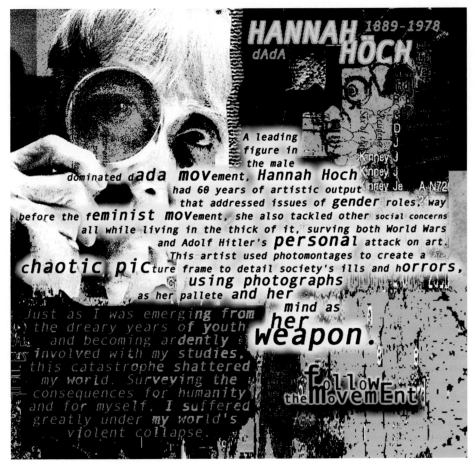

12-9
Adam McKee's Web site includes research on Dada artist Hannah Hoch, as well as a highly individual surface treatment of type and image.

glossary

ABSTRACTION   Simplification of existing shapes.

ACETATE OVERLAY   Clear plastic overlay that permits the positioning of units on a pasteup that cannot be put together on a single sheet.

ADDITIVE PRIMARIES   Red, blue, and green, which combine to produce white light.

AERIAL PERSPECTIVE   Creation of a sense of depth and distance through softening edges and decreasing value contrast.

ALIASING   Visual effect that occurs on a computer's visual display screen whenever the detail in the image exceeds the resolution available. It looks like a "stair stepping."

ANALOG   Signal that may be varied continuously. Computers cannot process this kind of signal, so their information must be converted to digital. Analog refers to everything in the real, non-computerized world.

ANALOGOUS COLORS   Hues that lie next to one another on the color wheel.

APPLIED ART AND DESIGN   Disciplines that use the principles and elements of design to create functional pieces for commercial use.

ASCENDER   Section of a lower case letter that extends above the x-height.

ASYMMETRICAL BALANCE   Distribution of shapes of different visual weights over a picture plane to create an overall impression of balance.

BALANCE   Distribution of the visual weight of design elements.

BIT   Abbreviation of Binary Digit. The most basic unit of digital information. A bit can be expressed in only one of two states, 0 or 1, meaning on or off, yes or no. This is actually the only information that a computer can process. Eight bits are required to store one alphabet character.

BITMAP   Text character or image comprised of dots. A bit map is the set of bits representing the position of items forming an image on the display screen.

BITMAPPED   Font or image comprised of dots (pixels), as distinct from an object-oriented graphic. Characterized by jagged edges. Also known as a raster image.

BLEED   Part of an image that extends beyond the edge of a page and is trimmed off.

BODY TYPE   Type smaller than 14 point, generally used for the main body of text. Also called text type.

BOLDFACE   Heavy version of a typeface.

BYTE   Unit of information made up of eight bits. Bytes are commonly used to represent alpha-numeric characters or the integers from 0 to 255.

CAD/CAM   Stands for computer-aided design/computer-aided manufacturing.

CAMERA-READY ART   Artwork that has been assembled and prepared for reproduction on a process camera.

CD-ROM   Compact disk-read only memory. A storage system of large capacity.

CENTERED TYPE   Lines of type of varying length that have been centered over one another.

CENTRAL PROCESSING UNIT (CPU)   Part of a computer system that contains the circuits that control and execute all data.

CHARACTER COUNT   Number of characters in a piece of copy. This number is used in copyfitting calculations.

CHOKE   Method of altering the thickness of a letter or solid shape, used in trapping to ensure peoper registration of colors.

CLOSURE   When the eye completes a line or curve in order to form a familiar shape.

CMYK   Process colors of cyan, magenta, yellow, and black inks used in four-color printing.

COLOR   The way an object absorbs or reflects light.

COLOR WHEEL   Part of color theory that demonstrates color relationships on a circle.

COMBINATION MARK   Trademark that combines symbol and logo.

COMPLEMENTARY HUES   Colors that are opposite one another on the color wheel.

COMPREHENSIVE (COMP)   Highly finished layout for presentation.

COMPUTER GRAPHICS   Branch of computer science that deals with creating and modifying pictorial data.

CONTINUATION   When the eye is carried smoothly into the line or curve of an adjoining object.

CONTINUOUS TONE   Illustration that contains continuous shades between the lightest and darkest tones without being broken up by the dots of a halftone screen or a digital file.

CONTINUOUS TONE ART   Art, such as illustrations or photographs, with a range of values. Must be reproduced with a halftone screen.

COPYFITTING   Process of determining the amount of space it will take to set copy in a specific type size and style.

CORPORATE IDENTITY   Elements of design by which an organization establishes a consistent identity through various forms of printed materials and promotions.

COUNTERS   White shapes inside a letterform.

CROP   To eliminate the unwanted sections of image area.

CROPMARKS   Short fine lines drawn on the image to indicate a cropped area, or at the corners of a pasteup to indicate where printed sheet will be trimmed. When used to indicate trim size, they can be called trim marks.

DIGITAL Signal that can only be in one of two states, on or off. Information, such as sound or image that is in a form that can be electronically manipulated.

DIMM Dual in-line memory module.

DIRECT ADVERTISING   Any form of advertising issued directly to the prospect through any means that does not involve the traditional mass media.

DIRECT MAIL   Advertising in which the advertiser acts as the publisher.

DIRECT MARKETING   Sale of goods and services direct to the consumer without intermediaries. Can include door-to-door sales.

DISK   Off-system data storage device for computers, consisting of one or more flat circular plates coated with magnetized material.

DISPLAY TYPE   Any type larger than 14 point.

DOT GAIN   Aberration that can occur in a printed image, caused by the tendency of halftone dots to grow in size. This can lead to inaccurate and coarsely printed results.

DPI   Dots per inch. This refers to the number of dots (resolution) a device is capable of producing.

DROPOUT   Copy that is reversed out of a halftone or a tint screen background.

DUOTONE   Two-color halftone reproduction made from one-color, continuous tone artwork.

EGYPTIAN   A slab-serif type category.

E-MAIL   Electronic mail sent between computers either over a network or with a modem over phone lines.

EPS   Encapsulated PostScript, a standard graphics file format based on vectors, or object-oriented information.

FIGURE/GROUND Relationship between the figure and the background of an image.

FOCAL POINT Area of a design toward which the viewer's eye is primarily drawn.

FONT Complete set of type of one size and one variation of a typeface.

FOUR-COLOR PROCESS Printing process that reproduces full-color images by using cyan, magenta and yellow plus black for added density.

GESTALT Unified configuration having properties that cannot be derived from simple addition of its parts.

GIF Graphic Interchange Format. A file format used for transferring graphics files between different computer systems via the internet. It creates very small data files.

GIGABYTE Unit of measure to describe 1,024 megabytes.

GRIPPER EDGE Leading edge of paper as it feeds into a press. Usually it calls for an unprinted margin of about 3/8" (1cm).

GUTTER Inner section of a page caught in the center binding.

HALFTONE Reproduction of continuous-tone art, such as a photograph, through a screen that converts it into dots of various sizes.

HARD COPY Printed copy of an image produced on a computer screen.

HARDWARE Physical components of a computer graphics system, including all mechanical, magnetic, and electronic parts.

HLS Hue, lightness and saturation. A color model.

HORIZONTAL BALANCE Visual balancing of the left and right sides of a composition.

HOT TYPE Typesetting in which the type is cast in molten metal.

HUE Name of a given color. Hue is one of the three properties of color.

INTENSITY Saturation or brightness of a color. Intensity is decreased by the addition of a gray or a complement.

INTERNET Electronic network that spans the globe.

JPEG Joint Photographic Experts Group, a lossy data compression file format that creates small compressed files by discarding part of the data before compressing. The reconstructed file usually looks quite good on photographic images.

JUSTIFY To align lines of type that are equal in length so both edges of the column are straight.

KERNING Selectively altering the spaces between letter combinations for a better fit.

KEYLINING drawing an outline on a finished pasteup to indicate the exact position for art that will be stripped in by the printer. Used when hairline registration is important.

LAYOUT Hand-rendered plan for a piece to be printed.

LEADING Amount of space placed vertically between lines of type.

LINE ART Black and white copy with no variations in value. Suitable for reproduction without a halftone screen.

LOGO Tademark of unique type or lettering, spelling out the name of a company or product.

LOWERCASE Small letters of an alphabet.

LPI Lines per inch. Printing term referring to the resolution of an image.

MASTER PAGE Page to which certain attributes can be given, which can then be applied to any other page in a document.

MECHANICAL Camera-ready pasteup, which contains all copy pasted in position for printing.

MENU-DRIVEN Computer graphics system that operates when a user selects options from those displayed on the monitor.

MODERN Type category that has great variation between thick and thin strokes and thin, unbracketed serifs.

MONOCHROMATIC COLOR Use of a single hue in varying values.x

NETWORK   Connection of two or more computers. This assemblage of computer hardware and software allows computers to share data, software, and other resources.

NONOBJECTIVE SHAPES   Shapes that are pure design elements, not related to any pictorial source.

OBJECT-ORIENTED   Graphics applications that allow the selection and manipulation of individual portions of an illustration or design. This is a characteristic of a vector graphic file and is the opposite of bitmapped graphics.

OLD STYLE TYPE   Type category characterized by mild contrast between thicks and thins, and by bracketed serifs.

PASTEUP   Assemblage of the elements of a layout, prepared for reproduction.

PHOSPHOR   Material coating the inside of a picture tube. When an electron beam hits this coating, the phosphor emits light in proportion to the voltage of the beam.

PICA   Typographic measurement of 1/16" (0.4cm).

PICTOGRAM   Symbol used to cross language barriers for international signage.

PICTURE PLANE   Flat surface of a two-dimensional design, possessing height and width, but no depth.

PIXEL   Individual picture element. It is the smallest element of a computer image that can be separately addressed.

POINT   Typographic measurement of 1/72 inch, or 1/12 pica.

POSTSCRIPT   Page-description language used to describe how a page is built up of copy, lines, images, and so on, for output to laser printers and high-resolution imagesetters.

PRESEPARATED ART   Art that has been separated onto acetate overlays by the pasteup artist before being sent to the printer.

PRIMARY COLORS   Three basic pigment colors of light—red, blue, and green—from which all other colors can be made are called "additive" primaries because when added together they produce white light.   "Subtractive" primaries are the magenta, cyan, and yellow of process printing.

PROCESS CAMERA   Large graphic arts camera used to make film negatives and positives for platemaking.

PROXIMITY   Visually grouping by similarity in spatial location.

RAGGED RIGHT (OR LEFT)   Unjustified column of type in which lines of varying length are aligned on either the right or left side.

RAM   Random access memory.

RASTER GRAPHICS   Computer graphics comprised of bitmaps that create a grid of individual picture elements (pixels).

REBUILD DESKTOP   Rebuilding the desktop gets rid of obsolete material that builds up as a computer is used. Doing this on a regular basis improves the operation of the computer. The desktop is rebuilt by holding down Option-Command while restarting the system.

REGISTRATION   Fitting two or more printing images on the same paper in exact alignment.

RESOLUTION   Ability of a computer graphics system to make distinguishable the individual parts of an image.

REVERSAL   Change to opposite tonal values, as when black type is altered to white.

REVERSIBLE FIGURE/GROUND   Relationship in which it is likely that figure and ground can be focused on equally.

ROM   Read-Only Memory. ROM resides in a chip on the motherboard. This memory can be read from, but cannot be written to.

ROUGH   Layout plan that comes after preliminary thumbnails and is usually executed in half or full size.

RUNAROUND   Type fitted around a piece of artwork.

SANS SERIF   Letterforms without serifs. *See* Serif.

SATURATION   Intensity or brightness of a color. Saturation is decreased by the addition of gray or a complementary color.

SCAN LINE   On a raster-scan computer monitor, one traversal of an electronic beam across the picture.

SECONDARY COLORS   Hues obtained by mixing two primary colors.

SERIF   Stroke that projects off the main stroke of a letter at the bottom or the top.

SERVICE BUREAU   Company used by designers for high-resolution imagesetting, it provides an array of computer services from file conversions to scanning. Service bureaus RIP the information from disk onto film, for offset reproduction. Some printing companies do this work in house.

SHADE   Darker value of a hue, created by adding black.

SHADING FILM   Commercially available textured screens of line art on a transfer sheet.

SHAPE   Figure that has visually definable edges.

SIMILARITY GROUPING   Visual grouping of images with similar shape, size, and color.

SIMM   Single in-line memory module. This plug-in board contains the chips some computers use for RAM.

SOFTWARE   Computer programs.

SPEC   Short for "specifying." To write type specifications (line length, size, style, leading) on copy.

STABLE FIGURE/GROUND   The unambiguous relationship of an object to background.

STET   Latin word used when marking up copy to signify "let it stand."

STRESS   The distribution of weight through the thinnest part of a letterform.

SUBTRACTIVE PRIMARIES   Magenta, cyan, and yellow—the colors left after subtracting one additive primary from white light.

SURPRINT   Line art superimposed over a screened area of the same color.

SYMBOL   Type of trademark to identify a company or product. It is abstract or pictorial but does not include letterforms.

SYMMETRICAL BALANCE   Formal placement of design elements to create a mirror image on either side. A less common form of symmetrical balance also creates the mirror image vertically.

TERTIARY COLORS   Hues I obtained by mixing primary color with a secondary color.

THUMBNAIL   First-stage miniature plan for a layout.

TIFF   Tagged Image File Format. This widely used file format is used for saving scanned, bitmapped images.

TINT   Light value of a hue, created by adding white.

TINT SCREEN   Flat, unmodulated light value made of evenly dispersed dots, usually achieved by stripping a piece of halftone film into the area on the negative that the artist has masked out.

TONE   Hue that has been decreased in intensity by the addition of black or a complement.

TRACKING   Adjustment of space between characters throughout a range of text.

TRADEMARK   Any unique name or symbol used by a corporation of manufacturer to identify a product and to distinguish it from other products.

TRANSITIONAL TYPE   Category of type that blends old style and modern, with emphasis on thick and thin contrast and gracefully bracketed serifs.

TRAPPING   Slight overlap of two colors to eliminate gaps that can occur due to normal registration problems during printing.

TYPEFACE   Style of lettering. Each family of typefaces may contain variations on that typeface, like "italic."

TYPE FAMILY   Complete range of sizes and variations of a typeface.

TYPESETTING   Composition of type by any method.

UNJUSTIFIED TYPE   Lines of type set with equal word spacing and uneven length.

UPPERCASE   Capital letters.

VALUE   Lightness or darkness of a color or a tone of gray.

VARIETY   Variations on a visual theme causing contrast in a design.

VECTOR GRAPHICS   Type of computer graphics in which graphic data are represented by lines drawn from coordinate point to coordinate point.

VERTICAL BALANCE   Visual balancing of the upper and lower portions of a composition.

VISUAL TEXTURE   Visual creation of an implied tactile texture.

WEIGHT   Lightness or heaviness of a visual image.

WIDOW   Short line at the end of a paragraph that falls at the top or bottom of a column page, or a single word on a line by itself at the end of a paragraph. Also called an *orphan*.

WINDOWS   Solid black or red areas of the pasteup that will convert into clear areas on the negative for a screen to be stripped onto.

WORD SPACING   The varying space between words, often adjusted to create a justified line of copy.

X-HEIGHT   Height of the body of a lowercase letter like an *a*, with no ascenders or descenders.

bibliography

Topics are listed by chapters.

Chapter 1
Applying the Art of Design

Albers, Josef, *Interaction of Color.* New Haven, Conn.: Yale University Press, 1972.

Baumgartner, Victor, *Graphic Games.* Englewood Cliffs, N.J.: Prentice-Hall, 1983.

Behrens, Roy, *Design in the Visual Arts.* Englewood Cliffs, N.J.: Prentice-Hall, 1984.

Bevlin, Marjorie, *Design Through Discovery.* New York: Holt, Rinehart and Winston, 1985.

Buchanan, Margolin, *Discovering Design,* University of Chicago Press, 1995.

Itten, Johannes, *The Art of Color.* New York: Van Nostrand Reinhold, 1974.

Kepes, Gyorgy, *Language of Vision.* Chicago: Paul Theobald, 1969.

Lauer, David, *Design Basics.* Harcourt Brace, 1995.

McKim, Robert H., *Experiences in Visual Thinking.* Monterey, Calif.: Brooks, Cole, 1980.

Rand, Paul, *Design Form and Chaos,* New Haven and London: Yale University Press, 1993.

Supon Design Group, *International Women in Design,* New York: Madison Square Press, Distributed by Van Nostrand Reinhart, 1993.

Chapter 2
Graphic Design History

Aynsley, Jeremy, A Century of Graphic Design,Hauppauge, NY: Barrons, 2001

Bayer, Herbert, et al., eds., *Bauhaus 1919–1928.* New York: Museum of Modern Art, 1938.

Berryman, Gregg, *Notes on Graphic Design and Visual Communication.* Los Altos, Calif.: William Kaufmann, 1990.

Cirker, Hayward, and Blanche Cirker, *Golden Age of the Poster.* New York: Dover, 1971.

Craig, James, *Graphic Design Career Guide.* New York: Watson-Guptill Publications, 1983.

Friedman, Mildred, and Joseph Giovannini, eds., *Graphic Design in America: A Visual Language History.* New York: Harry Abrams, 1989.

Garner, Philippe, *Sixties Design,* Taschen, 1996.

Glaser, Milton, *Milton Glaser: Graphic Design.* Woodstock, N.Y.: The Overlook Press, Walker Art Center, 1983.

Green, Oliver, *Underground Art*, London, England: Studio Vista 1990

Grieman, April, *Hybrid Imagery. The Fusion of Technology and Graphic Design,* New York: Watson Guptil, 1990.

Heller, Steven & Pettit, Elinor, *Graphic Design Timeline*, New York, NY: Allworth Press, 2000

Boswell/Makela*, The Photomontages of Hannah Hoch*, Minneapolis, MN: Walker Art Center, 1997

Hoffman, Armin, *Graphic Design Manual.* New York: Van Nostrand Reinhold, 1965.

Hurlburt, Allen, *Layout: The Design of the Printed Page.* New York: Watson-Guptill Publications, 1977.

Jackson, Lesley, *The New Look and Design in the Fifties,* New York: Thames and Hudson, 1991.

Meggs, Philip, *A History of Graphic Design,* New York: Van Nostrand Reinhold, 1998.

Motherwell, Robert, *Dada Painters and Poets.* New York: Wittenborn, Schultz, 1951.

Müller-Brockmann, Josef, *The Graphic Artist and His Design Problems.* New York: Hastings House, 1961.

Müller-Brockmann, Josef, *A History of Visual Communication.* New York: Hastings House, 1971.

Nelson, Roy Paul, *Publication Design.* Dubuque, Iowa: William C. Brown, 1991.

Pesch and Weisbeck, *Technostyle,* Zurich: Olms, 1995.

Rand, Paul, *A Designer's Art.* New Haven, Conn.: Yale University Press, 1985.

Rand, Paul, *Thoughts on Design.* New York: Van Nostrand Reinhold, 1971.

Scheidig, Walter, *Crafts of the Weimar Bauhaus 1919–1924.* New York: Reinhold Publishing, 1967.

Schwartz, Lillian, *The Computer Artist's Handbook, Concepts, Techniques and Applications,* New York: W.W. Norton & Co., 1992.

Snyder, Peckolick, *Herb Lubalin.* New York: American Showcase, 1985.

Varnedoe, Gapnik, *High & Low: Modern Art and Popular Culture.* New York: Museum of Modern Art, 1991.

Velthoven and Seijdel, *Multi Media Graphics, The Best of Global Hyperdesign,* Chronicle Books, 1997.

Wrede, Stuart, *The Modern Poster.* New York: The Museum of Modern Art, 1988.

Chapters 3–5
Perception

Arnheim, Rudolf, *Art and Visual Perception.* Berkeley: University of California Press, 1974.

Behrens, Roy,False Colors: Art, Design and Modern Camouflage. 2002 X Ave., Dysart, Iowa,: Bobolink Books, 2002.

Bloomer, Carolyn M., *Principles of Visual Perception.* New York: Van Nostrand Reinhold, 1976.

Gombrich, E. H., *Art and Illusion: A Study in the Psychology of Pictorial Representation.* New York: Pantheon Books, 1960.

Gombrich, E. H., Julian Hochberg, and Max Black, *Art, Perception, and Reality.* Baltimore: Johns Hopkins University Press, 1972.

Goodman, Nelson, *Languages of Art.* Indianapolis: Bobbs-Merrill, 1968.

Graphis Letterhead, An International Compilation of Letterhead Design, Zurich, Switzerland: Graphis Press, 1996.

Graphis Logo, An International Compilation of Logos, Zurich, Switzerland: Graphis Press, 1996.

Gregory, R. L., *Eye and Brain.* New York: McGraw-Hill, 1966.

Gregory, R. L., *The Intelligent Eye.* New York: McGraw-Hill, 1970.

Letterhead and Logo Design, Creating the Corporate Image, Rockport, Mass.: Rockport Publishers, Distributed by North Light Books, 1996.

Meggs and Carter, *Typographic Specimens and the Great Typefaces,* New York: Van Nostrand Reinhold, 1993.

Steuer, Sharon, *The Illustrator Wow! Book,* Berkeley, CA: Peachpit Press, 1995.

Zakia, Richard, *Perception and Photography.* Rochester, N.Y.: Light Impressions Corporation, 1979.

Chapters 6–7
Text type

Carter, Rob, et al., *Typographic Design: Form and Communication.* New York: Van Nostrand Reinhold, 1985.

Craig, James, *Designing with Type.* New York: Watson-Guptill Publications, 1992.

Dair, Carl, *Design with Type.* Toronto: University of Toronto Press, 1982.

Dürer, Albrecht, *On the Just Shaping of Letters.* Mineola, N.Y.: Dover, 1965.

Graphis Book Design II, Zurich, Switzerland: Graphis Press, 1995.

Graphis Brochures, *An International Compilation of Brochure Design,* Zurich, Switzerland: Graphis Press, 1996.

McLean, Ruari, *Jan Tschichold: Typographer.* Boston: David R. Godine, 1975.

Mossin, *Letter and Image.* New York: Van Nostrand Reinhold, 1970.

Ruder, Emil, *Typography.* New York: Hastings House, 1981.

The Whole Mac Solutions for the Creative Professional, Indianapolis, Indiana: Hayden Books, 1996.

Tschichold, Jan, *Asymmetric Typography.* New York: Van Nostrand Reinhold, 1980.

Chapters 8–9
Illustration, Photography, Advertising

Cabarga, Leslie, *Dynamic Black & White Illustration,* Glenbrook, CT:Art Direction Book Co, 1997

Cassandre, A. M., *A. M. Cassandre.* St. Gall, Switzerland: Zollikoffer & Company, 1948.

Douglas, Torin, *The Complete Guide to Advertising.* New York: Chartwell Books, Inc., 1984.

Dover Pictorial Archives. Mineola, N.Y.: Dover, 1979.

Graphis Advertising, The International Annual of Advertising, Zurich, Switzerland: Graphis Press, 1996.

Graphis Poster Design, The International Annual of Poster Art, Zurich, Switzerland: Graphis Press, 1996.

Haller, Lynn, *Fresh Ideas in Promotion,* Cincinnati, Ohio: North Light Books, 1994.

Heller/Arisman, *The Education of an Illustrator*, New York, NY: Allworth Press, 2000

Howell-Koehler, Nancy, *Vietnam, The Battle Comes Home: Photos by Gordon Baer.* Dobbs Ferry, N.Y.: Morgan & Morgan, 1984.

Hurley, McDougall, *Visual Impact in Print.* Chicago: Visual Impact, Inc., 1971.

Kerlow, Isaac V., and Judson Rosebush, *Computer Graphics for Artists and Designers.* New York: Van Nostrand Reinhold, 1994.

Leland, Karyn, *Licensing Art & Design.* Cincinnati, Ohio: North Light Books, 1990.

Nyman, Mattias, *Four Colors/One Image,* Berkeley, Calif.: Peachpit Press, 1993.

Pitz, Henry, *200 Years of American Illustration.* New York: Random House, 1977.

Steuer, Sharon, *The Illustrator Wow! Book,* Berkeley, CA: Peachpit Press, 1995.

The Creative Illustration Book #7, New York: The Black Book, 1996.

Vaizey, Marina, *The Artist as Photographer.* New York: Holt, Rinehart and Winston, 1982.

Whelan, Richard, *Double Take.* New York: Clarkson N. Potter, 1981.

Wilson, Stephen, *Using Computers to Create Art.* Englewood Cliffs, N.J.: Prentice-Hall, 1986.

Ziegler, Kathleen, *Digitaline Digital Design and Advertising,* Southhampton, PA, Dimensionals Illustrators, Inc., Distributed by North Light Books, 1996.

Chapters 10–12
Color, Production, Web Design

Blatner, David and Steve Roth, *Real World Scanning and Halftones,* Berkeley, CA: Peachpit Press, 1993.

Chartier and Mason, *Creating Great Designs on a Limited Budget,* Cincinnati, OH, North Light Books, 1995.

Dennis, Odesina and Wilson, *Lithographic Technology in Transition,* Delmar, 1997.

Evans, Poppy, *The Graphic Designer's Source Book...An Indispensable Treasury of Suppliers,* Cincinnati, OH, North Light Books, 1996.

Graphic Artists Guild Handbook: Pricing and Ethical Guidelines. New York: Graphic Artists Guild, 2002.

Hillman Curtis, *Flash Web Design.* Indianapolis, Indiana: New Riders, 2000

Niederst, Jennifer, *Web Design In A Nutshell*, Sebastopol, CA: O'Reilly & Associates, 1999

Pocket Pal. New York: International Paper Company, 2002..

Siegel, David*, Creating Killer Web Sites*, Indianpolis, IN: Hayden Books, 1997

The Whole Mac Solutions for the Creative Professional, Indianapolis, Indiana: Hayden Books, 1996.

Ulrich, Katherine, *Flash for Windows & Macintosh*, Visual Quickstart Guide, Berkeley, CA: Peachpit Press 1999

Towers, J. Tarin, *Dreamweaver for Windows & Macintosh*, Visual Quickstart Guide, Berkeley, CA: Peachpit Press 2002

Periodicals and Annuals

AIGA Graphic Design, USA. New York: Watson-Guptill Publications, annual, 1980–present.

Artists' Market: Where and How to Sell Your Artwork. Cincinnati, Ohio: Writers Digest Books.

AV Video. Torrance, Calif.: Montage Publishing, Inc.

Ballast. Roy Behrens, ed., 2002 X Avenue, Dysart, Iowa: Boblink Books

Communication Arts. Palo Alto, Calif.: Coyne & Blanchard, Inc.

Fine Print. San Francisco, California.

Graphic Artists' Guild. *Handbook of Pricing & Ethical Guidelines.* Cincinnati, Ohio: Writers Digest Books.

Graphis. Zurich, Switzerland: Walter Herdig.

How. New York: RC Publications.

Print. Washington, D.C.: RC Publications.

Print Casebooks. Washington, D.C.: RC Publications, six annual volumes, 1975–present.

Step-by-Step Graphics. Peoria, Ill.: Dynamic Graphics Educational Foundation (DGEF).

index